Cogl 2.0 Reference Manual

A catalogue record for this book is available from the Hong Kong Public Libraries.

Published in Hong Kong by Samurai Media Limited.

Email: info@samuraimedia.org

ISBN 978-988-8406-84-5

Contents

Chapter 1

Cogl - a modern 3D graphics API

1.1 About Cogl

Cogl is a modern 3D graphics API with associated utility APIs designed to expose the features of 3D graphics hardware using a more object oriented design than OpenGL. The library has primarily been driven by the practical needs of Clutter but it is not tied to any one toolkit or even constrained to developing UI toolkits.

1.2 General API concepts

1.2.1 The Object Interface

The Object Interface —

Functions

void *	cogl_object_ref ()
void	cogl_object_unref ()
void *	cogl_object_get_user_data ()
void	cogl_object_set_user_data ()

Types and Values

	CoglObject
	CoglUserDataKey
typedef	CoglUserDataDestroyCallback

Description

Functions

cogl_object_ref ()

```
void~*
cogl_object_ref (void *object);
```

Increases the reference count of *object* by 1

Parameters

| object | a CoglObject | |

Returns

the *object* , with its reference count increased

cogl_object_unref ()

```
void
cogl_object_unref (void *object);
```

Drecreases the reference count of *object* by 1; if the reference count reaches 0, the resources allocated by *object* will be freed

Parameters

| object | a CoglObject | |

cogl_object_get_user_data ()

```
void~*
cogl_object_get_user_data (CoglObject *object,
                           CoglUserDataKey *key);
```

Finds the user data previously associated with *object* using the given *key* . If no user data has been associated with *object* for the given *key* this function returns NULL.

Parameters

| object | The object with associated private data to query | |
| key | The address of a CoglUserDataKey which provides a unique value with which to index the private data. | |

Returns

The user data previously associated with *object* using the given *key* ; or NULL if no associated data is found.

[transfer none]

Since 1.4

cogl_object_set_user_data ()

```
void
cogl_object_set_user_data (CoglObject *object,
                           CoglUserDataKey *key,
                           void *user_data,
                           CoglUserDataDestroyCallback destroy);
```

Associates some private *user_data* with a given CoglObject. To later remove the association call cogl_object_set_user_data() with the same *key* but NULL for the *user_data* .

Parameters

object	The object to associate private data with	
key	The address of a CoglUserDataKey which provides a unique value with which to index the private data.	
user_data	The data to associate with the given object, or NULL to remove a previous association.	
destroy	A CoglUserDataDestroy-Callback to call if the object is destroyed or if the association is removed by later setting NULL data for the same key.	

Since 1.4

Types and Values

CoglObject

```
typedef struct _CoglObject CoglObject;
```

CoglUserDataKey

```
typedef struct {
  int unused;
} CoglUserDataKey;
```

A CoglUserDataKey is used to declare a key for attaching data to a CoglObject using cogl_object_set_user_data. The typedef only exists as a formality to make code self documenting since only the unique address of a CoglUserDataKey is used.

Typically you would declare a static CoglUserDataKey and set private data on an object something like this:

```
static CoglUserDataKey path_private_key;

static void
destroy_path_private_cb (void *data)
{
  g_free (data);
}

static void
my_path_set_data (CoglPath *path, void *data)
{
  cogl_object_set_user_data (COGL_OBJECT (path),
                             &private_key,
                             data,
```

```
                                   destroy_path_private_cb);
}
```

Members

int *unused*; | ignored.

Since 1.4

CoglUserDataDestroyCallback

```
typedef GDestroyNotify CoglUserDataDestroyCallback;
```

When associating private data with a CoglObject a callback can be given which will be called either if the object is destroyed or if cogl_object_set_user_data() is called with NULL user_data for the same key.

Since 1.4

1.2.2   Exception handling

Exception handling — A way for Cogl to throw exceptions

Functions

CoglBool	cogl_error_matches ()
void	cogl_error_free ()
CoglError *	cogl_error_copy ()
#define	COGL_GLIB_ERROR()

Types and Values

| CoglError

Description

As a general rule Cogl shields non-recoverable errors from developers, such as most heap allocation failures (unless for exceptionally large resources which we might reasonably expect to fail) and this reduces the burden on developers.

There are some Cogl apis though that can fail for exceptional reasons that can also potentially be recovered from at runtime and for these apis we use a standard convention for reporting runtime recoverable errors.

As an example if we look at the cogl_context_new() api which takes an error argument:

```
CoglContext *
cogl_context_new (CoglDisplay *display, CoglError **error);
```

A caller interested in catching any runtime error when creating a new CoglContext would pass the address of a CoglError pointer that has first been initialized to NULL as follows:

```
CoglError *error = NULL;
CoglContext *context;

context = cogl_context_new (NULL, &error);
```

The return status should usually be enough to determine if there was an error set (in this example we can check if context ==
NULL) but if it's not possible to tell from the function's return status you can instead look directly at the error pointer which you
initialized to NULL. In this example we now check the error, report any error to the user, free the error and then simply abort
without attempting to recover.

```
if (context == NULL)
  {
    fprintf (stderr, "Failed to create a Cogl context: %s\n",
             error->message);
    cogl_error_free (error);
    abort ();
  }
```

All Cogl APIs that accept an error argument can also be passed a NULL pointer. In this case if an exceptional error condition is
hit then Cogl will simply log the error message and abort the application. This can be compared to language execeptions where
the developer has not attempted to catch the exception. This means the above example is essentially redundant because it's what
Cogl would have done automatically and so, similarly, if your application has no way to recover from a particular error you might
just as well pass a NULL CoglError pointer to save a bit of typing.

Note If you are used to using the GLib API you will probably recognize that CoglError is just like a GError. In fact if Cogl has
been built with --enable-glib then it is safe to cast a CoglError to a GError.

Note An important detail to be aware of if you are used to using GLib's GError API is that Cogl deviates from the GLib GError
conventions in one noteable way which is that a NULL error pointer does not mean you want to ignore the details of an error, it
means you are not trying to catch any exceptional errors the function might throw which will result in the program aborting with
a log message if an error is thrown.

Functions

cogl_error_matches ()

```
CoglBool
cogl_error_matches (CoglError *error,
                    uint32_t domain,
                    int code);
```

Returns TRUE if error matches *domain* and *code* , FALSE otherwise. In particular, when error is NULL, FALSE will be
returned.

Parameters

error	A CoglError thrown by the Cogl api or NULL	
domain	The error domain	
code	The error code	

Returns

whether the *error* corresponds to the given *domain* and *code* .

cogl_error_free ()

```
void
cogl_error_free (CoglError *error);
```

Frees a CoglError and associated resources.

Parameters

error	A CoglError thrown by the Cogl api

cogl_error_copy ()

```
CoglError~*
cogl_error_copy (CoglError *error);
```

Makes a copy of *error* which can later be freed using cogl_error_free().

Parameters

error	A CoglError thrown by the Cogl api

Returns

A newly allocated CoglError initialized to match the contents of *error* .

COGL_GLIB_ERROR()

```
#define COGL_GLIB_ERROR(COGL_ERROR) ((CoglError *)COGL_ERROR)
```

Simply casts a CoglError to a CoglError

If Cogl is built with GLib support then it can safely be assumed that a CoglError is a GError and can be used directly with the GError api.

Parameters

COGL_ERROR	A CoglError thrown by the Cogl api or NULL

Types and Values

CoglError

```
typedef struct {
  uint32_t domain;
  int code;
  char *message;
} CoglError;
```

Members

uint32_t *domain*;	A high-level domain identifier for the error
int *code*;	A specific error code within a specified domain
char **message*;	A human readable error message

1.2.3 Common Types

Common Types — Types used throughout the library

Functions

| void | (*CoglFuncPtr) () |

Types and Values

	CoglVertexP2
	CoglVertexP3
	CoglVertexP2C4
	CoglVertexP3C4
	CoglVertexP2T2
	CoglVertexP3T2
	CoglVertexP2T2C4
	CoglVertexP3T2C4
enum	CoglVerticesMode

enum	CoglPixelFormat
enum	CoglBufferTarget
enum	CoglBufferBit
enum	CoglAttributeType
enum	CoglColorMask
typedef	CoglBool

Description

General types used by various Cogl functions.

Functions

CoglFuncPtr ()

```
void
(*CoglFuncPtr) (void);
```

The type used by cogl for function pointers, note that this type is used as a generic catch-all cast for function pointers and the actual arguments and return type may be different.

Types and Values

CoglVertexP2

```
typedef struct {
   float x, y;
} CoglVertexP2;
```

A convenience vertex definition that can be used with cogl_primitive_new_p2().

Members

float *x*;	The x component of a position attribute
float *y*;	The y component of a position attribute

Since 1.6

Stability Level: Unstable

CoglVertexP3

```
typedef struct {
   float x, y, z;
} CoglVertexP3;
```

A convenience vertex definition that can be used with cogl_primitive_new_p3().

Members

float *x*;	The x component of a position attribute
float *y*;	The y component of a position attribute
float *z*;	The z component of a position attribute

Since 1.6

Stability Level: Unstable

CoglVertexP2C4

```
typedef struct {
    float x, y;
    uint8_t r, g, b, a;
} CoglVertexP2C4;
```

A convenience vertex definition that can be used with cogl_primitive_new_p2c4().

Members

float *x*;	The x component of a position attribute
float *y*;	The y component of a position attribute
uint8_t *r*;	The red component of a color attribute
uint8_t *g*;	The blue component of a color attribute

	The green component of a color attribute
uint8_t *b*;	
uint8_t *a*;	The alpha component of a color attribute

Since 1.6

Stability Level: Unstable

CoglVertexP3C4

```
typedef struct {
   float x, y, z;
   uint8_t r, g, b, a;
} CoglVertexP3C4;
```

A convenience vertex definition that can be used with cogl_primitive_new_p3c4().

Members

	The x component of a position attribute
float *x*;	

float y;	The y component of a position attribute
float z;	The z component of a position attribute
uint8_t r;	The red component of a color attribute
uint8_t g;	The blue component of a color attribute
uint8_t b;	The green component of a color attribute

	The alpha component of a color attribute
uint8_t a;	

Since 1.6

Stability Level: Unstable

CoglVertexP2T2

```
typedef struct {
   float x, y;
   float s, t;
} CoglVertexP2T2;
```

A convenience vertex definition that can be used with cogl_primitive_new_p2t2().

Members

	The x component of a position attribute
float x;	
float y;	The y component of a position attribute

float *s*;	The s com- po- nent of a tex- ture co- or- di- nate at- tribute
float *t*;	The t com- po- nent of a tex- ture co- or- di- nate at- tribute

Since 1.6

Stability Level: Unstable

CoglVertexP3T2

```
typedef struct {
    float x, y, z;
    float s, t;
} CoglVertexP3T2;
```

A convenience vertex definition that can be used with cogl_primitive_new_p3t2().

Members

float *x*;	The x component of a position attribute
float *y*;	The y component of a position attribute
float *z*;	The z component of a position attribute
float *s*;	The s component of a texture coordinate attribute

	The t component of a texture coordinate attribute
float *t*;	

Since 1.6

Stability Level: Unstable

CoglVertexP2T2C4

```
typedef struct {
    float x, y;
    float s, t;
    uint8_t r, g, b, a;
} CoglVertexP2T2C4;
```

A convenience vertex definition that can be used with cogl_primitive_new_p3t2c4().

Members

	The x component of a position attribute
float *x*;	
float *y*;	The y component of a position attribute

float *s*;	The *s* component of a texture co-ordinate attribute
float *t*;	The *t* component of a texture co-ordinate attribute
uint8_t *r*;	The red component of a color attribute
uint8_t *g*;	The blue component of a color attribute

	The green component of a color attribute
uint8_t *b*;	
uint8_t *a*;	The alpha component of a color attribute

Since 1.6

Stability Level: Unstable

CoglVertexP3T2C4

```
typedef struct {
   float x, y, z;
   float s, t;
   uint8_t r, g, b, a;
} CoglVertexP3T2C4;
```

A convenience vertex definition that can be used with cogl_primitive_new_p3t2c4().

Members

	The x component of a position attribute
float *x*;	

float y;	The y component of a position attribute
float z;	The z component of a position attribute
float s;	The s component of a texture coordinate attribute
float t;	The t component of a texture coordinate attribute

uint8_t r;	The red component of a color attribute
uint8_t g;	The blue component of a color attribute
uint8_t b;	The green component of a color attribute
uint8_t a;	The alpha component of a color attribute

Since 1.6

Stability Level: Unstable

enum CoglVerticesMode

Different ways of interpreting vertices when drawing.

Members

COGL_VERTICES_MODE_POINTS	FIXME, equivalent to GL_POINTS
COGL_VERTICES_MODE_LINES	FIXME, equivalent to GL_LINES
COGL_VERTICES_MODE_LINE_LOOP	FIXME, equivalent to GL_LINE_LOOP
COGL_VERTICES_MODE_LINE_STRIP	FIXME, equivalent to GL_LINE_STRIP

COGL_VERTICES_MODE_TRIANGLES	FIXME, equiv-a-lent to GL_TRIANGLES
COGL_VERTICES_MODE_TRIANGLE_STRIP	FIXME, equiv-a-lent to GL_TRIANGLE_STRIP
COGL_VERTICES_MODE_TRIANGLE_FAN	FIXME, equiv-a-lent to GL_TRIANGLE_FAN

Since 1.0

enum CoglPixelFormat

Pixel formats used by Cogl. For the formats with a byte per component, the order of the components specify the order in increasing memory addresses. So for example COGL_PIXEL_FORMAT_RGB_888 would have the red component in the lowest address, green in the next address and blue after that regardless of the endianness of the system.

For the formats with non byte aligned components the component order specifies the order within a 16-bit or 32-bit number from most significant bit to least significant. So for COGL_PIXEL_FORMAT_RGB_565, the red component would be in bits 11-15, the green component would be in 6-11 and the blue component would be in 1-5. Therefore the order in memory depends on the endianness of the system.

Members

COGL_PIXEL_FORMAT_ANY	Any format
COGL_PIXEL_FORMAT_A_8	8 bits alpha mask
COGL_PIXEL_FORMAT_RG_88	RG, 16 bits. Note that red-green textures are only available if COGL_FEATURE_ID_TEXTURE_RG is advertised. See cogl_texture_set_components() for details.
COGL_PIXEL_FORMAT_RGB_565	RGB, 16 bits
COGL_PIXEL_FORMAT_RGBA_4444	RGBA, 16 bits
COGL_PIXEL_FORMAT_RGBA_4444_PRE	Premultiplied RGBA, 16 bits
COGL_PIXEL_FORMAT_RGBA_5551	RGBA, 16 bits
COGL_PIXEL_FORMAT_RGBA_5551_PRE	Premultiplied RGBA, 16 bits

COGL_PIXEL_FORMAT_RGB_888	RGB, 24 bits
COGL_PIXEL_FORMAT_BGR_888	BGR, 24 bits
COGL_PIXEL_FORMAT_RGBA_8888	RGBA, 32 bits
COGL_PIXEL_FORMAT_BGRA_8888	BGRA, 32 bits
COGL_PIXEL_FORMAT_ARGB_8888	ARGB, 32 bits
COGL_PIXEL_FORMAT_ABGR_8888	ABGR, 32 bits
COGL_PIXEL_FORMAT_RGBA_8888_PRE	Premultiplied RGBA, 32 bits
COGL_PIXEL_FORMAT_BGRA_8888_PRE	Premultiplied BGRA, 32 bits
COGL_PIXEL_FORMAT_ARGB_8888_PRE	Premultiplied ARGB, 32 bits
COGL_PIXEL_FORMAT_ABGR_8888_PRE	Premultiplied ABGR, 32 bits
COGL_PIXEL_FORMAT_RGBA_1010102	RGBA, 32 bits, 10 bpc
COGL_PIXEL_FORMAT_BGRA_1010102	BGRA, 32 bits, 10 bpc
COGL_PIXEL_FORMAT_ARGB_2101010	ARGB, 32 bits, 10 bpc
COGL_PIXEL_FORMAT_ABGR_2101010	ABGR, 32 bits, 10 bpc

COGL_PIXEL_FORMAT_RGBA_1010102_PRE	Premultiplied RGBA, 32 bits, 10 bpc
COGL_PIXEL_FORMAT_BGRA_1010102_PRE	Premultiplied BGRA, 32 bits, 10 bpc
COGL_PIXEL_FORMAT_ARGB_2101010_PRE	Premultiplied ARGB, 32 bits, 10 bpc
COGL_PIXEL_FORMAT_ABGR_2101010_PRE	Premultiplied ABGR, 32 bits, 10 bpc
COGL_PIXEL_FORMAT_DEPTH_16	Depth, 16 bits
COGL_PIXEL_FORMAT_DEPTH_32	Depth, 32 bits
COGL_PIXEL_FORMAT_DEPTH_24_STENCIL_8	Depth/Stencil, 24/8 bits

Since 0.8

enum CoglBufferTarget

Target flags for FBOs.

Members

COGL_WINDOW_BUFFER	FIXME
COGL_OFFSCREEN_BUFFER	FIXME

Since 0.8

enum CoglBufferBit

Types of auxiliary buffers

Members

COGL_BUFFER_BIT_COLOR	Selects the primary color buffer
COGL_BUFFER_BIT_DEPTH	Selects the depth buffer
COGL_BUFFER_BIT_STENCIL	Selects the stencil buffer

Since 1.0

enum CoglAttributeType

Data types for the components of a vertex attribute.

Members

COGL_ATTRIBUTE_TYPE_BYTE	Data is the same size of a byte
COGL_ATTRIBUTE_TYPE_UNSIGNED_BYTE	Data is the same size of an unsigned byte
COGL_ATTRIBUTE_TYPE_SHORT	Data is the same size of a short integer

| COGL_ATTRIBUTE_TYPE_UNSIGNED_SHORT | Data is the same size of an unsigned short integer |
| COGL_ATTRIBUTE_TYPE_FLOAT | Data is the same size of a float |

Since 1.0

enum CoglColorMask

Defines a bit mask of color channels. This can be used with cogl_pipeline_set_color_mask() for example to define which color channels should be written to the current framebuffer when drawing something.

Members

COGL_COLOR_MASK_NONE	None of the color channels are masked
COGL_COLOR_MASK_RED	Masks the red color channel
COGL_COLOR_MASK_GREEN	Masks the green color channel

COGL_COLOR_MASK_BLUE	Masks the blue color channel
COGL_COLOR_MASK_ALPHA	Masks the alpha color channel
COGL_COLOR_MASK_ALL	All of the color channels are masked

CoglBool

```
typedef int CoglBool;
```

A boolean data type used throughout the Cogl C api. This should be used in conjunction with the TRUE and FALSE macro defines for setting and testing boolean values.

Since 2.0

Stability Level: Stable

1.3   Setting Up A Drawing Context

1.3.1   CoglRenderer: Connect to a backend renderer

CoglRenderer: Connect to a backend renderer — Choosing a means to render

Functions

CoglBool	cogl_is_renderer ()
CoglRenderer *	cogl_renderer_new ()
int	cogl_renderer_get_n_fragment_texture_units ()
CoglBool	cogl_renderer_connect ()
void	cogl_renderer_set_winsys_id ()
CoglWinsysID	cogl_renderer_get_winsys_id ()
void	cogl_renderer_add_constraint ()
void	cogl_renderer_remove_constraint ()
void	cogl_xlib_renderer_set_foreign_display ()
Display *	cogl_xlib_renderer_get_foreign_display ()
CoglFilterReturn	(*CoglXlibFilterFunc) ()
void	cogl_xlib_renderer_add_filter ()
void	cogl_xlib_renderer_remove_filter ()

CoglFilterReturn	cogl_xlib_renderer_handle_event ()
CoglFilterReturn	(*CoglWin32FilterFunc) ()
void	cogl_win32_renderer_add_filter ()
void	cogl_win32_renderer_remove_filter ()
CoglFilterReturn	cogl_win32_renderer_handle_event ()
void	cogl_win32_renderer_set_event_retrieval_enabled ()
void	cogl_wayland_renderer_set_foreign_display ()
void	cogl_wayland_renderer_set_event_dispatch_enabled ()
struct wl_display *	cogl_wayland_renderer_get_display ()

Types and Values

	CoglRenderer
enum	CoglWinsysID
enum	CoglRendererConstraint
enum	CoglFilterReturn

Description

A CoglRenderer represents a means to render. It encapsulates the selection of an underlying driver, such as OpenGL or OpenGL-ES and a selection of a window system binding API such as GLX, or EGL or WGL.

A CoglRenderer has two states, "unconnected" and "connected". When a renderer is first instantiated using cogl_renderer_new() it is unconnected so that it can be configured and constraints can be specified for how the backend driver and window system should be chosen.

After configuration a CoglRenderer can (optionally) be explicitly connected using cogl_renderer_connect() which allows for the handling of connection errors so that fallback configurations can be tried if necessary. Applications that don't support any fallbacks though can skip using cogl_renderer_connect() and leave Cogl to automatically connect the renderer.

Once you have a configured CoglRenderer it can be used to create a CoglDisplay object using cogl_display_new().

> **Note** Many applications don't need to explicitly use cogl_renderer_new() or cogl_display_new() and can just jump straight to cogl_context_new() and pass a NULL display argument so Cogl will automatically connect and setup a renderer and display.

Functions

cogl_is_renderer ()

```
CoglBool
cogl_is_renderer (void *object);
```

Determines if the given *object* is a CoglRenderer

Parameters

| object | A CoglObject pointer | |

Returns

TRUE if *object* is a CoglRenderer, else FALSE.

Since 1.10

Stability Level: Unstable

cogl_renderer_new ()

```
CoglRenderer~*
cogl_renderer_new (void);
```

Instantiates a new (unconnected) CoglRenderer object. A CoglRenderer represents a means to render. It encapsulates the selection of an underlying driver, such as OpenGL or OpenGL-ES and a selection of a window system binding API such as GLX, or EGL or WGL.

While the renderer is unconnected it can be configured so that applications may specify backend constraints, such as "must use x11" for example via cogl_renderer_add_constraint().

There are also some platform specific configuration apis such as cogl_xlib_renderer_set_foreign_display() that may also be used while the renderer is unconnected.

Once the renderer has been configured, then it may (optionally) be explicitly connected using cogl_renderer_connect() which allows errors to be handled gracefully and potentially fallback configurations can be tried out if there are initial failures.

If a renderer is not explicitly connected then cogl_display_new() will automatically connect the renderer for you. If you don't have any code to deal with error/fallback situations then its fine to just let Cogl do the connection for you.

Once you have setup your renderer then the next step is to create a CoglDisplay using cogl_display_new().

Note Many applications don't need to explicitly use cogl_renderer_new() or cogl_display_new() and can just jump straight to cogl_context_new() and pass a NULL display argument so Cogl will automatically connect and setup a renderer and display.

Returns

A newly created CoglRenderer.

[transfer full]

Since 1.10

Stability Level: Unstable

cogl_renderer_get_n_fragment_texture_units ()

```
int
cogl_renderer_get_n_fragment_texture_units
                        (CoglRenderer *renderer);
```

Queries how many texture units can be used from fragment programs

Parameters

| renderer | A CoglRenderer | |

Returns

the number of texture image units.

Since 1.8

Stability Level: Unstable

cogl_renderer_connect ()

```
CoglBool
cogl_renderer_connect (CoglRenderer *renderer,
                       CoglError **error);
```

Connects the configured *renderer*. Renderer connection isn't a very active process, it basically just means validating that any given constraint criteria can be satisfied and that a usable driver and window system backend can be found.

Parameters

renderer	An unconnected CoglRenderer	
error	a pointer to a CoglError for reporting exceptions	

Returns

TRUE if there was no error while connecting the given *renderer*. FALSE if there was an error.

Since 1.10

Stability Level: Unstable

cogl_renderer_set_winsys_id ()

```
void
cogl_renderer_set_winsys_id (CoglRenderer *renderer,
                             CoglWinsysID winsys_id);
```

This allows you to explicitly select a winsys backend to use instead of letting Cogl automatically select a backend.

if you select an unsupported backend then cogl_renderer_connect() will fail and report an error.

This may only be called on an un-connected CoglRenderer.

Parameters

renderer	A CoglRenderer	
winsys_id	An ID of the winsys you explicitly want to use.	

cogl_renderer_get_winsys_id ()

```
CoglWinsysID
cogl_renderer_get_winsys_id (CoglRenderer *renderer);
```

Queries which window system backend Cogl has chosen to use.

This may only be called on a connected CoglRenderer.

Parameters

renderer	A CoglRenderer	

Returns

The CoglWinsysID corresponding to the chosen window system backend.

cogl_renderer_add_constraint ()

```
void
cogl_renderer_add_constraint (CoglRenderer *renderer,
                              CoglRendererConstraint constraint);
```

This adds a renderer selection *constraint* .

Applications should ideally minimize how many of these constraints they depend on to ensure maximum portability.

Parameters

renderer	An unconnected CoglRenderer	
constraint	A CoglRendererConstraint to add	

Since 1.10

Stability Level: Unstable

cogl_renderer_remove_constraint ()

```
void
cogl_renderer_remove_constraint (CoglRenderer *renderer,
                                 CoglRendererConstraint constraint);
```

This removes a renderer selection *constraint* .

Applications should ideally minimize how many of these constraints they depend on to ensure maximum portability.

Parameters

renderer	An unconnected CoglRenderer	
constraint	A CoglRendererConstraint to remove	

Since 1.10

Stability Level: Unstable

cogl_xlib_renderer_set_foreign_display ()

```
void
cogl_xlib_renderer_set_foreign_display
                              (CoglRenderer *renderer,
                               Display *display);
```

cogl_xlib_renderer_get_foreign_display ()

```
Display~*
cogl_xlib_renderer_get_foreign_display
                          (CoglRenderer *renderer);
```

CoglXlibFilterFunc ()

```
CoglFilterReturn
(*CoglXlibFilterFunc) (XEvent *event,
                       void *data);
```

cogl_xlib_renderer_add_filter ()

```
void
cogl_xlib_renderer_add_filter (CoglRenderer *renderer,
                               CoglXlibFilterFunc func,
                               void *data);
```

cogl_xlib_renderer_remove_filter ()

```
void
cogl_xlib_renderer_remove_filter (CoglRenderer *renderer,
                                  CoglXlibFilterFunc func,
                                  void *data);
```

cogl_xlib_renderer_handle_event ()

```
CoglFilterReturn
cogl_xlib_renderer_handle_event (CoglRenderer *renderer,
                                 XEvent *event);
```

CoglWin32FilterFunc ()

```
CoglFilterReturn
(*CoglWin32FilterFunc) (MSG *message,
                        void *data);
```

A callback function that can be registered with cogl_win32_renderer_add_filter(). The function should return COGL_FILTER_REMOVE if it wants to prevent further processing or COGL_FILTER_CONTINUE otherwise.

Parameters

message	A pointer to a win32 MSG struct
data	The data that was given when the filter was added

cogl_win32_renderer_add_filter ()

```
void
cogl_win32_renderer_add_filter (CoglRenderer *renderer,
                                CoglWin32FilterFunc func,
                                void *data);
```

Adds a callback function that will receive all native events. The function can stop further processing of the event by return COGL_FILTER_REMOVE.

Parameters

renderer	a CoglRenderer	
func	the callback function	
data	user data passed to *func* when called	

cogl_win32_renderer_remove_filter ()

```
void
cogl_win32_renderer_remove_filter (CoglRenderer *renderer,
                                   CoglWin32FilterFunc func,
                                   void *data);
```

Removes a callback that was previously added with cogl_win32_renderer_add_filter().

Parameters

renderer	a CoglRenderer	
func	the callback function	
data	user data given when the callback was installed	

cogl_win32_renderer_handle_event ()

```
CoglFilterReturn
cogl_win32_renderer_handle_event (CoglRenderer *renderer,
                                  MSG *message);
```

This function processes a single event; it can be used to hook into external event retrieval (for example that done by Clutter or GDK).

Parameters

renderer	a CoglRenderer	
message	A pointer to a win32 MSG struct	

Returns

CoglFilterReturn. COGL_FILTER_REMOVE indicates that Cogl has internally handled the event and the caller should do no further processing. COGL_FILTER_CONTINUE indicates that Cogl is either not interested in the event, or has used the event to update internal state without taking any exclusive action.

cogl_win32_renderer_set_event_retrieval_enabled ()

```
void
cogl_win32_renderer_set_event_retrieval_enabled
                                (CoglRenderer *renderer,
                                 CoglBool enable);
```

Sets whether Cogl should automatically retrieve messages from Windows. It defaults to TRUE. It can be set to FALSE if the application wants to handle its own message retrieval. Note that Cogl still needs to see all of the messages to function properly so the application should call cogl_win32_renderer_handle_event() for each message if it disables automatic event retrieval.

Parameters

renderer	a CoglRenderer	
enable	The new value	

Since 1.16

Stability Level: Unstable

cogl_wayland_renderer_set_foreign_display ()

```
void
cogl_wayland_renderer_set_foreign_display
                                (CoglRenderer *renderer,
                                 struct wl_display *display);
```

Allows you to explicitly control what Wayland display you want Cogl to work with instead of leaving Cogl to automatically connect to a wayland compositor.

Parameters

renderer	A CoglRenderer	
display	A Wayland display	

Since 1.8

Stability Level: Unstable

cogl_wayland_renderer_set_event_dispatch_enabled ()

```
void
cogl_wayland_renderer_set_event_dispatch_enabled
                                (CoglRenderer *renderer,
                                 CoglBool enable);
```

Sets whether Cogl should handle calling wl_display_dispatch() and wl_display_flush() as part of its main loop integration via cogl_poll_renderer_get_info() and cogl_poll_renderer_dispatch(). The default value is TRUE. When it is enabled the application can register listeners for Wayland interfaces and the callbacks will be invoked during cogl_poll_renderer_dispatch(). If the application wants to integrate with its own code that is already handling reading from the Wayland display socket, it should disable this to avoid having competing code read from the socket.

Parameters

renderer	A CoglRenderer	
enable	The new value	

Since 1.16

Stability Level: Unstable

cogl_wayland_renderer_get_display ()

```
struct wl_display~*
cogl_wayland_renderer_get_display (CoglRenderer *renderer);
```

Retrieves the Wayland display that Cogl is using. If a foreign display has been specified using cogl_wayland_renderer_set_foreign_display then that display will be returned. If no foreign display has been specified then the display that Cogl creates internally will be returned unless the renderer has not yet been connected (either implicitly or explicitly by calling cogl_renderer_connect()) in which case NULL is returned.

Parameters

renderer	A CoglRenderer	

Returns

The wayland display currently associated with *renderer* , or NULL if the renderer hasn't yet been connected and no foreign display has been specified.

Since 1.8

Stability Level: Unstable

Types and Values

CoglRenderer

```
typedef struct _CoglRenderer CoglRenderer;
```

enum CoglWinsysID

Identifies specific window system backends that Cogl supports.

These can be used to query what backend Cogl is using or to try and explicitly select a backend to use.

Members

COGL_WINSYS_ID_ANY	Implies no preference for which backend is used
COGL_WINSYS_ID_STUB	Use the no-op stub backend
COGL_WINSYS_ID_GLX	Use the GLX window system binding API
COGL_WINSYS_ID_EGL_XLIB	Use EGL with the X window system via XLib
COGL_WINSYS_ID_EGL_NULL	Use EGL with the PowerVR NULL window system
COGL_WINSYS_ID_EGL_GDL	Use EGL with the GDL platform

COGL_WINSYS_ID_EGL_WAYLAND	Use EGL with the Wayland window system
COGL_WINSYS_ID_EGL_KMS	Use EGL with the KMS platform
COGL_WINSYS_ID_EGL_ANDROID	Use EGL with the Android platform
COGL_WINSYS_ID_WGL	Use the Microsoft Windows WGL binding API
COGL_WINSYS_ID_SDL	Use the SDL window system

enum CoglRendererConstraint

These constraint flags are hard-coded features of the different renderer backends. Sometimes a platform may support multiple rendering options which Cogl will usually choose from automatically. Some of these features are important to higher level applications and frameworks though, such as whether a renderer is X11 based because an application might only support X11 based input handling. An application might also need to ensure EGL is used internally too if they depend on access to an EGLDisplay for some purpose.

Applications should ideally minimize how many of these constraints they depend on to ensure maximum portability.

Members

COGL_RENDERER_CONSTRAINT_USES_X11	Require the renderer to be X11 based
COGL_RENDERER_CONSTRAINT_USES_XLIB	Require the renderer to be X11 based and use Xlib
COGL_RENDERER_CONSTRAINT_USES_EGL	Require the renderer to be EGL based

COGL_RENDERER_CONSTRAINT_SUPPORTS_COGL_GLES2	Require that the renderer supports creating a CoglGLES2Context via cogl_gles2_context_new(). This can be used to integrate GLES 2.0 code into Cogl based applications.

Since 1.10

Stability Level: Unstable

enum CoglFilterReturn

Return values for the CoglXlibFilterFunc and CoglWin32FilterFunc functions.

Members

COGL_FILTER_CONTINUE	The event was not handled, continues the processing

COGL_FILTER_REMOVE	Remove the event, stops the pro- cess- ing

Stability Level: Unstable

1.3.2 CoglOnscreenTemplate: Describe a template for onscreen framebuffers

CoglOnscreenTemplate: Describe a template for onscreen framebuffers —

Functions

CoglBool	cogl_is_onscreen_template ()
CoglOnscreenTemplate *	cogl_onscreen_template_new ()
void	cogl_onscreen_template_set_has_alpha ()
void	cogl_onscreen_template_set_swap_throttled ()
void	cogl_onscreen_template_set_samples_per_pixel ()

Types and Values

	CoglOnscreenTemplate

Description

Functions

cogl_is_onscreen_template ()

```
CoglBool
cogl_is_onscreen_template (void *object);
```

Gets whether the given object references a CoglOnscreenTemplate.

Parameters

object	A CoglObject pointer	

Returns

TRUE if the object references a CoglOnscreenTemplate and FALSE otherwise.

Since 1.10

Stability Level: Unstable

cogl_onscreen_template_new ()

```
CoglOnscreenTemplate~*
cogl_onscreen_template_new (void);
```

cogl_onscreen_template_set_has_alpha ()

```
void
cogl_onscreen_template_set_has_alpha (CoglOnscreenTemplate *onscreen_template,
                                      CoglBool has_alpha);
```

Requests that any future CoglOnscreen framebuffers derived from this template should have an alpha channel if `has_alpha` is TRUE. If `has_alpha` is FALSE then future framebuffers derived from this template aren't required to have an alpha channel, although Cogl may choose to ignore this and allocate a redundant alpha channel.

By default a template does not request an alpha component.

Parameters

onscreen_template	A CoglOnscreenTemplate template framebuffer	
has_alpha	Whether an alpha channel is required	

Since 1.16

Stability Level: Unstable

cogl_onscreen_template_set_swap_throttled ()

```
void
cogl_onscreen_template_set_swap_throttled
                          (CoglOnscreenTemplate *onscreen_template,
                           CoglBool throttled);
```

Requests that any future CoglOnscreen framebuffers derived from this template should enable or disable swap throttling according to the given `throttled` argument.

Parameters

onscreen_template	A CoglOnscreenTemplate template framebuffer	
throttled	Whether throttling should be enabled	

Since 1.10

Stability Level: Unstable

cogl_onscreen_template_set_samples_per_pixel ()

```
void
cogl_onscreen_template_set_samples_per_pixel
                          (CoglOnscreenTemplate *onscreen_template,
                           int n);
```

Requires that any future CoglOnscreen framebuffers derived from this template must support making at least n samples per pixel which will all contribute to the final resolved color for that pixel.

By default this value is usually set to 0 and that is referred to as "single-sample" rendering. A value of 1 or greater is referred to as "multisample" rendering.

Note There are some semantic differences between single-sample rendering and multisampling with just 1 point sample such as it being redundant to use the cogl_framebuffer_resolve_samples() and cogl_framebuffer_resolve_samples_region() apis with single-sample rendering.

Parameters

onscreen_template	A CoglOnscreenTemplate template framebuffer	
n	The minimum number of samples per pixel	

Since 1.10

Stability Level: Unstable

Types and Values

CoglOnscreenTemplate

```
typedef struct _CoglOnscreenTemplate CoglOnscreenTemplate;
```

1.3.3 CoglDisplay: Setup a display pipeline

CoglDisplay: Setup a display pipeline — Common aspects of a display pipeline

Functions

CoglBool	cogl_is_display ()
CoglDisplay *	cogl_display_new ()
CoglRenderer *	cogl_display_get_renderer ()
CoglBool	cogl_display_setup ()
void	cogl_gdl_display_set_plane ()
void	cogl_wayland_display_set_compositor_display ()

Types and Values

	CoglDisplay

Description

The basic intention for this object is to let the application configure common display preferences before creating a context, and there are a few different aspects to this...

Firstly there are options directly relating to the physical display pipeline that is currently being used including the digital to analogue conversion hardware and the screens the user sees.

Another aspect is that display options may constrain or affect how onscreen framebuffers should later be configured. The original rationale for the display object in fact was to let us handle GLX and EGLs requirements that framebuffers must be "compatible" with the config associated with the current context meaning we have to force the user to describe how they would like to create their onscreen windows before we can choose a suitable fbconfig and create a GLContext.

Functions

cogl_is_display ()

```
CoglBool
cogl_is_display (void *object);
```

Gets whether the given object references a CoglDisplay.

Parameters

object	A CoglObject pointer	

Returns

TRUE if the object references a CoglDisplay and FALSE otherwise.

Since 1.10

Stability Level: Unstable

cogl_display_new ()

```
CoglDisplay~*
cogl_display_new (CoglRenderer *renderer,
                  CoglOnscreenTemplate *onscreen_template);
```

Explicitly allocates a new CoglDisplay object to encapsulate the common state of the display pipeline that applies to the whole application.

Note Many applications don't need to explicitly use cogl_display_new() and can just jump straight to cogl_context_new() and pass a NULL display argument so Cogl will automatically connect and setup a renderer and display.

A *display* can only be made for a specific choice of renderer which is why this takes the *renderer* argument.

A common use for explicitly allocating a display object is to define a template for allocating onscreen framebuffers which is what the *onscreen_template* argument is for, or alternatively you can use cogl_display_set_onscreen_template().

When a display is first allocated via cogl_display_new() it is in a mutable configuration mode. It's designed this way so we can extend the apis available for configuring a display without requiring huge numbers of constructor arguments.

When you have finished configuring a display object you can optionally call cogl_display_setup() to explicitly apply the configuration and check for errors. Alternaitvely you can pass the display to cogl_context_new() and Cogl will implicitly apply your configuration but if there are errors then the application will abort with a message. For simple applications with no fallback options then relying on the implicit setup can be fine.

Parameters

renderer	A CoglRenderer	
onscreen_template	A CoglOnscreenTemplate	

Returns

A newly allocated CoglDisplay object in a mutable configuration mode.

[transfer full]

Since 1.10

Stability Level: Unstable

cogl_display_get_renderer ()

```
CoglRenderer~*
cogl_display_get_renderer (CoglDisplay *display);
```

Queries the CoglRenderer associated with the given `display` .

Parameters

display	a CoglDisplay	

Returns

The associated CoglRenderer.

[transfer none]

Since 1.10

Stability Level: Unstable

cogl_display_setup ()

```
CoglBool
cogl_display_setup (CoglDisplay *display,
                    CoglError **error);
```

Explicitly sets up the given `display` object. Use of this api is optional since Cogl will internally setup the display if not done explicitly.

When a display is first allocated via cogl_display_new() it is in a mutable configuration mode. This allows us to extend the apis available for configuring a display without requiring huge numbers of constructor arguments.

Its possible to request a configuration that might not be supportable on the current system and so this api provides a means to apply the configuration explicitly but if it fails then an exception will be returned so you can handle the error gracefully and perhaps fall back to an alternative configuration.

If you instead rely on Cogl implicitly calling cogl_display_setup() for you then if there is an error with the configuration you won't get an opportunity to handle that and the application may abort with a message. For simple applications that don't have any fallback options this behaviour may be fine.

Parameters

display	a CoglDisplay	
error	return location for a CoglError	

Returns

Returns TRUE if there was no error, else it returns FALSE and returns an exception via `error`.

Since 1.10

Stability Level: Unstable

cogl_gdl_display_set_plane ()

```
void
cogl_gdl_display_set_plane (CoglDisplay *display,
                            gdl_plane_id_t plane);
```

Request that Cogl output to a specific GDL overlay `plane`.

Parameters

display	a CoglDisplay	
plane	the GDL plane id	

Since 1.10

Stability Level: Unstable

cogl_wayland_display_set_compositor_display ()

```
void
cogl_wayland_display_set_compositor_display
                            (CoglDisplay *display,
                             struct wl_display *wayland_display);
```

Informs Cogl of a compositor's Wayland display pointer. This enables Cogl to register private wayland extensions required to pass buffers between the clients and compositor.

Parameters

display	a CoglDisplay	
wayland_display	A compositor's Wayland display pointer	

Since 1.10

Stability Level: Unstable

Types and Values

CoglDisplay

```
typedef struct _CoglDisplay CoglDisplay;
```

1.3.4 The Top-Level Context

The Top-Level Context — The top level application context.

Functions

CoglBool	cogl_is_context ()
CoglContext *	cogl_context_new ()
CoglDisplay *	cogl_context_get_display ()
CoglBool	cogl_has_feature ()
CoglBool	cogl_has_features ()
void	(*CoglFeatureCallback) ()
void	cogl_foreach_feature ()

Types and Values

	CoglContext
enum	CoglFeatureID
enum	CoglReadPixelsFlags

Description

A CoglContext is the top most sandbox of Cogl state for an application or toolkit. Its main purpose is to act as a sandbox for the memory management of state objects. Normally an application will only create a single context since there is no way to share resources between contexts.

For those familiar with OpenGL or perhaps Cairo it should be understood that unlike these APIs a Cogl context isn't a rendering context as such. In other words Cogl doesn't aim to provide a state machine style model for configuring rendering parameters. Most rendering state in Cogl is directly associated with user managed objects called pipelines and geometry is drawn with a specific pipeline object to a framebuffer object and those 3 things fully define the state for drawing. This is an important part of Cogl's design since it helps you write orthogonal rendering components that can all access the same GPU without having to worry about what state other components have left you with.

Note
Cogl does not maintain internal references to the context for resources that depend on the context so applications. This is to help applications control the lifetime a context without us needing to introduce special api to handle the breakup of internal circular references due to internal resources and caches associated with the context. One a context has been destroyed then all directly or indirectly dependant resources will be in an inconsistent state and should not be manipulated or queried in any way. For applications that rely on the operating system to clean up resources this policy shouldn't affect them, but for applications that need to carefully destroy and re-create Cogl contexts multiple times throughout their lifetime (such as Android applications) they should be careful to destroy all context dependant resources, such as framebuffers or textures etc before unrefing and destroying the context.

Functions

cogl_is_context ()

```
CoglBool
cogl_is_context (void *object);
```

Gets whether the given object references an existing context object.

Parameters

object	An object or NULL	

Returns

TRUE if the `object` references a CoglContext, FALSE otherwise

Since 1.10

Stability Level: Unstable

cogl_context_new ()

```
CoglContext~*
cogl_context_new (CoglDisplay *display,
                  CoglError **error);
```

Creates a new CoglContext which acts as an application sandbox for any state objects that are allocated.

Parameters

display	A CoglDisplay pointer.	*[allow-none]*
error	A CoglError return location.	

Returns

A newly allocated CoglContext.

[transfer full]

Since 1.8

Stability Level: Unstable

cogl_context_get_display ()

```
CoglDisplay~*
cogl_context_get_display (CoglContext *context);
```

Retrieves the CoglDisplay that is internally associated with the given `context` . This will return the same CoglDisplay that was passed to cogl_context_new() or if NULL was passed to cogl_context_new() then this function returns a pointer to the display that was automatically setup internally.

Parameters

context	A CoglContext pointer	

Returns

The CoglDisplay associated with the given `context` .

[transfer none]

Since 1.8

Stability Level: Unstable

cogl_has_feature ()

```
CoglBool
cogl_has_feature (CoglContext *context,
                  CoglFeatureID feature);
```

Checks if a given *feature* is currently available

Cogl does not aim to be a lowest common denominator API, it aims to expose all the interesting features of GPUs to application which means applications have some responsibility to explicitly check that certain features are available before depending on them.

Parameters

context	A CoglContext pointer	
feature	A CoglFeatureID	

Returns

TRUE if the *feature* is currently supported or FALSE if not.

Since 1.10

Stability Level: Unstable

cogl_has_features ()

```
CoglBool
cogl_has_features (CoglContext *context,
                   ...);
```

Checks if a list of features are all currently available.

This checks all of the listed features using cogl_has_feature() and returns TRUE if all the features are available or FALSE otherwise.

Parameters

context	A CoglContext pointer	
...	A 0 terminated list of CoglFeatureIDs	

Returns

TRUE if all the features are available, FALSE otherwise.

Since 1.10

Stability Level: Unstable

CoglFeatureCallback ()

```
void
(*CoglFeatureCallback) (CoglFeatureID feature,
                        void *user_data);
```

A callback used with cogl_foreach_feature() for enumerating all context level features supported by Cogl.

Parameters

feature	A single feature currently supported by Cogl	
user_data	A private pointer passed to cogl_foreach_feature().	

Since 0.10

Stability Level: Unstable

cogl_foreach_feature ()

```
void
cogl_foreach_feature (CoglContext *context,
                      CoglFeatureCallback callback,
                      void *user_data);
```

Iterates through all the context level features currently supported for a given *context* and for each feature *callback* is called.

Parameters

context	A CoglContext pointer	
callback	A CoglFeatureCallback called for each supported feature.	*[scope call]*
user_data	Private data to pass to the callback.	*[closure]*

Since 1.10

Stability Level: Unstable

Types and Values

CoglContext

```
typedef struct _CoglContext CoglContext;
```

enum CoglFeatureID

All the capabilities that can vary between different GPUs supported by Cogl. Applications that depend on any of these features should explicitly check for them using cogl_has_feature() or cogl_has_features().

Members

COGL_FEATURE_ID_TEXTURE_NPOT_BASIC	The hardware supports non power of two textures, but you also need to check the COGL_FEATURE_ID_TEXTURE_NPOT_MIPMAP and COGL_FEATURE_ID_TEXTURE_NPOT_REPEAT features to know if the hardware supports npot texture mipmaps or repeat modes other than COGL_PIPELINE_WRAP_MODE_CLAMP_TO_EDGE respectively.

COGL_FEATURE_ID_TEXTURE_NPOT_MIPMAP	Mipmapping is supported in conjuntion with non power of two textures.
COGL_FEATURE_ID_TEXTURE_NPOT_REPEAT	Repeat modes other than COGL_PIPELINE_WRAP_MODE_CLAMP_TO_ED are supported by the hardware.
COGL_FEATURE_ID_TEXTURE_NPOT	Non power of two textures are supported by the hardware. This is a equivalent to the COGL_FEATURE_ID_TEXTURE_NPOT_BASIC, COGL_FEATURE_ID_TEXTURE_NPOT_MIPMAP and COGL_FEATURE_ID_TEXTURE_NPOT_REPEAT features combined.

COGL_FEATURE_ID_TEXTURE_RECTANGLE	Support for rectangular textures with non-normalized texture coordinates.
COGL_FEATURE_ID_TEXTURE_3D	3D texture support
COGL_FEATURE_ID_GLSL	GLSL support
COGL_FEATURE_ID_OFFSCREEN	Offscreen rendering support
COGL_FEATURE_ID_OFFSCREEN_MULTISAMPLE	Multisample support for offscreen framebuffers
COGL_FEATURE_ID_ONSCREEN_MULTIPLE	Multiple onscreen framebuffers supported.
COGL_FEATURE_ID_UNSIGNED_INT_INDICES	Set if COGL_INDICES_TYPE_UNSIGNED_INT is supported in cogl_indices_new().
COGL_FEATURE_ID_DEPTH_RANGE	cogl_pipeline_set_depth_range() support

COGL_FEATURE_ID_POINT_SPRITE	Whether cogl_pipeline_set_layer_point_sprite_coords_enabled() is supported.
COGL_FEATURE_ID_MAP_BUFFER_FOR_READ	Whether cogl_buffer_map() is supported with CoglBufferAccess including read support.
COGL_FEATURE_ID_MAP_BUFFER_FOR_WRITE	Whether cogl_buffer_map() is supported with CoglBufferAccess including write support.
COGL_FEATURE_ID_MIRRORED_REPEAT	Whether COGL_PIPELINE_WRAP_MODE_MIRRORED_REP is supported.
COGL_FEATURE_ID_GLES2_CONTEXT	Whether creating new GLES2 contexts is suported.

COGL_FEATURE_ID_DEPTH_TEXTURE	Whether CoglFramebuffer support rendering the depth buffer to a texture.
COGL_FEATURE_ID_PRESENTATION_TIME	Whether frame presentation time stamps will be recorded in CoglFrameInfo objects.
COGL_FEATURE_ID_FENCE	
COGL_FEATURE_ID_PER_VERTEX_POINT_SIZE	Whether cogl_point_size_in can be used as an attribute to set a per-vertex point size.

COGL_FEATURE_ID_TEXTURE_RG	Support for COGL_TEXTURE_COMPONENTS_RG as the internal components of a texture.

Since 1.10

enum CoglReadPixelsFlags

Flags for cogl_framebuffer_read_pixels_into_bitmap()

Members

COGL_READ_PIXELS_COLOR_BUFFER	Read from the color buffer

Since 1.0

1.4   Setting Up A GPU Pipeline

1.4.1   Blend Strings

Blend Strings — A simple syntax and grammar for describing blending and texture combining functions.

Cogl Blend Strings

Describing GPU blending and texture combining states is rather awkward to do in a consise but also readable fashion. Cogl helps by supporting string based descriptions using a simple syntax.

1.4.2   Some examples

Here is an example used for blending:

```
"RGBA = ADD (SRC_COLOR * (SRC_COLOR[A]), DST_COLOR * (1-SRC_COLOR[A]))"
```

In OpenGL terms this replaces glBlendFunc[Separate] and glBlendEquation[Separate]

Actually in this case it's more verbose than the GL equivalent:

```
glBlendFunc (GL_SRC_ALPHA, GL_ONE_MINUS_SRC_ALPHA);
```

But unless you are familiar with OpenGL or refer to its API documentation you wouldn't know that the default function used by OpenGL is GL_FUNC_ADD nor would you know that the above arguments determine what the source color and destination color will be multiplied by before being adding.

Here is an example used for texture combining:

```
"RGB = REPLACE (PREVIOUS)"
"A = MODULATE (PREVIOUS, TEXTURE)"
```

In OpenGL terms this replaces glTexEnv, and the above example is equivalent to this OpenGL code:

```
glTexEnvi (GL_TEXTURE_ENV, GL_TEXTURE_ENV_MODE, GL_COMBINE);
glTexEnvi (GL_TEXTURE_ENV, GL_COMBINE_RGB, GL_REPLACE);
glTexEnvi (GL_TEXTURE_ENV, GL_SRC0_RGB, GL_PREVIOUS);
glTexEnvi (GL_TEXTURE_ENV, GL_OPERAND0_RGB, GL_SRC_COLOR);
glTexEnvi (GL_TEXTURE_ENV, GL_COMBINE_ALPHA, GL_MODULATE);
glTexEnvi (GL_TEXTURE_ENV, GL_SRC0_ALPHA, GL_PREVIOUS);
glTexEnvi (GL_TEXTURE_ENV, GL_OPERAND0_ALPHA, GL_SRC_COLOR);
glTexEnvi (GL_TEXTURE_ENV, GL_SRC1_ALPHA, GL_TEXTURE);
glTexEnvi (GL_TEXTURE_ENV, GL_OPERAND1_ALPHA, GL_SRC_COLOR);
```

1.4.3 Here's the syntax

```
<statement>:
  <channel-mask>=<function-name>(<arg-list>)

  You can either use a single statement with an RGBA channel-mask or you can use
  two statements; one with an A channel-mask and the other with an RGB
  channel-mask.

<channel-mask>:
  A or RGB or RGBA

<function-name>:
  [A-Za-z_]*

<arg-list>:
  <arg>,<arg>
  or <arg>
  or ""

  I.e. functions may take 0 or more arguments

<arg>:
  <color-source>
  1 - <color-source>            : Only intended for texture combining
  <color-source> * ( <factor> ) : Only intended for blending
  0                             : Only intended for blending

  See the blending or texture combining sections for further notes and examples.

<color-source>:
  <source-name>[<channel-mask>]
  <source-name>

  See the blending or texture combining sections for the list of source-names
  valid in each context.
```

If a channel mask is not given then the channel mask of the statement
is assumed instead.

```
<factor>:
  0
  1
  <color-source>
  1-<color-source>
  SRC_ALPHA_SATURATE
```

1.4.4 Pipeline

Pipeline — Functions for creating and manipulating the GPU pipeline

Functions

CoglPipeline *	cogl_pipeline_new ()
CoglPipeline *	cogl_pipeline_copy ()
CoglBool	cogl_is_pipeline ()
void	cogl_pipeline_set_color ()
void	cogl_pipeline_set_color4ub ()
void	cogl_pipeline_set_color4f ()
void	cogl_pipeline_get_color ()
void	cogl_pipeline_set_alpha_test_function ()
#define	COGL_BLEND_STRING_ERROR
CoglBool	cogl_pipeline_set_blend ()
void	cogl_pipeline_set_blend_constant ()
void	cogl_pipeline_set_point_size ()
float	cogl_pipeline_get_point_size ()
CoglBool	cogl_pipeline_set_per_vertex_point_size ()
CoglBool	cogl_pipeline_get_per_vertex_point_size ()
CoglColorMask	cogl_pipeline_get_color_mask ()
void	cogl_pipeline_set_color_mask ()
CoglBool	cogl_pipeline_set_depth_state ()
void	cogl_pipeline_get_depth_state ()
void	cogl_pipeline_set_cull_face_mode ()
void	cogl_pipeline_set_front_face_winding ()
void	cogl_pipeline_set_layer_texture ()
void	cogl_pipeline_set_layer_null_texture ()
CoglTexture *	cogl_pipeline_get_layer_texture ()
void	cogl_pipeline_set_layer_filters ()
CoglPipelineFilter	cogl_pipeline_get_layer_min_filter ()
CoglPipelineFilter	cogl_pipeline_get_layer_mag_filter ()
void	cogl_pipeline_set_layer_wrap_mode ()
void	cogl_pipeline_set_layer_wrap_mode_s ()
void	cogl_pipeline_set_layer_wrap_mode_t ()
void	cogl_pipeline_set_layer_wrap_mode_p ()
CoglBool	cogl_pipeline_set_layer_combine ()
void	cogl_pipeline_set_layer_combine_constant ()
CoglBool	cogl_pipeline_set_layer_point_sprite_coords_enabled ()
CoglBool	cogl_pipeline_get_layer_point_sprite_coords_enabled ()
void	cogl_pipeline_remove_layer ()
int	cogl_pipeline_get_n_layers ()

CoglBool	(*CoglPipelineLayerCallback) ()
void	cogl_pipeline_foreach_layer ()
int	cogl_pipeline_get_uniform_location ()
void	cogl_pipeline_set_uniform_1f ()
void	cogl_pipeline_set_uniform_1i ()
void	cogl_pipeline_set_uniform_float ()
void	cogl_pipeline_set_uniform_int ()
void	cogl_pipeline_set_uniform_matrix ()
void	cogl_pipeline_add_snippet ()
void	cogl_pipeline_add_layer_snippet ()

Types and Values

	CoglPipeline
enum	CoglPipelineAlphaFunc
enum	CoglBlendStringError
enum	CoglPipelineCullFaceMode
enum	CoglWinding
enum	CoglPipelineFilter
enum	CoglPipelineWrapMode

Description

Cogl allows creating and manipulating objects representing the full configuration of the GPU pipeline. In simplified terms the GPU pipeline takes primitive geometry as the input, it first performs vertex processing, allowing you to deform your geometry, then rasterizes that (turning it from pure geometry into fragments) then performs fragment processing including depth testing and texture mapping. Finally it blends the result with the framebuffer.

Functions

cogl_pipeline_new ()

```
CoglPipeline~*
cogl_pipeline_new (CoglContext *context);
```

Allocates and initializes a default simple pipeline that will color a primitive white.

Parameters

context	a CoglContext	

Returns

a pointer to a new CoglPipeline

Since 2.0

Stability Level: Unstable

cogl_pipeline_copy ()

```
CoglPipeline~*
cogl_pipeline_copy (CoglPipeline *source);
```

Creates a new pipeline with the configuration copied from the source pipeline.

We would strongly advise developers to always aim to use cogl_pipeline_copy() instead of cogl_pipeline_new() whenever there will be any similarity between two pipelines. Copying a pipeline helps Cogl keep track of a pipelines ancestry which we may use to help minimize GPU state changes.

Parameters

source	a CoglPipeline object to copy

Returns

a pointer to the newly allocated CoglPipeline

Since 2.0

Stability Level: Unstable

cogl_is_pipeline ()

```
CoglBool
cogl_is_pipeline (void *object);
```

Gets whether the given object references an existing pipeline object.

Parameters

object	A CoglObject

Returns

TRUE if the object references a CoglPipeline, FALSE otherwise

Since 2.0

Stability Level: Unstable

cogl_pipeline_set_color ()

```
void
cogl_pipeline_set_color (CoglPipeline *pipeline,
                         const CoglColor *color);
```

Sets the basic color of the pipeline, used when no lighting is enabled.

Note that if you don't add any layers to the pipeline then the color will be blended unmodified with the destination; the default blend expects premultiplied colors: for example, use (0.5, 0.0, 0.0, 0.5) for semi-transparent red. See cogl_color_premultiply().

The default value is (1.0, 1.0, 1.0, 1.0)

Parameters

pipeline	A CoglPipeline object	
color	The components of the color	

Since 2.0

Stability Level: Unstable

cogl_pipeline_set_color4ub ()

```
void
cogl_pipeline_set_color4ub (CoglPipeline *pipeline,
                            uint8_t red,
                            uint8_t green,
                            uint8_t blue,
                            uint8_t alpha);
```

Sets the basic color of the pipeline, used when no lighting is enabled.

The default value is (0xff, 0xff, 0xff, 0xff)

Parameters

pipeline	A CoglPipeline object	
red	The red component	
green	The green component	
blue	The blue component	
alpha	The alpha component	

Since 2.0

Stability Level: Unstable

cogl_pipeline_set_color4f ()

```
void
cogl_pipeline_set_color4f (CoglPipeline *pipeline,
                           float red,
                           float green,
                           float blue,
                           float alpha);
```

Sets the basic color of the pipeline, used when no lighting is enabled.

The default value is (1.0, 1.0, 1.0, 1.0)

Parameters

pipeline	A CoglPipeline object	
red	The red component	
green	The green component	
blue	The blue component	
alpha	The alpha component	

Since 2.0

Stability Level: Unstable

cogl_pipeline_get_color ()

```
void
cogl_pipeline_get_color (CoglPipeline *pipeline,
                         CoglColor *color);
```

Retrieves the current pipeline color.

Parameters

pipeline	A CoglPipeline object	
color	The location to store the color.	[out]

Since 2.0

Stability Level: Unstable

cogl_pipeline_set_alpha_test_function ()

```
void
cogl_pipeline_set_alpha_test_function (CoglPipeline *pipeline,
                                       CoglPipelineAlphaFunc alpha_func,
                                       float alpha_reference);
```

Before a primitive is blended with the framebuffer, it goes through an alpha test stage which lets you discard fragments based on the current alpha value. This function lets you change the function used to evaluate the alpha channel, and thus determine which fragments are discarded and which continue on to the blending stage.

The default is COGL_PIPELINE_ALPHA_FUNC_ALWAYS

Parameters

pipeline	A CoglPipeline object	
alpha_func	A *CoglPipelineAlphaFunc* constant	
alpha_reference	A reference point that the chosen alpha function uses to compare incoming fragments to.	

Since 2.0

Stability Level: Unstable

COGL_BLEND_STRING_ERROR

```
#define COGL_BLEND_STRING_ERROR (cogl_blend_string_error_domain ())
```

CoglError domain for blend string parser errors

Since 1.0

cogl_pipeline_set_blend ()

```
CoglBool
cogl_pipeline_set_blend (CoglPipeline *pipeline,
                         const char *blend_string,
                         CoglError **error);
```

If not already familiar; please refer here for an overview of what blend strings are, and their syntax.

Blending occurs after the alpha test function, and combines fragments with the framebuffer.

Currently the only blend function Cogl exposes is ADD(). So any valid blend statements will be of the form:

```
<channel-mask>=ADD(SRC_COLOR*(<factor>), DST_COLOR*(<factor>))
```

This is the list of source-names usable as blend factors:

- SRC_COLOR: The color of the in comming fragment

- DST_COLOR: The color of the framebuffer

- CONSTANT: The constant set via cogl_pipeline_set_blend_constant()

The source names can be used according to the color-source and factor syntax,

so for example "(1-SRC_COLOR[A])" would be a valid factor, as would "(CONSTANT[RGB])"

These can also be used as factors:

- 0: (0, 0, 0, 0)

- 1: (1, 1, 1, 1)

- SRC_ALPHA_SATURATE_FACTOR: (f,f,f,1) where f = MIN(SRC_COLOR[A],1-DST_COLOR[A])

Note Remember; all color components are normalized to the range [0, 1] before computing the result of blending.

Example 1.1 Blend Strings/1

Blend a non-premultiplied source over a destination with premultiplied alpha:

```
"RGB = ADD(SRC_COLOR*(SRC_COLOR[A]), DST_COLOR*(1-SRC_COLOR[A]))"
"A   = ADD(SRC_COLOR, DST_COLOR*(1-SRC_COLOR[A]))"
```

Example 1.2 Blend Strings/2

Blend a premultiplied source over a destination with premultiplied alpha

```
"RGBA = ADD(SRC_COLOR, DST_COLOR*(1-SRC_COLOR[A]))"
```

The default blend string is:

```
    RGBA = ADD (SRC_COLOR, DST_COLOR*(1-SRC_COLOR[A]))
```

That gives normal alpha-blending when the calculated color for the pipeline is in premultiplied form.

Parameters

pipeline	A CoglPipeline object	
blend_string	A Cogl blend string describing the desired blend function.	
error	return location for a CoglError that may report lack of driver support if you give separate blend string statements for the alpha channel and RGB channels since some drivers, or backends such as GLES 1.1, don't support this feature. May be NULL, in which case a warning will be printed out using GLib's logging facilities if an error is encountered.	

Returns

TRUE if the blend string was successfully parsed, and the described blending is supported by the underlying driver/hardware. If there was an error, FALSE is returned and *error* is set accordingly (if present).

Since 2.0

Stability Level: Unstable

cogl_pipeline_set_blend_constant ()

```
void
cogl_pipeline_set_blend_constant (CoglPipeline *pipeline,
                                  const CoglColor *constant_color);
```

When blending is setup to reference a CONSTANT blend factor then blending will depend on the constant set with this function.

Parameters

pipeline	A CoglPipeline object	
constant_color	The constant color you want	

Since 2.0

Stability Level: Unstable

cogl_pipeline_set_point_size ()

```
void
cogl_pipeline_set_point_size (CoglPipeline *pipeline,
                              float point_size);
```

Changes the size of points drawn when COGL_VERTICES_MODE_POINTS is used with the attribute buffer API. Note that typically the GPU will only support a limited minimum and maximum range of point sizes. If the chosen point size is outside that range then the nearest value within that range will be used instead. The size of a point is in screen space so it will be the same regardless of any transformations.

If the point size is set to 0.0 then drawing points with the pipeline will have undefined results. This is the default value so if an application wants to draw points it must make sure to use a pipeline that has an explicit point size set on it.

Parameters

pipeline	a CoglPipeline pointer	
point_size	the new point size.	

Since 2.0

Stability Level: Unstable

cogl_pipeline_get_point_size ()

```
float
cogl_pipeline_get_point_size (CoglPipeline *pipeline);
```

Get the size of points drawn when COGL_VERTICES_MODE_POINTS is used with the vertex buffer API.

Parameters

pipeline	a CoglPipeline pointer	

Returns

the point size of the *pipeline* .

Since 2.0

Stability Level: Unstable

cogl_pipeline_set_per_vertex_point_size ()

```
CoglBool
cogl_pipeline_set_per_vertex_point_size
                              (CoglPipeline *pipeline,
                               CoglBool enable,
                               CoglError **error);
```

Sets whether to use a per-vertex point size or to use the value set by cogl_pipeline_set_point_size(). If per-vertex point size is enabled then the point size can be set for an individual point either by drawing with a CoglAttribute with the name 'cogl_point_size_in' or by writing to the GLSL builtin 'cogl_point_size_out' from a vertex shader snippet.

If per-vertex point size is enabled and this attribute is not used and cogl_point_size_out is not written to then the results are undefined.

Note that enabling this will only work if the COGL_FEATURE_ID_PER_VERTEX_POINT_SIZE feature is available. If this is not available then the function will return FALSE and set a CoglError.

Parameters

pipeline	a CoglPipeline pointer	

enable	whether to enable per-vertex point size	
error	a location to store a CoglError if the change failed	

Returns

TRUE if the change suceeded or FALSE otherwise

Since 2.0

Stability Level: Unstable

cogl_pipeline_get_per_vertex_point_size ()

```
CoglBool
cogl_pipeline_get_per_vertex_point_size
                           (CoglPipeline *pipeline);
```

Parameters

pipeline	a CoglPipeline pointer	

Returns

TRUE if the pipeline has per-vertex point size enabled or FALSE otherwise. The per-vertex point size can be enabled with cogl_pipeline_set_per_vertex_point_size().

Since 2.0

Stability Level: Unstable

cogl_pipeline_get_color_mask ()

```
CoglColorMask
cogl_pipeline_get_color_mask (CoglPipeline *pipeline);
```

Gets the current CoglColorMask of which channels would be written to the current framebuffer. Each bit set in the mask means that the corresponding color would be written.

Parameters

pipeline	a CoglPipeline object.	

Returns

A CoglColorMask

Since 1.8

Stability Level: Unstable

cogl_pipeline_set_color_mask ()

```
void
cogl_pipeline_set_color_mask (CoglPipeline *pipeline,
                              CoglColorMask color_mask);
```

Defines a bit mask of which color channels should be written to the current framebuffer. If a bit is set in *color_mask* that means that color will be written.

Parameters

pipeline	a CoglPipeline object.	
color_mask	A CoglColorMask of which color channels to write to the current framebuffer.	

Since 1.8

Stability Level: Unstable

cogl_pipeline_set_depth_state ()

```
CoglBool
cogl_pipeline_set_depth_state (CoglPipeline *pipeline,
                              const CoglDepthState *state,
                              CoglError **error);
```

This commits all the depth state configured in *state* struct to the given *pipeline* . The configuration values are copied into the pipeline so there is no requirement to keep the CoglDepthState struct around if you don't need it any more.

Note: Since some platforms do not support the depth range feature it is possible for this function to fail and report an *error* .

Parameters

pipeline	A CoglPipeline object	
state	A CoglDepthState struct	
error	A CoglError to report failures to setup the given *state* .	

Returns

TRUE if the GPU supports all the given *state* else FALSE and returns an *error* .

Since 2.0

Stability Level: Unstable

cogl_pipeline_get_depth_state ()

```
void
cogl_pipeline_get_depth_state (CoglPipeline *pipeline,
                              CoglDepthState *state_out);
```

Retrieves the current depth state configuration for the given *pipeline* as previously set using cogl_pipeline_set_depth_state().

Parameters

pipeline	A CoglPipeline object	
state_out	A destination CoglDepthState struct.	*[out]*

Since 2.0

Stability Level: Unstable

cogl_pipeline_set_cull_face_mode ()

```
void
cogl_pipeline_set_cull_face_mode (CoglPipeline *pipeline,
                                  CoglPipelineCullFaceMode cull_face_mode);
```

Sets which faces will be culled when drawing. Face culling can be used to increase efficiency by avoiding drawing faces that would get overridden. For example, if a model has gaps so that it is impossible to see the inside then faces which are facing away from the screen will never be seen so there is no point in drawing them. This can be acheived by setting the cull face mode to COGL_PIPELINE_CULL_FACE_MODE_BACK.

Face culling relies on the primitives being drawn with a specific order to represent which faces are facing inside and outside the model. This order can be specified by calling cogl_pipeline_set_front_face_winding().

Status: Unstable

Parameters

pipeline	A CoglPipeline	
cull_face_mode	The new mode to set	

Since 2.0

cogl_pipeline_set_front_face_winding ()

```
void
cogl_pipeline_set_front_face_winding (CoglPipeline *pipeline,
                                      CoglWinding front_winding);
```

The order of the vertices within a primitive specifies whether it is considered to be front or back facing. This function specifies which order is considered to be the front faces. COGL_WINDING_COUNTER_CLOCKWISE sets the front faces to primitives with vertices in a counter-clockwise order and COGL_WINDING_CLOCKWISE sets them to be clockwise. The default is COGL_WINDING_COUNTER_CLOCKWISE.

Status: Unstable

Parameters

pipeline	a CoglPipeline	
front_winding	the winding order	

Since 2.0

cogl_pipeline_set_layer_texture ()

```
void
cogl_pipeline_set_layer_texture (CoglPipeline *pipeline,
                                 int layer_index,
                                 CoglTexture *texture);
```

cogl_pipeline_set_layer_null_texture ()

```
void
cogl_pipeline_set_layer_null_texture (CoglPipeline *pipeline,
                                      int layer_index,
                                      CoglTextureType texture_type);
```

Sets the texture for this layer to be the default texture for the given type. This is equivalent to calling cogl_pipeline_set_layer_texture() with NULL for the texture argument except that you can also specify the type of default texture to use. The default texture is a 1x1 pixel white texture.

This function is mostly useful if you want to create a base pipeline that you want to create multiple copies from using cogl_pipeline_copy(). In that case this function can be used to specify the texture type so that any pipeline copies can share the internal texture type state for efficiency.

Parameters

pipeline	A CoglPipeline	
layer_index	The layer number to modify	
texture_type	The type of the default texture to use	

Since 1.10

Stability Level: Unstable

cogl_pipeline_get_layer_texture ()

```
CoglTexture~*
cogl_pipeline_get_layer_texture (CoglPipeline *pipeline,
                                 int layer_index);
```

Parameters

pipeline	A CoglPipeline object	
layer_index	the index of the layer	

Returns

the texture that was set for the given layer of the pipeline or NULL if no texture was set.

Since 1.10

Stability Level: Unstable

cogl_pipeline_set_layer_filters ()

```
void
cogl_pipeline_set_layer_filters (CoglPipeline *pipeline,
                                 int layer_index,
                                 CoglPipelineFilter min_filter,
                                 CoglPipelineFilter mag_filter);
```

Changes the decimation and interpolation filters used when a texture is drawn at other scales than 100%.

Note It is an error to pass anything other than COGL_PIPELINE_FILTER_NEAREST or COGL_PIPELINE_FILTER_LINEAR as magnification filters since magnification doesn't ever need to reference values stored in the mipmap chain.

Parameters

pipeline	A CoglPipeline object	
layer_index	the layer number to change.	
min_filter	the filter used when scaling a texture down.	
mag_filter	the filter used when magnifying a texture.	

Since 1.10

Stability Level: Unstable

cogl_pipeline_get_layer_min_filter ()

```
CoglPipelineFilter
cogl_pipeline_get_layer_min_filter (CoglPipeline *pipeline,
                                    int layer_index);
```

Retrieves the currently set minification CoglPipelineFilter set on the specified layer. The miniifcation filter determines how the layer should be sampled when down-scaled.

The default filter is COGL_PIPELINE_FILTER_LINEAR but this can be changed using cogl_pipeline_set_layer_filters().

Parameters

pipeline	A CoglPipeline object	
layer_index	the layer number to change.	

Returns

The minification CoglPipelineFilter for the specified layer.

Since 1.10

Stability Level: Unstable

cogl_pipeline_get_layer_mag_filter ()

```
CoglPipelineFilter
cogl_pipeline_get_layer_mag_filter (CoglPipeline *pipeline,
                                    int layer_index);
```

Retrieves the currently set magnification CoglPipelineFilter set on the specified layer. The magnification filter determines how the layer should be sampled when up-scaled.

The default filter is COGL_PIPELINE_FILTER_LINEAR but this can be changed using cogl_pipeline_set_layer_filters().

Parameters

pipeline	A CoglPipeline object	
layer_index	the layer number to change.	

Returns

The magnification CoglPipelineFilter for the specified layer.

Since 1.10

Stability Level: Unstable

cogl_pipeline_set_layer_wrap_mode ()

```
void
cogl_pipeline_set_layer_wrap_mode (CoglPipeline *pipeline,
                                   int layer_index,
                                   CoglPipelineWrapMode mode);
```

Sets the wrap mode for all three coordinates of texture lookups on this layer. This is equivalent to calling cogl_pipeline_set_layer_wrap_mode_s cogl_pipeline_set_layer_wrap_mode_t() and cogl_pipeline_set_layer_wrap_mode_p() separately.

Parameters

pipeline	A CoglPipeline object	
layer_index	the layer number to change.	
mode	the new wrap mode	

Since 2.0

Stability Level: Unstable

cogl_pipeline_set_layer_wrap_mode_s ()

```
void
cogl_pipeline_set_layer_wrap_mode_s (CoglPipeline *pipeline,
                                     int layer_index,
                                     CoglPipelineWrapMode mode);
```

Sets the wrap mode for the 's' coordinate of texture lookups on this layer.

Parameters

pipeline	A CoglPipeline object	
layer_index	the layer number to change.	
mode	the new wrap mode	

Since 2.0

Stability Level: Unstable

cogl_pipeline_set_layer_wrap_mode_t ()

```
void
cogl_pipeline_set_layer_wrap_mode_t (CoglPipeline *pipeline,
                                     int layer_index,
                                     CoglPipelineWrapMode mode);
```

Sets the wrap mode for the 't' coordinate of texture lookups on this layer.

Parameters

pipeline	A CoglPipeline object	
layer_index	the layer number to change.	
mode	the new wrap mode	

Since 2.0

Stability Level: Unstable

cogl_pipeline_set_layer_wrap_mode_p ()

```
void
cogl_pipeline_set_layer_wrap_mode_p (CoglPipeline *pipeline,
                                     int layer_index,
                                     CoglPipelineWrapMode mode);
```

Sets the wrap mode for the 'p' coordinate of texture lookups on this layer. 'p' is the third coordinate.

Parameters

pipeline	A CoglPipeline object	
layer_index	the layer number to change.	
mode	the new wrap mode	

Since 2.0

Stability Level: Unstable

cogl_pipeline_set_layer_combine ()

```
CoglBool
cogl_pipeline_set_layer_combine (CoglPipeline *pipeline,
                                 int layer_index,
                                 const char *blend_string,
                                 CoglError **error);
```

If not already familiar; you can refer here for an overview of what blend

strings are and there syntax.

These are all the functions available for texture combining:

- REPLACE(arg0) = arg0

- MODULATE(arg0, arg1) = arg0 x arg1

- ADD(arg0, arg1) = arg0 + arg1

- ADD_SIGNED(arg0, arg1) = arg0 + arg1 - 0.5

- INTERPOLATE(arg0, arg1, arg2) = arg0 x arg2 + arg1 x (1 - arg2)

- SUBTRACT(arg0, arg1) = arg0 - arg1

-
  ```
  DOT3_RGB(arg0, arg1) = 4 x ((arg0[R] - 0.5)) * (arg1[R] - 0.5) +
                              (arg0[G] - 0.5)) * (arg1[G] - 0.5) +
                              (arg0[B] - 0.5)) * (arg1[B] - 0.5))
  ```

-
  ```
  DOT3_RGBA(arg0, arg1) = 4 x ((arg0[R] - 0.5)) * (arg1[R] - 0.5) +
                               (arg0[G] - 0.5)) * (arg1[G] - 0.5) +
                               (arg0[B] - 0.5)) * (arg1[B] - 0.5))
  ```

Refer to the color-source syntax for

describing the arguments. The valid source names for texture combining are:

TEXTURE Use the color from the current texture layer

TEXTURE_0, TEXTURE_1, etc Use the color from the specified texture layer

CONSTANT Use the color from the constant given with cogl_pipeline_set_layer_combine_constant()

PRIMARY Use the color of the pipeline as set with cogl_pipeline_set_color()

PREVIOUS Either use the texture color from the previous layer, or if this is layer 0, use the color of the pipeline as set with cogl_pipeline_set_color()

Layer Combine Examples

This is effectively what the default blending is:

```
RGBA = MODULATE (PREVIOUS, TEXTURE)
```

This could be used to cross-fade between two images, using the alpha component of a constant as the interpolator. The constant color is given by calling cogl_pipeline_set_layer_combine_constant().

```
RGBA = INTERPOLATE (PREVIOUS, TEXTURE, CONSTANT[A])
```

Note You can't give a multiplication factor for arguments as you can with blending.

Parameters

pipeline	A CoglPipeline object	
layer_index	Specifies the layer you want define a combine function for	
blend_string	A Cogl blend string describing the desired texture combine function.	

	A CoglError that may report parse errors or lack of GPU/driver support. May be NULL, in which case a warning will be printed out if an error is encountered.
error	

Returns

TRUE if the blend string was successfully parsed, and the described texture combining is supported by the underlying driver and or hardware. On failure, FALSE is returned and *error* is set

Since 2.0

Stability Level: Unstable

cogl_pipeline_set_layer_combine_constant ()

```
void
cogl_pipeline_set_layer_combine_constant
                          (CoglPipeline *pipeline,
                           int layer_index,
                           const CoglColor *constant);
```

When you are using the 'CONSTANT' color source in a layer combine description then you can use this function to define its value.

Parameters

pipeline	A CoglPipeline object	
layer_index	Specifies the layer you want to specify a constant used for texture combining	
constant	The constant color you want	

Since 2.0

Stability Level: Unstable

cogl_pipeline_set_layer_point_sprite_coords_enabled ()

```
CoglBool
cogl_pipeline_set_layer_point_sprite_coords_enabled
                          (CoglPipeline *pipeline,
                           int layer_index,
                           CoglBool enable,
                           CoglError **error);
```

When rendering points, if *enable* is TRUE then the texture coordinates for this layer will be replaced with coordinates that vary from 0.0 to 1.0 across the primitive. The top left of the point will have the coordinates 0.0,0.0 and the bottom right will have 1.0,1.0. If *enable* is FALSE then the coordinates will be fixed for the entire point.

This function will only work if COGL_FEATURE_ID_POINT_SPRITE is available. If the feature is not available then the function will return FALSE and set *error* .

Parameters

pipeline	A CoglPipeline object	
layer_index	the layer number to change.	
enable	whether to enable point sprite coord generation.	
error	A return location for a CoglError, or NULL to ignore errors.	

Returns

TRUE if the function succeeds, FALSE otherwise.

Since 2.0

Stability Level: Unstable

cogl_pipeline_get_layer_point_sprite_coords_enabled ()

```
CoglBool
cogl_pipeline_get_layer_point_sprite_coords_enabled
                          (CoglPipeline *pipeline,
                           int layer_index);
```

Gets whether point sprite coordinate generation is enabled for this texture layer.

Parameters

pipeline	A CoglPipeline object	
layer_index	the layer number to check.	

Returns

whether the texture coordinates will be replaced with point sprite coordinates.

Since 2.0

Stability Level: Unstable

cogl_pipeline_remove_layer ()

```
void
cogl_pipeline_remove_layer (CoglPipeline *pipeline,
                            int layer_index);
```

This function removes a layer from your pipeline

Parameters

pipeline	A CoglPipeline object	
layer_index	Specifies the layer you want to remove	

Since 1.10

Stability Level: Unstable

cogl_pipeline_get_n_layers ()

```
int
cogl_pipeline_get_n_layers (CoglPipeline *pipeline);
```

Retrieves the number of layers defined for the given *pipeline*

Parameters

pipeline	A CoglPipeline object	

Returns

the number of layers

Since 2.0

Stability Level: Unstable

CoglPipelineLayerCallback ()

```
CoglBool
(*CoglPipelineLayerCallback) (CoglPipeline *pipeline,
                              int layer_index,
                              void *user_data);
```

The callback prototype used with cogl_pipeline_foreach_layer() for iterating all the layers of a *pipeline* .

Parameters

pipeline	The CoglPipeline whos layers are being iterated	
layer_index	The current layer index	
user_data	The private data passed to cogl_pipeline_foreach_layer()	

Since 2.0

Stability Level: Unstable

cogl_pipeline_foreach_layer ()

```
void
cogl_pipeline_foreach_layer (CoglPipeline *pipeline,
                             CoglPipelineLayerCallback callback,
                             void *user_data);
```

Iterates all the layer indices of the given *pipeline* .

Parameters

pipeline	A CoglPipeline object	
callback	A CoglPipelineLayerCallback to be called for each layer index.	*[scope call]*
user_data	Private data that will be passed to the callback.	*[closure]*

Since 2.0

Stability Level: Unstable

cogl_pipeline_get_uniform_location ()

```
int
cogl_pipeline_get_uniform_location (CoglPipeline *pipeline,
                                    const char *uniform_name);
```

This is used to get an integer representing the uniform with the name *uniform_name* . The integer can be passed to functions such as cogl_pipeline_set_uniform_1f() to set the value of a uniform.

This function will always return a valid integer. Ie, unlike OpenGL, it does not return -1 if the uniform is not available in this pipeline so it can not be used to test whether uniforms are present. It is not necessary to set the program on the pipeline before calling this function.

Parameters

| pipeline | A CoglPipeline object | |
| uniform_name | The name of a uniform | |

Returns

A integer representing the location of the given uniform.

Since 2.0

Stability Level: Unstable

cogl_pipeline_set_uniform_1f ()

```
void
cogl_pipeline_set_uniform_1f (CoglPipeline *pipeline,
                              int uniform_location,
                              float value);
```

Sets a new value for the uniform at *uniform_location* . If this pipeline has a user program attached and is later used as a source for drawing, the given value will be assigned to the uniform which can be accessed from the shader's source. The value for *uniform_location* should be retrieved from the string name of the uniform by calling cogl_pipeline_get_uniform_location().

This function should be used to set uniforms that are of type float. It can also be used to set a single member of a float array uniform.

Parameters

| pipeline | A CoglPipeline object | |

uniform_location	The uniform's location identifier	
value	The new value for the uniform	

Since 2.0

Stability Level: Unstable

cogl_pipeline_set_uniform_1i ()

```
void
cogl_pipeline_set_uniform_1i (CoglPipeline *pipeline,
                              int uniform_location,
                              int value);
```

Sets a new value for the uniform at *uniform_location*. If this pipeline has a user program attached and is later used as a source for drawing, the given value will be assigned to the uniform which can be accessed from the shader's source. The value for *uniform_location* should be retrieved from the string name of the uniform by calling cogl_pipeline_get_uniform_location().

This function should be used to set uniforms that are of type int. It can also be used to set a single member of a int array uniform or a sampler uniform.

Parameters

pipeline	A CoglPipeline object	
uniform_location	The uniform's location identifier	
value	The new value for the uniform	

Since 2.0

Stability Level: Unstable

cogl_pipeline_set_uniform_float ()

```
void
cogl_pipeline_set_uniform_float (CoglPipeline *pipeline,
                                 int uniform_location,
                                 int n_components,
                                 int count,
                                 const float *value);
```

Sets new values for the uniform at *uniform_location*. If this pipeline has a user program attached and is later used as a source for drawing, the given values will be assigned to the uniform which can be accessed from the shader's source. The value for *uniform_location* should be retrieved from the string name of the uniform by calling cogl_pipeline_get_uniform_location().

This function can be used to set any floating point type uniform, including float arrays and float vectors. For example, to set a single vec4 uniform you would use 4 for *n_components* and 1 for *count*. To set an array of 8 float values, you could use 1 for *n_components* and 8 for *count*.

Parameters

pipeline	A CoglPipeline object	

uniform_location	The uniform's location identifier	
n_components	The number of components in the corresponding uniform's type	
count	The number of values to set	
value	Pointer to the new values to set	

Since 2.0

Stability Level: Unstable

cogl_pipeline_set_uniform_int ()

```
void
cogl_pipeline_set_uniform_int (CoglPipeline *pipeline,
                               int uniform_location,
                               int n_components,
                               int count,
                               const int *value);
```

Sets new values for the uniform at *uniform_location* . If this pipeline has a user program attached and is later used as a source for drawing, the given values will be assigned to the uniform which can be accessed from the shader's source. The value for *uniform_location* should be retrieved from the string name of the uniform by calling cogl_pipeline_get_uniform_location().

This function can be used to set any integer type uniform, including int arrays and int vectors. For example, to set a single ivec4 uniform you would use 4 for *n_components* and 1 for *count* . To set an array of 8 int values, you could use 1 for *n_components* and 8 for *count* .

Parameters

pipeline	A CoglPipeline object	
uniform_location	The uniform's location identifier	
n_components	The number of components in the corresponding uniform's type	
count	The number of values to set	
value	Pointer to the new values to set	

Since 2.0

Stability Level: Unstable

cogl_pipeline_set_uniform_matrix ()

```
void
cogl_pipeline_set_uniform_matrix (CoglPipeline *pipeline,
                                  int uniform_location,
                                  int dimensions,
                                  int count,
                                  CoglBool transpose,
                                  const float *value);
```

Sets new values for the uniform at `uniform_location`. If this pipeline has a user program attached and is later used as a source for drawing, the given values will be assigned to the uniform which can be accessed from the shader's source. The value for `uniform_location` should be retrieved from the string name of the uniform by calling cogl_pipeline_get_uniform_location().

This function can be used to set any matrix type uniform, including matrix arrays. For example, to set a single mat4 uniform you would use 4 for `dimensions` and 1 for `count`. To set an array of 8 mat3 values, you could use 3 for `dimensions` and 8 for `count`.

If `transpose` is FALSE then the matrix is expected to be in column-major order or if it is TRUE then the matrix is in row-major order. You can pass a CoglMatrix by calling by passing the result of cogl_matrix_get_array() in `value` and setting `transpose` to FALSE.

Parameters

pipeline	A CoglPipeline object	
uniform_location	The uniform's location identifier	
dimensions	The size of the matrix	
count	The number of values to set	
transpose	Whether to transpose the matrix	
value	Pointer to the new values to set	

Since 2.0

Stability Level: Unstable

cogl_pipeline_add_snippet ()

```
void
cogl_pipeline_add_snippet (CoglPipeline *pipeline,
                           CoglSnippet *snippet);
```

Adds a shader snippet to `pipeline`. The snippet will wrap around or replace some part of the pipeline as defined by the hook point in `snippet`. Note that some hook points are specific to a layer and must be added with cogl_pipeline_add_layer_snippet() instead.

Parameters

pipeline	A CoglPipeline	
snippet	The CoglSnippet to add to the vertex processing hook	

Since 1.10

Stability Level: Unstable

cogl_pipeline_add_layer_snippet ()

```
void
cogl_pipeline_add_layer_snippet (CoglPipeline *pipeline,
                                 int layer,
                                 CoglSnippet *snippet);
```

Adds a shader snippet that will hook on to the given layer of the pipeline. The exact part of the pipeline that the snippet wraps around depends on the hook that is given to cogl_snippet_new(). Note that some hooks can't be used with a layer and need to be added with cogl_pipeline_add_snippet() instead.

Parameters

pipeline	A CoglPipeline	
layer	The layer to hook the snippet to	
snippet	A CoglSnippet	

Since 1.10

Stability Level: Unstable

Types and Values

CoglPipeline

```
typedef struct _CoglPipeline CoglPipeline;
```

enum CoglPipelineAlphaFunc

Alpha testing happens before blending primitives with the framebuffer and gives an opportunity to discard fragments based on a comparison with the incoming alpha value and a reference alpha value. The CoglPipelineAlphaFunc determines how the comparison is done.

Members

COGL_PIPELINE_ALPHA_FUNC_NEVER	Never let the fragment through.

COGL_PIPELINE_ALPHA_FUNC_LESS	Let the fragment through if the incoming alpha value is less than the reference alpha value
COGL_PIPELINE_ALPHA_FUNC_EQUAL	Let the fragment through if the incoming alpha value equals the reference alpha value

| COGL_PIPELINE_ALPHA_FUNC_LEQUAL | Let the fragment through if the incoming alpha value is less than or equal to the reference alpha value |
| COGL_PIPELINE_ALPHA_FUNC_GREATER | Let the fragment through if the incoming alpha value is greater than the reference alpha value |

COGL_PIPELINE_ALPHA_FUNC_NOTEQUAL	Let the fragment through if the incoming alpha value does not equal the reference alpha value
COGL_PIPELINE_ALPHA_FUNC_GEQUAL	Let the fragment through if the incoming alpha value is greater than or equal to the reference alpha value.
COGL_PIPELINE_ALPHA_FUNC_ALWAYS	Always let the fragment through.

enum CoglBlendStringError

Error enumeration for the blend strings parser

Members

COGL_BLEND_STRING_ERROR_PARSE_ERROR	Generic parse error
COGL_BLEND_STRING_ERROR_ARGUMENT_PARSE_ERROR	Argument parse error
COGL_BLEND_STRING_ERROR_INVALID_ERROR	Internal parser error
COGL_BLEND_STRING_ERROR_GPU_UNSUPPORTED_ERROR	Blend string not supported by the GPU

Since 1.0

enum CoglPipelineCullFaceMode

Specifies which faces should be culled. This can be set on a pipeline using cogl_pipeline_set_cull_face_mode().

Members

COGL_PIPELINE_CULL_FACE_MODE_NONE	Neither face will be culled. This is the default.
COGL_PIPELINE_CULL_FACE_MODE_FRONT	Front faces will be culled.
COGL_PIPELINE_CULL_FACE_MODE_BACK	Back faces will be culled.

| COGL_PIPELINE_CULL_FACE_MODE_BOTH | All faces will be culled. |

enum CoglWinding

Enum used to represent the two directions of rotation. This can be used to set the front face for culling by calling cogl_pipeline_set_front_

Members

COGL_WINDING_CLOCKWISE	Vertices are in a clock-wise or-der
COGL_WINDING_COUNTER_CLOCKWISE	Vertices are in a counter-clockwise or-der

enum CoglPipelineFilter

Texture filtering is used whenever the current pixel maps either to more than one texture element (texel) or less than one. These filter enums correspond to different strategies used to come up with a pixel color, by possibly referring to multiple neighbouring texels and taking a weighted average or simply using the nearest texel.

Members

COGL_PIPELINE_FILTER_NEAREST	Measuring in manhatten distance from the, current pixel center, use the nearest texture texel
COGL_PIPELINE_FILTER_LINEAR	Use the weighted average of the 4 texels nearest the current pixel center

COGL_PIPELINE_FILTER_NEAREST_MIPMAP_NEAREST	Select the mimap level whose texel size most closely matches the current pixel, and use the COGL_PIPELINE_FILTER_NEAREST criterion
COGL_PIPELINE_FILTER_LINEAR_MIPMAP_NEAREST	Select the mimap level whose texel size most closely matches the current pixel, and use the COGL_PIPELINE_FILTER_LINEAR criterion

COGL_PIPELINE_FILTER_NEAREST_MIPMAP_LINEAR	Select the two mimap levels whose texel size most closely matches the current pixel, use the COGL_PIPELINE_FILTER_NEAREST criterion on each one and take their weighted average

COGL_PIPELINE_FILTER_LINEAR_MIPMAP_LINEAR	Select the two mimap levels whose texel size most closely matches the current pixel, use the COGL_PIPELINE_FILTER_LINEAR criterion on each one and take their weighted average

enum CoglPipelineWrapMode

The wrap mode specifies what happens when texture coordinates outside the range $0 \to 1$ are used. Note that if the filter mode is anything but COGL_PIPELINE_FILTER_NEAREST then texels outside the range $0 \to 1$ might be used even when the coordinate is exactly 0 or 1 because OpenGL will try to sample neighbouring pixels. For example if you are trying to render the full texture then you may get artifacts around the edges when the pixels from the other side are merged in if the wrap mode is set to repeat.

Members

COGL_PIPELINE_WRAP_MODE_REPEAT	The texture will be repeated. This is useful for example to draw a tiled background.
COGL_PIPELINE_WRAP_MODE_MIRRORED_REPEAT	

COGL_PIPELINE_WRAP_MODE_CLAMP_TO_EDGE

The co-or-di-nates out-side the range $0 \rightarrow 1$ will sam-ple copies of the edge pix-els of the tex-ture. This is use-ful to avoid ar-ti-facts if only one copy of the tex-ture is be-ing ren-dered.

COGL_PIPELINE_WRAP_MODE_AUTOMATIC

Cogl will try to automatically decide which of the above two to use. For cogl_framebuffer_draw_rectangle(), it will use repeat mode if any of the texture coordinates are outside the range 0→1, otherwise it will use clamp to edge. For cogl_framebuffer_draw_attributes() or cogl_primitive_draw() it will use repeat mode except

Since 2.0

1.4.5 Depth State

Depth State — Functions for describing the depth testing state of your GPU.

Functions

void	cogl_depth_state_init ()
void	cogl_depth_state_set_test_enabled ()
CoglBool	cogl_depth_state_get_test_enabled ()
void	cogl_depth_state_set_test_function ()
CoglDepthTestFunction	cogl_depth_state_get_test_function ()
void	cogl_depth_state_set_write_enabled ()
CoglBool	cogl_depth_state_get_write_enabled ()
void	cogl_depth_state_set_range ()
void	cogl_depth_state_get_range ()

Types and Values

	CoglDepthState
enum	CoglDepthTestFunction

Description

Functions

cogl_depth_state_init ()

```
void
cogl_depth_state_init (CoglDepthState *state);
```

Initializes the members of *state* to their default values.

You should never pass an un initialized CoglDepthState structure to cogl_pipeline_set_depth_state().

Parameters

state	A CoglDepthState struct

Since 2.0

Stability Level: Unstable

cogl_depth_state_set_test_enabled ()

```
void
cogl_depth_state_set_test_enabled (CoglDepthState *state,
                                   CoglBool enable);
```

Enables or disables depth testing according to the value of *enable* .

If depth testing is enable then the CoglDepthTestFunction set using cogl_depth_state_set_test_function() us used to evaluate the depth value of incoming fragments against the corresponding value stored in the current depth buffer, and if the test passes then the fragments depth value is used to update the depth buffer. (unless you have disabled depth writing via cogl_depth_state_set_write_enabled())

By default depth testing is disabled.

NB: this won't directly affect the state of the GPU. You have to then set the state on a CoglPipeline using cogl_pipeline_set_depth_state()

Parameters

state	A CoglDepthState struct	
enable	The enable state you want	

Since 2.0

Stability Level: Unstable

cogl_depth_state_get_test_enabled ()

```
CoglBool
cogl_depth_state_get_test_enabled (CoglDepthState *state);
```

Gets the current depth test enabled state as previously set by cogl_depth_state_set_test_enabled().

Parameters

state	A CoglDepthState struct	

Returns

The pipeline's current depth test enabled state.

Since 2.0

Stability Level: Unstable

cogl_depth_state_set_test_function ()

```
void
cogl_depth_state_set_test_function (CoglDepthState *state,
                                    CoglDepthTestFunction function);
```

Sets the CoglDepthTestFunction used to compare the depth value of an incoming fragment against the corresponding value in the current depth buffer.

By default the depth test function is COGL_DEPTH_TEST_FUNCTION_LESS

NB: this won't directly affect the state of the GPU. You have to then set the state on a CoglPipeline using cogl_pipeline_set_depth_state()

Parameters

state	A CoglDepthState struct	
function	The CoglDepthTestFunction to set	

Since 2.0

Stability Level: Unstable

cogl_depth_state_get_test_function ()

```
CoglDepthTestFunction
cogl_depth_state_get_test_function (CoglDepthState *state);
```

Gets the current depth test enable state as previously set via cogl_depth_state_set_test_enabled().

Parameters

state	A CoglDepthState struct

Returns

The current depth test enable state.

Since 2.0

Stability Level: Unstable

cogl_depth_state_set_write_enabled ()

```
void
cogl_depth_state_set_write_enabled (CoglDepthState *state,
                                    CoglBool enable);
```

Enables or disables depth buffer writing according to the value of enable . Normally when depth testing is enabled and the comparison between a fragment's depth value and the corresponding depth buffer value passes then the fragment's depth is written to the depth buffer unless writing is disabled here.

By default depth writing is enabled

NB: this won't directly affect the state of the GPU. You have to then set the state on a CoglPipeline using cogl_pipeline_set_depth_state()

Parameters

state	A CoglDepthState struct
enable	The enable state you want

Since 2.0

Stability Level: Unstable

cogl_depth_state_get_write_enabled ()

```
CoglBool
cogl_depth_state_get_write_enabled (CoglDepthState *state);
```

Gets the depth writing enable state as set by the corresponding cogl_depth_state_set_write_enabled().

Parameters

| state | A CoglDepthState struct | |

Returns

The current depth writing enable state

Since 2.0

Stability Level: Unstable

cogl_depth_state_set_range ()

```
void
cogl_depth_state_set_range (CoglDepthState *state,
                            float near_val,
                            float far_val);
```

Sets the range to map depth values in normalized device coordinates to before writing out to a depth buffer.

After your geometry has be transformed, clipped and had perspective division applied placing it in normalized device coordinates all depth values between the near and far z clipping planes are in the range -1 to 1. Before writing any depth value to the depth buffer though the value is mapped into the range [0, 1].

With this function you can change the range which depth values are mapped too although the range must still lye within the range [0, 1].

If your driver does not support this feature (for example you are using GLES 1 drivers) then if you don't use the default range values you will get an error reported when calling cogl_pipeline_set_depth_state(). You can check ahead of time for the COGL_FEATURE_ID_DEPTH_RANGE feature with cogl_has_feature() to know if this function will succeed.

By default normalized device coordinate depth values are mapped to the full range of depth buffer values, [0, 1].

NB: this won't directly affect the state of the GPU. You have to then set the state on a CoglPipeline using cogl_pipeline_set_depth_state().

Parameters

state	A CoglDepthState object	
near_val	The near component of the desired depth range which will be clamped to the range [0, 1]	
far_val	The far component of the desired depth range which will be clamped to the range [0, 1]	

Since 2.0

Stability Level: Unstable

cogl_depth_state_get_range ()

```
void
cogl_depth_state_get_range (CoglDepthState *state,
                            float *near_val,
                            float *far_val);
```

Gets the current range to which normalized depth values are mapped before writing to the depth buffer. This corresponds to the range set with cogl_depth_state_set_range().

Parameters

state	A CoglDepthState object	
near_val	A pointer to store the near component of the depth range	
far_val	A pointer to store the far component of the depth range	

Since 2.0

Stability Level: Unstable

Types and Values

CoglDepthState

```
typedef struct {
} CoglDepthState;
```

Since 2.0

enum CoglDepthTestFunction

When using depth testing one of these functions is used to compare the depth of an incoming fragment against the depth value currently stored in the depth buffer. The function is changed using cogl_depth_state_set_test_function().

The test is only done when depth testing is explicitly enabled. (See cogl_depth_state_set_test_enabled())

Members

COGL_DEPTH_TEST_FUNCTION_NEVER	Never passes.
COGL_DEPTH_TEST_FUNCTION_LESS	Passes if the fragment's depth value is less than the value currently in the depth buffer.

COGL_DEPTH_TEST_FUNCTION_EQUAL	Passes if the fragment's depth value is equal to the value currently in the depth buffer.
COGL_DEPTH_TEST_FUNCTION_LEQUAL	Passes if the fragment's depth value is less or equal to the value currently in the depth buffer.
COGL_DEPTH_TEST_FUNCTION_GREATER	Passes if the fragment's depth value is greater than the value currently in the depth buffer.

COGL_DEPTH_TEST_FUNCTION_NOTEQUAL	Passes if the fragment's depth value is not equal to the value currently in the depth buffer.
COGL_DEPTH_TEST_FUNCTION_GEQUAL	Passes if the fragment's depth value greater than or equal to the value currently in the depth buffer.
COGL_DEPTH_TEST_FUNCTION_ALWAYS	Always passes.

1.4.6 Shader snippets

Shader snippets — Functions for creating and manipulating shader snippets

Functions

CoglSnippet *	cogl_snippet_new ()
CoglSnippetHook	cogl_snippet_get_hook ()
CoglBool	cogl_is_snippet ()
void	cogl_snippet_set_declarations ()
const char *	cogl_snippet_get_declarations ()
void	cogl_snippet_set_pre ()
const char *	cogl_snippet_get_pre ()

void	cogl_snippet_set_replace ()
const char *	cogl_snippet_get_replace ()
void	cogl_snippet_set_post ()
const char *	cogl_snippet_get_post ()

Types and Values

	CoglSnippet
enum	CoglSnippetHook

Description

CoglSnippets are used to modify or replace parts of a CoglPipeline using GLSL. GLSL is a programming language supported by OpenGL on programmable hardware to provide a more flexible description of what should be rendered. A description of GLSL itself is outside the scope of this documentation but any good OpenGL book should help to describe it.

Unlike in OpenGL, when using GLSL with Cogl it is possible to write short snippets to replace small sections of the pipeline instead of having to replace the whole of either the vertex or fragment pipelines. Of course it is also possible to replace the whole of the pipeline if needed.

Each snippet is a standalone chunk of code which would attach to the pipeline at a particular point. The code is split into four separate strings (all of which are optional):

declarations

> The code in this string will be inserted outside of any function in the global scope of the shader. This can be used to declare uniforms, attributes, varyings and functions to be used by the snippet.

pre

> The code in this string will be inserted before the hook point.

post

> The code in this string will be inserted after the hook point. This can be used to modify the results of the builtin generated code for that hook point.

replace

> If present the code in this string will replace the generated code for the hook point.

All of the strings apart from the declarations string of a pipeline are generated in a single function so they can share variables declared from one string in another. The scope of the code is limited to each snippet so local variables declared in the snippet will not collide with variables declared in another snippet. However, code in the 'declarations' string is global to the shader so it is the application's responsibility to ensure that variables declared here will not collide with those from other snippets.

The snippets can be added to a pipeline with cogl_pipeline_add_snippet() or cogl_pipeline_add_layer_snippet(). Which function to use depends on which hook the snippet is targetting. The snippets are all generated in the order they are added to the pipeline. That is, the post strings are executed in the order they are added to the pipeline and the pre strings are executed in reverse order. If any replace strings are given for a snippet then any other snippets with the same hook added before that snippet will be ignored. The different hooks are documented under CoglSnippetHook.

For portability with GLES2, it is recommended not to use the GLSL builtin names such as gl_FragColor. Instead there are replacement names under the cogl_* namespace which can be used instead. These are:

uniform mat4 *cogl_modelview_matrix*

> The current modelview matrix. This is equivalent to gl_ModelViewMatrix.

uniform mat4 *cogl_projection_matrix*

> The current projection matrix. This is equivalent to gl_ProjectionMatrix.

uniform mat4 *cogl_modelview_projection_matrix*

> The combined modelview and projection matrix. A vertex shader would typically use this to transform the incoming vertex position. The separate modelview and projection matrices are usually only needed for lighting calculations. This is equivalent to gl_ModelViewProjectionMatrix.

In a vertex shader, the following are also available:

attribute vec4 *cogl_position_in*

> The incoming vertex position. This is equivalent to gl_Vertex.

attribute vec4 *cogl_color_in*

> The incoming vertex color. This is equivalent to gl_Color.

attribute vec4 *cogl_tex_coord_in*

> The texture coordinate for layer 0. This is an alternative name for cogl_tex_coord0_in.

attribute vec4 *cogl_tex_coord0_in*

> The texture coordinate for the layer 0. This is equivalent to gl_MultiTexCoord0. There will also be cogl_tex_coord1_in and so on if more layers are added to the pipeline.

attribute vec3 *cogl_normal_in*

> The normal of the vertex. This is equivalent to gl_Normal.

vec4 *cogl_position_out*

> The calculated position of the vertex. This must be written to in all vertex shaders. This is equivalent to gl_Position.

float *cogl_point_size_in*

> The incoming point size from the cogl_point_size_in attribute. This is only available if cogl_pipeline_set_per_vertex_point_size() is set on the pipeline.

float *cogl_point_size_out*

> The calculated size of a point. This is equivalent to gl_PointSize.

varying vec4 *cogl_color_out*

> The calculated color of a vertex. This is equivalent to gl_FrontColor.

varying vec4 *cogl_tex_coord0_out*

> The calculated texture coordinate for layer 0 of the pipeline. This is equivalent to gl_TexCoord[0]. There will also be cogl_tex_coord1_out and so on if more layers are added to the pipeline. In the fragment shader, this varying is called cogl_tex_coord0_in.

In a fragment shader, the following are also available:

varying vec4 *cogl_color_in*

> The calculated color of a vertex. This is equivalent to gl_FrontColor.

varying vec4 *cogl_tex_coord0_in*

> The texture coordinate for layer 0. This is equivalent to gl_TexCoord[0]. There will also be cogl_tex_coord1_in and so on if more layers are added to the pipeline.

vec4 *cogl_color_out*

> The final calculated color of the fragment. All fragment shaders must write to this variable. This is equivalent to gl_FrontColor.

float *cogl_depth_out*

> An optional output variable specifying the depth value to use for this fragment. This is equivalent to gl_FragDepth.

bool *cogl_front_facing*

>   A readonly variable that will be true if the current primitive is front facing. This can be used to implement two-sided coloring algorithms. This is equivalent to gl_FrontFacing.

vec2 *cogl_point_coord*

>   When rendering points, this will contain a vec2 which represents the position within the point of the current fragment. vec2(0.0,0.0) will be the topleft of the point and vec2(1.0,1.0) will be the bottom right. Note that there is currently a bug in Cogl where when rendering to an offscreen buffer these coordinates will be upside-down. The value is undefined when not rendering points. This builtin can only be used if the COGL_FEATURE_ID_POINT_SPRITE feature is available.

Here is an example of using a snippet to add a desaturate effect to the generated color on a pipeline.

```
CoglPipeline *pipeline = cogl_pipeline_new ();

/* Set up the pipeline here, ie by adding a texture or other
   layers */

/* Create the snippet. The first string is the declarations which
   we will use to add a uniform. The second is the 'post' string which
   will contain the code to perform the desaturation. */
CoglSnippet *snippet =
  cogl_snippet_new (COGL_SNIPPET_HOOK_FRAGMENT,
                    "uniform float factor;",
                    "float gray = dot (vec3 (0.299, 0.587, 0.114), "
                    "                  cogl_color_out.rgb);"
                    "cogl_color_out.rgb = mix (vec3 (gray),"
                    "                          cogl_color_out.rgb,"
                    "                          factor);");

/* Add it to the pipeline */
cogl_pipeline_add_snippet (pipeline, snippet);
/* The pipeline keeps a reference to the snippet
   so we don't need to */
cogl_object_unref (snippet);

/* Update the custom uniform on the pipeline */
int location = cogl_pipeline_get_uniform_location (pipeline, "factor");
cogl_pipeline_set_uniform_1f (pipeline, location, 0.5f);

/* Now we can render with the snippet as usual */
cogl_framebuffer_draw_rectangle (fb, pipeline, 0, 0, 10, 10);
```

Functions

cogl_snippet_new ()

```
CoglSnippet~*
cogl_snippet_new (CoglSnippetHook hook,
                  const char *declarations,
                  const char *post);
```

Allocates and initializes a new snippet with the given source strings.

Parameters

hook	The point in the pipeline that this snippet will wrap around or replace.	
declarations	The source code for the declarations for this snippet or NULL. See cogl_snippet_set_declarations().	
post	The source code to run after the hook point where this shader snippet is attached or NULL. See cogl_snippet_set_post().	

Returns

a pointer to a new CoglSnippet

Since 1.10

Stability Level: Unstable

cogl_snippet_get_hook ()

```
CoglSnippetHook
cogl_snippet_get_hook (CoglSnippet *snippet);
```

Parameters

snippet	A CoglSnippet	

Returns

the hook that was set when cogl_snippet_new() was called.

Since 1.10

Stability Level: Unstable

cogl_is_snippet ()

```
CoglBool
cogl_is_snippet (void *object);
```

Gets whether the given *object* references an existing snippet object.

Parameters

object	A CoglObject pointer	

Returns

TRUE if the *object* references a CoglSnippet, FALSE otherwise

Since 1.10

Stability Level: Unstable

cogl_snippet_set_declarations ()

```
void
cogl_snippet_set_declarations (CoglSnippet *snippet,
                               const char *declarations);
```

Sets a source string that will be inserted in the global scope of the generated shader when this snippet is used on a pipeline. This string is typically used to declare uniforms, attributes or functions that will be used by the other parts of the snippets.

This function should only be called before the snippet is attached to its first pipeline. After that the snippet should be considered immutable.

Parameters

snippet	A CoglSnippet	
declarations	The new source string for the declarations section of this snippet.	

Since 1.10

Stability Level: Unstable

cogl_snippet_get_declarations ()

```
const char~*
cogl_snippet_get_declarations (CoglSnippet *snippet);
```

Parameters

snippet	A CoglSnippet	

Returns

the source string that was set with cogl_snippet_set_declarations() or NULL if none was set.

Since 1.10

Stability Level: Unstable

cogl_snippet_set_pre ()

```
void
cogl_snippet_set_pre (CoglSnippet *snippet,
                      const char *pre);
```

Sets a source string that will be inserted before the hook point in the generated shader for the pipeline that this snippet is attached to. Please see the documentation of each hook point in CoglPipeline for a description of how this string should be used.

This function should only be called before the snippet is attached to its first pipeline. After that the snippet should be considered immutable.

Parameters

snippet	A CoglSnippet	
pre	The new source string for the pre section of this snippet.	

Since 1.10

Stability Level: Unstable

cogl_snippet_get_pre ()

```
const char~*
cogl_snippet_get_pre (CoglSnippet *snippet);
```

Parameters

snippet	A CoglSnippet	

Returns

the source string that was set with cogl_snippet_set_pre() or NULL if none was set.

Since 1.10

Stability Level: Unstable

cogl_snippet_set_replace ()

```
void
cogl_snippet_set_replace (CoglSnippet *snippet,
                          const char *replace);
```

Sets a source string that will be used instead of any generated source code or any previous snippets for this hook point. Please see the documentation of each hook point in CoglPipeline for a description of how this string should be used.

This function should only be called before the snippet is attached to its first pipeline. After that the snippet should be considered immutable.

Parameters

snippet	A CoglSnippet	
replace	The new source string for the replace section of this snippet.	

Since 1.10

Stability Level: Unstable

cogl_snippet_get_replace ()

```
const char~*
cogl_snippet_get_replace (CoglSnippet *snippet);
```

Parameters

snippet	A CoglSnippet	

Returns

the source string that was set with cogl_snippet_set_replace() or NULL if none was set.

Since 1.10

Stability Level: Unstable

cogl_snippet_set_post ()

```
void
cogl_snippet_set_post (CoglSnippet *snippet,
                       const char *post);
```

Sets a source string that will be inserted after the hook point in the generated shader for the pipeline that this snippet is attached to. Please see the documentation of each hook point in CoglPipeline for a description of how this string should be used.

This function should only be called before the snippet is attached to its first pipeline. After that the snippet should be considered immutable.

Parameters

snippet	A CoglSnippet	
post	The new source string for the post section of this snippet.	

Since 1.10

Stability Level: Unstable

cogl_snippet_get_post ()

```
const char~*
cogl_snippet_get_post (CoglSnippet *snippet);
```

Parameters

snippet	A CoglSnippet	

Returns

the source string that was set with cogl_snippet_set_post() or NULL if none was set.

Since 1.10

Stability Level: Unstable

Types and Values

CoglSnippet

```
typedef struct _CoglSnippet CoglSnippet;
```

enum CoglSnippetHook

CoglSnippetHook is used to specify a location within a CoglPipeline where the code of the snippet should be used when it is attached to a pipeline.

COGL_SNIPPET_HOOK_VERTEX_GLOBALS

Adds a shader snippet at the beginning of the global section of the shader for the vertex processing. Any declarations here can be shared with all other snippets that are attached to a vertex hook. Only the 'declarations' string is used and the other strings are ignored.

COGL_SNIPPET_HOOK_FRAGMENT_GLOBALS

Adds a shader snippet at the beginning of the global section of the shader for the fragment processing. Any declarations here can be shared with all other snippets that are attached to a fragment hook. Only the 'declarations' string is used and the other strings are ignored.

COGL_SNIPPET_HOOK_VERTEX

Adds a shader snippet that will hook on to the vertex processing stage of the pipeline. This gives a chance for the application to modify the vertex attributes generated by the shader. Typically the snippet will modify cogl_color_out or cogl_position_out builtins.

The 'declarations' string in *snippet* will be inserted in the global scope of the shader. Use this to declare any uniforms, attributes or functions that the snippet requires.

The 'pre' string in *snippet* will be inserted at the top of the main() function before any vertex processing is done.

The 'replace' string in *snippet* will be used instead of the generated vertex processing if it is present. This can be used if the application wants to provide a complete vertex shader and doesn't need the generated output from Cogl.

The 'post' string in *snippet* will be inserted after all of the standard vertex processing is done. This can be used to modify the outputs.

COGL_SNIPPET_HOOK_VERTEX_TRANSFORM

Adds a shader snippet that will hook on to the vertex transform stage. Typically the snippet will use the cogl_modelview_matrix, cogl_projection_matrix and cogl_modelview_projection_matrix matrices and the cogl_position_in attribute. The hook must write to cogl_position_out. The default processing for this hook will multiply cogl_position_in by the combined modelview-projection matrix and store it on cogl_position_out.

The 'declarations' string in *snippet* will be inserted in the global scope of the shader. Use this to declare any uniforms, attributes or functions that the snippet requires.

The 'pre' string in *snippet* will be inserted at the top of the main() function before the vertex transform is done.

The 'replace' string in *snippet* will be used instead of the generated vertex transform if it is present.

The 'post' string in *snippet* will be inserted after all of the standard vertex transformation is done. This can be used to modify the cogl_position_out in addition to the default processing.

COGL_SNIPPET_HOOK_POINT_SIZE

Adds a shader snippet that will hook on to the point size calculation step within the vertex shader stage. The snippet should write to the builtin cogl_point_size_out with the new point size. The snippet can either read cogl_point_size_in directly and write a new value or first read an existing value in cogl_point_size_out that would be set by a previous snippet. Note that this hook is only used if cogl_pipeline_set_per_vertex_point_size() is enabled on the pipeline.

The 'declarations' string in *snippet* will be inserted in the global scope of the shader. Use this to declare any uniforms, attributes or functions that the snippet requires.

The 'pre' string in `snippet` will be inserted just before calculating the point size.

The 'replace' string in `snippet` will be used instead of the generated point size calculation if it is present.

The 'post' string in `snippet` will be inserted after the standard point size calculation is done. This can be used to modify cogl_point_size_out in addition to the default processing.

COGL_SNIPPET_HOOK_FRAGMENT

Adds a shader snippet that will hook on to the fragment processing stage of the pipeline. This gives a chance for the application to modify the fragment color generated by the shader. Typically the snippet will modify cogl_color_out.

The 'declarations' string in `snippet` will be inserted in the global scope of the shader. Use this to declare any uniforms, attributes or functions that the snippet requires.

The 'pre' string in `snippet` will be inserted at the top of the main() function before any fragment processing is done.

The 'replace' string in `snippet` will be used instead of the generated fragment processing if it is present. This can be used if the application wants to provide a complete fragment shader and doesn't need the generated output from Cogl.

The 'post' string in `snippet` will be inserted after all of the standard fragment processing is done. At this point the generated value for the rest of the pipeline state will already be in cogl_color_out so the application can modify the result by altering this variable.

COGL_SNIPPET_HOOK_TEXTURE_COORD_TRANSFORM

Adds a shader snippet that will hook on to the texture coordinate transformation of a particular layer. This can be used to replace the processing for a layer or to modify the results.

Within the snippet code for this hook there is an extra variable called cogl_tex_coord and represents the incoming and outgoing texture coordinate. On entry to the hook, cogl_tex_coord contains the value of the corresponding texture coordinate attribute for this layer. The hook is expected to modify this variable. The output will be passed as a varying to the fragment processing stage. The default code will leave cogl_tex_coord untouched.

The 'declarations' string in `snippet` will be inserted in the global scope of the shader. Use this to declare any uniforms, attributes or functions that the snippet requires.

The 'pre' string in `snippet` will be inserted just before the fragment processing for this layer. At this point cogl_tex_coord still contains the value of the texture coordinate attribute.

If a 'replace' string is given then this will be used instead of the default fragment processing for this layer. The snippet can modify cogl_tex_coord or leave it as is to apply no transformation.

The 'post' string in `snippet` will be inserted just after the transformation. At this point cogl_tex_coord will contain the results of the transformation but it can be further modified by the snippet.

COGL_SNIPPET_HOOK_LAYER_FRAGMENT

Adds a shader snippet that will hook on to the fragment processing of a particular layer. This can be used to replace the processing for a layer or to modify the results.

Within the snippet code for this hook there is an extra vec4 variable called 'cogl_layer'. This contains the resulting color that will be used for the layer. This can be modified in the 'post' section or it the default processing can be replaced entirely using the 'replace' section.

The 'declarations' string in `snippet` will be inserted in the global scope of the shader. Use this to declare any uniforms, attributes or functions that the snippet requires.

The 'pre' string in `snippet` will be inserted just before the fragment processing for this layer.

If a 'replace' string is given then this will be used instead of the default fragment processing for this layer. The snippet must write to the 'cogl_layer' variable in that case.

The 'post' string in `snippet` will be inserted just after the fragment processing for the layer. The results can be modified by changing the value of the 'cogl_layer' variable.

COGL_SNIPPET_HOOK_TEXTURE_LOOKUP

Adds a shader snippet that will hook on to the texture lookup part of a given layer. This gives a chance for the application to modify the coordinates that will be used for the texture lookup or to alter the returned texel.

Within the snippet code for this hook there are three extra variables available. 'cogl_sampler' is a sampler object representing the sampler for the layer where the snippet is attached. 'cogl_tex_coord' is a vec4 which contains the texture coordinates that will be used for the texture lookup. This can be modified. 'cogl_texel' will contain the result of the texture lookup. This can also be modified.

The 'declarations' string in *snippet* will be inserted in the global scope of the shader. Use this to declare any uniforms, attributes or functions that the snippet requires.

The 'pre' string in *snippet* will be inserted at the top of the main() function before any fragment processing is done. This is a good place to modify the cogl_tex_coord variable.

If a 'replace' string is given then this will be used instead of a the default texture lookup. The snippet would typically use its own sampler in this case.

The 'post' string in *snippet* will be inserted after texture lookup has been preformed. Here the snippet can modify the cogl_texel variable to alter the returned texel.

Members

COGL_SNIPPET_HOOK_VERTEX	A hook for the entire vertex processing stage of the pipeline.
COGL_SNIPPET_HOOK_VERTEX_TRANSFORM	A hook for the vertex transformation.

COGL_SNIPPET_HOOK_VERTEX_GLOBALS	A hook for declaring global data that can be shared with all other snippets that are on a vertex hook.
COGL_SNIPPET_HOOK_POINT_SIZE	A hook for manipulating the point size of a vertex. This is only used if cogl_pipeline_set_per_vertex_point_size() is enabled on the pipeline.

COGL_SNIPPET_HOOK_FRAGMENT	A hook for the entire fragment processing stage of the pipeline.
COGL_SNIPPET_HOOK_FRAGMENT_GLOBALS	A hook for declaring global data wthat can be shared with all other snippets that are on a fragment hook.
COGL_SNIPPET_HOOK_TEXTURE_COORD_TRANSFORM	A hook for transforming the texture coordinates for a layer.

COGL_SNIPPET_HOOK_LAYER_FRAGMENT	A hook for the fragment processing of a particular layer.
COGL_SNIPPET_HOOK_TEXTURE_LOOKUP	A hook for the texture lookup stage of a given layer in a pipeline.

Since 1.10

Stability Level: Unstable

1.5 Allocating GPU Memory

1.5.1 CoglBuffer: The Buffer Interface

CoglBuffer: The Buffer Interface — Common buffer functions, including data upload APIs

Stability Level

Unstable, unless otherwise indicated

Functions

CoglBool	cogl_is_buffer ()
unsigned int	cogl_buffer_get_size ()
void	cogl_buffer_set_update_hint ()
CoglBufferUpdateHint	cogl_buffer_get_update_hint ()
void *	cogl_buffer_map ()

void *	cogl_buffer_map_range ()
void	cogl_buffer_unmap ()
CoglBool	cogl_buffer_set_data ()
CoglPixelBuffer *	cogl_pixel_buffer_new ()
CoglBool	cogl_is_pixel_buffer ()

Types and Values

typedef	CoglBuffer
enum	CoglBufferUpdateHint
enum	CoglBufferAccess
enum	CoglBufferMapHint
	CoglPixelBuffer

Description

The CoglBuffer API provides a common interface to manipulate buffers that have been allocated either via cogl_pixel_buffer_new() or cogl_attribute_buffer_new(). The API allows you to upload data to these buffers and define usage hints that help Cogl manage your buffer optimally.

Data can either be uploaded by supplying a pointer and size so Cogl can copy your data, or you can mmap() a CoglBuffer and then you can copy data to the buffer directly.

One of the most common uses for CoglBuffers is to upload texture data asynchronously since the ability to mmap the buffers into the CPU makes it possible for another thread to handle the IO of loading an image file and unpacking it into the mapped buffer without blocking other Cogl operations.

Functions

cogl_is_buffer ()

```
CoglBool
cogl_is_buffer (void *object);
```

Checks whether *buffer* is a buffer object.

Parameters

object	a buffer object	

Returns

TRUE if the handle is a CoglBuffer, and FALSE otherwise

Since 1.2

Stability Level: Unstable

cogl_buffer_get_size ()

```
unsigned int
cogl_buffer_get_size (CoglBuffer *buffer);
```

Retrieves the size of buffer

Parameters

buffer	a buffer object	

Returns

the size of the buffer in bytes

Since 1.2

Stability Level: Unstable

cogl_buffer_set_update_hint ()

```
void
cogl_buffer_set_update_hint (CoglBuffer *buffer,
                             CoglBufferUpdateHint hint);
```

Sets the update hint on a buffer. See CoglBufferUpdateHint for a description of the available hints.

Parameters

buffer	a buffer object	
hint	the new hint	

Since 1.2

Stability Level: Unstable

cogl_buffer_get_update_hint ()

```
CoglBufferUpdateHint
cogl_buffer_get_update_hint (CoglBuffer *buffer);
```

Retrieves the update hints set using cogl_buffer_set_update_hint()

Parameters

buffer	a buffer object	

Returns

the CoglBufferUpdateHint currently used by the buffer

Since 1.2

Stability Level: Unstable

cogl_buffer_map ()

```
void~*
cogl_buffer_map (CoglBuffer *buffer,
                 CoglBufferAccess access,
                 CoglBufferMapHint hints,
                 CoglError **error);
```

Maps the buffer into the application address space for direct access. This is equivalent to calling cogl_buffer_map_range() with zero as the offset and the size of the entire buffer as the size.

It is strongly recommended that you pass COGL_BUFFER_MAP_HINT_DISCARD as a hint if you are going to replace all the buffer's data. This way if the buffer is currently being used by the GPU then the driver won't have to stall the CPU and wait for the hardware to finish because it can instead allocate a new buffer to map.

The behaviour is undefined if you access the buffer in a way conflicting with the *access* mask you pass. It is also an error to release your last reference while the buffer is mapped.

Parameters

buffer	a buffer object	
access	how the mapped buffer will be used by the application	
hints	A mask of CoglBufferMapHints that tell Cogl how the data will be modified once mapped.	
error	A CoglError for catching exceptional errors	

Returns

A pointer to the mapped memory or NULL is the call fails.

[transfer none]

Since 1.2

Stability Level: Unstable

cogl_buffer_map_range ()

```
void~*
cogl_buffer_map_range (CoglBuffer *buffer,
                       size_t offset,
                       size_t size,
                       CoglBufferAccess access,
                       CoglBufferMapHint hints,
                       CoglError **error);
```

Maps a sub-region of the buffer into the application's address space for direct access.

It is strongly recommended that you pass COGL_BUFFER_MAP_HINT_DISCARD as a hint if you are going to replace all the buffer's data. This way if the buffer is currently being used by the GPU then the driver won't have to stall the CPU and wait for the hardware to finish because it can instead allocate a new buffer to map. You can pass COGL_BUFFER_MAP_HINT_DISCARD_RANGE instead if you want the regions outside of the mapping to be retained.

The behaviour is undefined if you access the buffer in a way conflicting with the *access* mask you pass. It is also an error to release your last reference while the buffer is mapped.

Parameters

buffer	a buffer object	
offset	Offset within the buffer to start the mapping	
size	The size of data to map	

access	how the mapped buffer will be used by the application	
hints	A mask of CoglBufferMapHints that tell Cogl how the data will be modified once mapped.	
error	A CoglError for catching exceptional errors	

Returns

A pointer to the mapped memory or NULL is the call fails.

[transfer none]

Since 2.0

Stability Level: Unstable

cogl_buffer_unmap ()

```
void
cogl_buffer_unmap (CoglBuffer *buffer);
```

Unmaps a buffer previously mapped by cogl_buffer_map().

Parameters

buffer	a buffer object	

Since 1.2

Stability Level: Unstable

cogl_buffer_set_data ()

```
CoglBool
cogl_buffer_set_data (CoglBuffer *buffer,
                      size_t offset,
                      const void *data,
                      size_t size,
                      CoglError **error);
```

Updates part of the buffer with new data from *data* . Where to put this new data is controlled by *offset* and *offset* + *data* should be less than the buffer size.

Parameters

buffer	a buffer object	
offset	destination offset (in bytes) in the buffer	
data	a pointer to the data to be copied into the buffer	
size	number of bytes to copy	
error	A CoglError for catching exceptional errors	

Returns

TRUE is the operation succeeded, FALSE otherwise

Since 1.2

Stability Level: Unstable

cogl_pixel_buffer_new ()

```
CoglPixelBuffer~*
cogl_pixel_buffer_new (CoglContext *context,
                       size_t size,
                       const void *data,
                       CoglError **error);
```

Declares a new CoglPixelBuffer of `size` bytes to contain arrays of pixels. Once declared, data can be set using cogl_buffer_set_data() or by mapping it into the application's address space using cogl_buffer_map().

If `data` isn't NULL then `size` bytes will be read from `data` and immediately copied into the new buffer.

Parameters

context	A CoglContext	
size	The number of bytes to allocate for the pixel data.	
data	An optional pointer to vertex data to upload immediately	
error	A CoglError for catching exceptional errors	

Returns

a newly allocated CoglPixelBuffer.

[transfer full]

Since 1.10

Stability Level: Unstable

cogl_is_pixel_buffer ()

```
CoglBool
cogl_is_pixel_buffer (void *object);
```

Checks whether `object` is a pixel buffer.

Parameters

object	a CoglObject to test	

Returns

TRUE if the `object` is a pixel buffer, and FALSE otherwise

Since 1.2

Stability Level: Unstable

Types and Values

CoglBuffer

```
typedef void CoglBuffer;
```

enum CoglBufferUpdateHint

The update hint on a buffer allows the user to give some detail on how often the buffer data is going to be updated.

Members

COGL_BUFFER_UPDATE_HINT_STATIC	the buffer will not change over time
COGL_BUFFER_UPDATE_HINT_DYNAMIC	the buffer will change from time to time
COGL_BUFFER_UPDATE_HINT_STREAM	the buffer will be used once or a cou-ple of times

Since 1.2

Stability Level: Unstable

enum CoglBufferAccess

The access hints for cogl_buffer_set_update_hint()

Members

COGL_BUFFER_ACCESS_READ	the buffer will be read
COGL_BUFFER_ACCESS_WRITE	the buffer will written to
COGL_BUFFER_ACCESS_READ_WRITE	the buffer will be used for both reading and writing

Since 1.2

Stability Level: Unstable

enum CoglBufferMapHint

Hints to Cogl about how you are planning to modify the data once it is mapped.

Members

| COGL_BUFFER_MAP_HINT_DISCARD | Tells Cogl that you plan to re-place all the buffer's con-tents. When this flag is used to map a buffer, the en-tire con-tents of the buffer be-come un-de-fined, even if only a sub-re-gion of the buffer is mapped. |

| COGL_BUFFER_MAP_HINT_DISCARD_RANGE | Tells Cogl that you plan to replace all the contents of the mapped region. The contents of the region specified are undefined after this flag is used to map a buffer. |

Since 1.4

Stability Level: Unstable

CoglPixelBuffer

```
typedef struct _CoglPixelBuffer CoglPixelBuffer;
```

1.5.2 CoglAttributeBuffer: Buffers of vertex attributes

CoglAttributeBuffer: Buffers of vertex attributes — Functions for creating and manipulating attribute buffers

Functions

CoglAttributeBuffer *	cogl_attribute_buffer_new_with_size ()
CoglAttributeBuffer *	cogl_attribute_buffer_new ()
CoglBool	cogl_is_attribute_buffer ()

Types and Values

	CoglAttributeBuffer

Description

FIXME

Functions

cogl_attribute_buffer_new_with_size ()

```
CoglAttributeBuffer~*
cogl_attribute_buffer_new_with_size (CoglContext *context,
                                     size_t bytes);
```

Describes a new CoglAttributeBuffer of `size` bytes to contain arrays of vertex attribute data. Afterwards data can be set using cogl_buffer_set_data() or by mapping it into the application's address space using cogl_buffer_map().

The underlying storage of this buffer isn't allocated by this function so that you have an opportunity to use the cogl_buffer_set_update_hi and cogl_buffer_set_usage_hint() functions which may influence how the storage is allocated. The storage will be allocated once you upload data to the buffer.

Note: You can assume this function always succeeds and won't return NULL

Parameters

context	A CoglContext	
bytes	The number of bytes to allocate for vertex attribute data.	

Returns

A newly allocated CoglAttributeBuffer. Never NULL.

[transfer full]

Stability Level: Unstable

cogl_attribute_buffer_new ()

```
CoglAttributeBuffer~*
cogl_attribute_buffer_new (CoglContext *context,
                           size_t bytes,
                           const void *data);
```

Describes a new CoglAttributeBuffer of `size` bytes to contain arrays of vertex attribute data and also uploads `size` bytes read from `data` to the new buffer.

You should never pass a NULL data pointer.

Note This function does not report out-of-memory errors back to the caller by returning NULL and so you can assume this function always succeeds.

Note In the unlikely case that there is an out of memory problem then Cogl will abort the application with a message. If your application needs to gracefully handle out-of-memory errors then you can use cogl_attribute_buffer_new_with_size() and then explicitly catch errors with cogl_buffer_set_data() or cogl_buffer_map().

Parameters

context	A CoglContext	
bytes	The number of bytes to allocate for vertex attribute data.	
data	An optional pointer to vertex data to upload immediately.	*[array length=bytes]*

Returns

A newly allocated CoglAttributeBuffer (never NULL).

[transfer full]

Since 1.4

Stability Level: Unstable

cogl_is_attribute_buffer ()

```
CoglBool
cogl_is_attribute_buffer (void *object);
```

Gets whether the given object references a CoglAttributeBuffer.

Parameters

object	A CoglObject	

Returns

TRUE if *object* references a CoglAttributeBuffer, FALSE otherwise

Since 1.4

Stability Level: Unstable

Types and Values

CoglAttributeBuffer

```
typedef struct _CoglAttributeBuffer CoglAttributeBuffer;
```

1.5.3 CoglIndexBuffer: Buffers of vertex indices

CoglIndexBuffer: Buffers of vertex indices — Functions for creating and manipulating vertex indices.

Functions

CoglIndexBuffer *	cogl_index_buffer_new ()
CoglBool	cogl_is_index_buffer ()

Types and Values

	CoglIndexBuffer

Description

FIXME

Functions

cogl_index_buffer_new ()

```
CoglIndexBuffer~*
cogl_index_buffer_new (CoglContext *context,
                       size_t bytes);
```

Declares a new CoglIndexBuffer of *size* bytes to contain vertex indices. Once declared, data can be set using cogl_buffer_set_data() or by mapping it into the application's address space using cogl_buffer_map().

Parameters

context	A CoglContext	
bytes	The number of bytes to allocate for vertex attribute data.	

Returns

A newly allocated CoglIndexBuffer.

[transfer full]

Since 1.4

Stability Level: Unstable

cogl_is_index_buffer ()

```
CoglBool
cogl_is_index_buffer (void *object);
```

Gets whether the given object references a CoglIndexBuffer.

Parameters

| object | A CoglObject | |

Returns

TRUE if the *object* references a CoglIndexBuffer, FALSE otherwise

Since 1.4

Stability Level: Unstable

Types and Values

CoglIndexBuffer

```
typedef struct _CoglIndexBuffer CoglIndexBuffer;
```

1.6 Describing the layout of GPU Memory

1.6.1 Vertex Attributes

Vertex Attributes — Functions for declaring and drawing vertex attributes

Functions

CoglAttribute *	cogl_attribute_new ()
CoglBool	cogl_is_attribute ()
void	cogl_attribute_set_normalized ()
CoglBool	cogl_attribute_get_normalized ()
CoglAttributeBuffer *	cogl_attribute_get_buffer ()
void	cogl_attribute_set_buffer ()

Types and Values

| | CoglAttribute |

Description

FIXME

Functions

cogl_attribute_new ()

```
CoglAttribute~*
cogl_attribute_new (CoglAttributeBuffer *attribute_buffer,
                    const char *name,
                    size_t stride,
                    size_t offset,
                    int components,
                    CoglAttributeType type);
```

Describes the layout for a list of vertex attribute values (For example, a list of texture coordinates or colors).

The *name* is used to access the attribute inside a GLSL vertex shader and there are some special names you should use if they are applicable:

- "cogl_position_in" (used for vertex positions)

- "cogl_color_in" (used for vertex colors)

- "cogl_tex_coord0_in", "cogl_tex_coord1", ... (used for vertex texture coordinates)

- "cogl_normal_in" (used for vertex normals)

- "cogl_point_size_in" (used to set the size of points per-vertex. Note this can only be used if COGL_FEATURE_ID_POINT_SIZE_AT" is advertised and cogl_pipeline_set_per_vertex_point_size() is called on the pipeline.

The attribute values corresponding to different vertices can either be tightly packed or interleaved with other attribute values. For example it's common to define a structure for a single vertex like:

```
typedef struct
{
  float x, y, z; /<!-- -->* position attribute *<!-- -->/
  float s, t; /<!-- -->* texture coordinate attribute *<!-- -->/
} MyVertex;
```

And then create an array of vertex data something like:

```
MyVertex vertices[100] = { .... }
```

In this case, to describe either the position or texture coordinate attribute you have to move `sizeof (MyVertex)` bytes to move from one vertex to the next. This is called the attribute *stride*. If you weren't interleving attributes and you instead had a packed array of float x, y pairs then the attribute stride would be `(2 * sizeof (float))`. So the *stride* is the number of bytes to move to find the attribute value of the next vertex.

Normally a list of attributes starts at the beginning of an array. So for the `MyVertex` example above the *offset* is the offset inside the `MyVertex` structure to the first component of the attribute. For the texture coordinate attribute the offset would be `offsetof (MyVertex, s)` or instead of using the offsetof macro you could use `sizeof (float) * 3`. If you've divided your *array* into blocks of non-interleved attributes then you will need to calculate the *offset* as the number of bytes in blocks preceding the attribute you're describing.

An attribute often has more than one component. For example a color is often comprised of 4 red, green, blue and alpha *components*, and a position may be comprised of 2 x and y *components*. You should aim to keep the number of components to a minimum as more components means more data needs to be mapped into the GPU which can be a bottlneck when dealing with a large number of vertices.

Finally you need to specify the component data type. Here you should aim to use the smallest type that meets your precision requirements. Again the larger the type then more data needs to be mapped into the GPU which can be a bottlneck when dealing with a large number of vertices.

Parameters

attribute_buffer	The CoglAttributeBuffer containing the actual attribute data	
name	The name of the attribute (used to reference it from GLSL)	
stride	The number of bytes to jump to get to the next attribute value for the next vertex. (Usually `sizeof (MyVertex)`)	

offset	The byte offset from the start of *attribute_buffer* for the first attribute value. (Usually `offsetof` `(MyVertex,` `component0)`	
components	The number of components (e.g. 4 for an rgba color or 3 for and (x,y,z) position)	
type	FIXME	

Returns

A newly allocated CoglAttribute describing the layout for a list of attribute values stored in `array` .

[transfer full]

Since 1.4

Stability Level: Unstable

cogl_is_attribute ()

```
CoglBool
cogl_is_attribute (void *object);
```

Gets whether the given object references a CoglAttribute.

Parameters

object	A CoglObject	

Returns

TRUE if the `object` references a CoglAttribute, FALSE otherwise

cogl_attribute_set_normalized ()

```
void
cogl_attribute_set_normalized (CoglAttribute *attribute,
                               CoglBool normalized);
```

Sets whether fixed point attribute types are mapped to the range 0→1. For example when this property is TRUE and a COGL_ATTRIBUTE_TYPE_UNSIGNED_BYTE type is used then the value 255 will be mapped to 1.0.

The default value of this property depends on the name of the attribute. For the builtin properties cogl_color_in and cogl_normal_in it will default to TRUE and for all other names it will default to FALSE.

Parameters

attribute	A CoglAttribute	
normalized	The new value for the normalized property.	

Since 1.10

Stability Level: Unstable

cogl_attribute_get_normalized ()

```
CoglBool
cogl_attribute_get_normalized (CoglAttribute *attribute);
```

Parameters

| attribute | A CoglAttribute | |

Returns

the value of the normalized property set with cogl_attribute_set_normalized().

Since 1.10

Stability Level: Unstable

cogl_attribute_get_buffer ()

```
CoglAttributeBuffer~*
cogl_attribute_get_buffer (CoglAttribute *attribute);
```

Parameters

| attribute | A CoglAttribute | |

Returns

the CoglAttributeBuffer that was set with cogl_attribute_set_buffer() or cogl_attribute_new().

[transfer none]

Since 1.10

Stability Level: Unstable

cogl_attribute_set_buffer ()

```
void
cogl_attribute_set_buffer (CoglAttribute *attribute,
                           CoglAttributeBuffer *attribute_buffer);
```

Sets a new CoglAttributeBuffer for the attribute.

Parameters

| attribute | A CoglAttribute | |
| attribute_buffer | A CoglAttributeBuffer | |

Since 1.10

Stability Level: Unstable

Types and Values

CoglAttribute

```
typedef struct _CoglAttribute CoglAttribute;
```

1.6.2 Indices

Indices — Describe vertex indices stored in a CoglIndexBuffer.

Functions

CoglBool	cogl_is_indices ()
CoglIndices *	cogl_indices_new ()
CoglIndices *	cogl_get_rectangle_indices ()

Types and Values

	CoglIndices
enum	CoglIndicesType

Description

Indices allow you to avoid duplicating vertices in your vertex data by virtualizing your data and instead providing a sequence of index values that tell the GPU which data should be used for each vertex.

If the GPU is given a sequence of indices it doesn't simply walk through each vertex of your data in order it will instead walk through the indices which can provide random access to the underlying data.

Since it's very common to have duplicate vertices when describing a shape as a list of triangles it can often be a significant space saving to describe geometry using indices. Reducing the size of your models can make it cheaper to map them into the GPU by reducing the demand on memory bandwidth and may help to make better use of your GPUs internal vertex caching.

For example, to describe a quadrilateral as 2 triangles for the GPU you could either provide data with 6 vertices or instead with indices you can provide vertex data for just 4 vertices and an index buffer that specfies the 6 vertices by indexing the shared vertices multiple times.

```
CoglVertex2f quad_vertices[] = {
  {x0, y0}, //0 = top left
  {x1, y1}, //1 = bottom left
  {x2, y2}, //2 = bottom right
  {x3, y3}, //3 = top right
};
//tell the gpu how to interpret the quad as 2 triangles...
unsigned char indices[] = {0, 1, 2, 0, 2, 3};
```

Even in the above illustration we see a saving of 10bytes for one quad compared to having data for 6 vertices and no indices but if you need to draw 100s or 1000s of quads then its really quite significant.

Something else to consider is that often indices can be defined once and remain static while the vertex data may change for animations perhaps. That means you may be able to ignore the negligable cost of mapping your indices into the GPU if they don't ever change.

The above illustration is actually a good example of static indices because it's really common that developers have quad mesh data that they need to display and we know exactly what that indices array needs to look like depending on the number of quads that need to be drawn. It doesn't matter how the quads might be animated and changed the indices will remain the same. Cogl even has a utility (cogl_get_rectangle_indices()) to get access to re-useable indices for drawing quads as above.

Functions

cogl_is_indices ()

```
CoglBool
cogl_is_indices (void *object);
```

Gets whether the given object references a CoglIndices.

Parameters

object	A CoglObject pointer

Returns

TRUE if the object references a CoglIndices and FALSE otherwise.

Since 1.10

Stability Level: Unstable

cogl_indices_new ()

```
CoglIndices~*
cogl_indices_new (CoglContext *context,
                  CoglIndicesType type,
                  const void *indices_data,
                  int n_indices);
```

cogl_get_rectangle_indices ()

```
CoglIndices~*
cogl_get_rectangle_indices (CoglContext *context,
                            int n_rectangles);
```

Types and Values

CoglIndices

```
typedef struct _CoglIndices CoglIndices;
```

enum CoglIndicesType

You should aim to use the smallest data type that gives you enough range, since it reduces the size of your index array and can help reduce the demand on memory bandwidth.

Note that COGL_INDICES_TYPE_UNSIGNED_INT is only supported if the COGL_FEATURE_ID_UNSIGNED_INT_INDICES feature is available. This should always be available on OpenGL but on OpenGL ES it will only be available if the GL_OES_element_ind extension is advertized.

Members

COGL_INDICES_TYPE_UNSIGNED_BYTE	Your indices are unsigned bytes
COGL_INDICES_TYPE_UNSIGNED_SHORT	Your indices are unsigned shorts
COGL_INDICES_TYPE_UNSIGNED_INT	Your indices are unsigned ints

1.7 Geometry

1.7.1 Primitives

Primitives — Functions for creating, manipulating and drawing primitives

Functions

CoglPrimitive *	cogl_primitive_new ()
CoglPrimitive *	cogl_primitive_new_with_attributes ()
CoglPrimitive *	cogl_primitive_new_p2 ()
CoglPrimitive *	cogl_primitive_new_p3 ()
CoglPrimitive *	cogl_primitive_new_p2c4 ()
CoglPrimitive *	cogl_primitive_new_p3c4 ()
CoglPrimitive *	cogl_primitive_new_p2t2 ()
CoglPrimitive *	cogl_primitive_new_p3t2 ()
CoglPrimitive *	cogl_primitive_new_p2t2c4 ()
CoglPrimitive *	cogl_primitive_new_p3t2c4 ()
CoglBool	cogl_is_primitive ()
int	cogl_primitive_get_first_vertex ()
void	cogl_primitive_set_first_vertex ()
int	cogl_primitive_get_n_vertices ()
void	cogl_primitive_set_n_vertices ()
CoglVerticesMode	cogl_primitive_get_mode ()
void	cogl_primitive_set_mode ()
void	cogl_primitive_set_attributes ()
CoglIndices *	cogl_primitive_get_indices ()
void	cogl_primitive_set_indices ()
CoglPrimitive *	cogl_primitive_copy ()

CoglBool	(*CoglPrimitiveAttributeCallback) ()
void	cogl_primitive_foreach_attribute ()
void	cogl_primitive_draw ()

Types and Values

| | CoglPrimitive |

Description

FIXME

Functions

cogl_primitive_new ()

```
CoglPrimitive~*
cogl_primitive_new (CoglVerticesMode mode,
                    int n_vertices,
                    ...);
```

Combines a set of CoglAttributes with a specific draw *mode* and defines a vertex count so a CoglPrimitive object can be retained and drawn later with no addition information required.

The value passed as *n_vertices* will simply update the CoglPrimitive *n_vertices* property as if cogl_primitive_set_n_vertices() were called. This property defines the number of vertices to read when drawing.

Parameters

mode	A CoglVerticesMode defining how to draw the vertices	
n_vertices	The number of vertices to process when drawing	
...	A NULL terminated list of attributes	

Returns

A newly allocated CoglPrimitive object.

[transfer full]

Since 1.6

Stability Level: Unstable

cogl_primitive_new_with_attributes ()

```
CoglPrimitive~*
cogl_primitive_new_with_attributes (CoglVerticesMode mode,
                                    int n_vertices,
                                    CoglAttribute **attributes,
                                    int n_attributes);
```

Combines a set of CoglAttributes with a specific draw *mode* and defines a vertex count so a CoglPrimitive object can be retained and drawn later with no addition information required.

The value passed as *n_vertices* will simply update the CoglPrimitive *n_vertices* property as if cogl_primitive_set_n_vertices() were called. This property defines the number of vertices to read when drawing.

Parameters

mode	A CoglVerticesMode defining how to draw the vertices	
n_vertices	The number of vertices to process when drawing	
attributes	An array of CoglAttribute	
n_attributes	The number of attributes	

Returns

A newly allocated CoglPrimitive object.

[transfer full]

Since 1.6

Stability Level: Unstable

cogl_primitive_new_p2 ()

```
CoglPrimitive~*
cogl_primitive_new_p2 (CoglContext *context,
                       CoglVerticesMode mode,
                       int n_vertices,
                       const CoglVertexP2 *data);
```

data : (array length=n_vertices): (type Cogl.VertexP2): An array of CoglVertexP2 vertices

Provides a convenient way to describe a primitive, such as a single triangle strip or a triangle fan, that will internally allocate the necessary CoglAttributeBuffer storage, describe the position attribute with a CoglAttribute and upload your data.

For example to draw a convex polygon you can do:

```
CoglVertexP2 triangle[] =
{
  { 0,    300 },
  { 150, 0,  },
  { 300, 300 }
};
prim = cogl_primitive_new_p2 (COGL_VERTICES_MODE_TRIANGLE_FAN,
                              3, triangle);
cogl_primitive_draw (prim);
```

The value passed as *n_vertices* is initially used to determine how much can be read from *data* but it will also be used to update the CoglPrimitive *n_vertices* property as if cogl_primitive_set_n_vertices() were called. This property defines the number of vertices to read when drawing.

Note The primitive API doesn't support drawing with high-level meta texture types such as CoglTexture2DSliced or CoglAtlasTexture so you need to ensure that only low-level textures that can be directly sampled by a GPU such as CoglTexture2D, CoglTextureRectangle or CoglTexture3D are associated with the layers of any pipeline used while drawing a primitive.

Parameters

context	A CoglContext	
mode	A CoglVerticesMode defining how to draw the vertices	
n_vertices	The number of vertices to read from *data* and also the number of vertices to read when later drawing.	

Returns

A newly allocated CoglPrimitive with a reference of 1. This can be freed using cogl_object_unref().

[transfer full]

Since 1.6

Stability Level: Unstable

cogl_primitive_new_p3 ()

```
CoglPrimitive~*
cogl_primitive_new_p3 (CoglContext *context,
                       CoglVerticesMode mode,
                       int n_vertices,
                       const CoglVertexP3 *data);
```

Provides a convenient way to describe a primitive, such as a single triangle strip or a triangle fan, that will internally allocate the necessary CoglAttributeBuffer storage, describe the position attribute with a CoglAttribute and upload your data.

For example to draw a convex polygon you can do:

```
CoglVertexP3 triangle[] =
{
  { 0,    300, 0 },
  { 150, 0,    0 },
  { 300, 300, 0 }
};
prim = cogl_primitive_new_p3 (COGL_VERTICES_MODE_TRIANGLE_FAN,
                              3, triangle);
cogl_primitive_draw (prim);
```

The value passed as *n_vertices* is initially used to determine how much can be read from *data* but it will also be used to update the CoglPrimitive *n_vertices* property as if cogl_primitive_set_n_vertices() were called. This property defines the number of vertices to read when drawing.

Note The primitive API doesn't support drawing with high-level meta texture types such as CoglTexture2DSliced or CoglAtlasTexture so you need to ensure that only low-level textures that can be directly sampled by a GPU such as CoglTexture2D, CoglTextureRectangle or CoglTexture3D are associated with the layers of any pipeline used while drawing a primitive.

Parameters

context	A CoglContext	

mode	A CoglVerticesMode defining how to draw the vertices	
n_vertices	The number of vertices to read from *data* and also the number of vertices to read when later drawing.	
data	(type Cogl.VertexP3): An array of CoglVertexP3 vertices.	*[array length=n_vertices]*

Returns

A newly allocated CoglPrimitive with a reference of 1. This can be freed using cogl_object_unref().

[transfer full]

Since 1.6

Stability Level: Unstable

cogl_primitive_new_p2c4 ()

```
CoglPrimitive~*
cogl_primitive_new_p2c4 (CoglContext *context,
                         CoglVerticesMode mode,
                         int n_vertices,
                         const CoglVertexP2C4 *data);
```

Provides a convenient way to describe a primitive, such as a single triangle strip or a triangle fan, that will internally allocate the necessary CoglAttributeBuffer storage, describe the position and color attributes with CoglAttributes and upload your data.

For example to draw a convex polygon with a linear gradient you can do:

```
CoglVertexP2C4 triangle[] =
{
  { 0,   300,  0xff, 0x00, 0x00, 0xff },
  { 150, 0,    0x00, 0xff, 0x00, 0xff },
  { 300, 300,  0xff, 0x00, 0x00, 0xff }
};
prim = cogl_primitive_new_p2c4 (COGL_VERTICES_MODE_TRIANGLE_FAN,
                                3, triangle);
cogl_primitive_draw (prim);
```

The value passed as *n_vertices* is initially used to determine how much can be read from *data* but it will also be used to update the CoglPrimitive *n_vertices* property as if cogl_primitive_set_n_vertices() were called. This property defines the number of vertices to read when drawing.

Note The primitive API doesn't support drawing with high-level meta texture types such as CoglTexture2DSliced or CoglAtlasTexture so you need to ensure that only low-level textures that can be directly sampled by a GPU such as CoglTexture2D, CoglTextureRectangle or CoglTexture3D are associated with the layers of any pipeline used while drawing a primitive.

Parameters

context	A CoglContext	
mode	A CoglVerticesMode defining how to draw the vertices	

n_vertices	The number of vertices to read from `data` and also the number of vertices to read when later drawing.	
data	(type Cogl.VertexP2C4): An array of CoglVertexP2C4 vertices.	*[array length=n_vertices]*

Returns

A newly allocated CoglPrimitive with a reference of 1. This can be freed using cogl_object_unref().

[transfer full]

Since 1.6

Stability Level: Unstable

cogl_primitive_new_p3c4 ()

```
CoglPrimitive~*
cogl_primitive_new_p3c4 (CoglContext *context,
                         CoglVerticesMode mode,
                         int n_vertices,
                         const CoglVertexP3C4 *data);
```

Provides a convenient way to describe a primitive, such as a single triangle strip or a triangle fan, that will internally allocate the necessary CoglAttributeBuffer storage, describe the position and color attributes with CoglAttributes and upload your data.

For example to draw a convex polygon with a linear gradient you can do:

```
CoglVertexP3C4 triangle[] =
{
  { 0,   300, 0,  0xff, 0x00, 0x00, 0xff },
  { 150, 0,   0,  0x00, 0xff, 0x00, 0xff },
  { 300, 300, 0,  0xff, 0x00, 0x00, 0xff }
};
prim = cogl_primitive_new_p3c4 (COGL_VERTICES_MODE_TRIANGLE_FAN,
                                3, triangle);
cogl_primitive_draw (prim);
```

The value passed as *n_vertices* is initially used to determine how much can be read from *data* but it will also be used to update the CoglPrimitive *n_vertices* property as if cogl_primitive_set_n_vertices() were called. This property defines the number of vertices to read when drawing.

Note The primitive API doesn't support drawing with high-level meta texture types such as CoglTexture2DSliced or CoglAtlasTexture so you need to ensure that only low-level textures that can be directly sampled by a GPU such as CoglTexture2D, CoglTextureRectangle or CoglTexture3D are associated with the layers of any pipeline used while drawing a primitive.

Parameters

context	A CoglContext	
mode	A CoglVerticesMode defining how to draw the vertices	

n_vertices	The number of vertices to read from *data* and also the number of vertices to read when later drawing.	
data	(type Cogl.VertexP3C4): An array of CoglVertexP3C4 vertices.	*[array length=n_vertices]*

Returns

A newly allocated CoglPrimitive with a reference of 1. This can be freed using cogl_object_unref().

[transfer full]

Since 1.6

Stability Level: Unstable

cogl_primitive_new_p2t2 ()

```
CoglPrimitive~*
cogl_primitive_new_p2t2 (CoglContext *context,
                         CoglVerticesMode mode,
                         int n_vertices,
                         const CoglVertexP2T2 *data);
```

Provides a convenient way to describe a primitive, such as a single triangle strip or a triangle fan, that will internally allocate the necessary CoglAttributeBuffer storage, describe the position and texture coordinate attributes with CoglAttributes and upload your data.

For example to draw a convex polygon with texture mapping you can do:

```
CoglVertexP2T2 triangle[] =
{
  { 0,   300,  0.0, 1.0},
  { 150, 0,    0.5, 0.0},
  { 300, 300,  1.0, 1.0}
};
prim = cogl_primitive_new_p2t2 (COGL_VERTICES_MODE_TRIANGLE_FAN,
                                3, triangle);
cogl_primitive_draw (prim);
```

The value passed as *n_vertices* is initially used to determine how much can be read from *data* but it will also be used to update the CoglPrimitive *n_vertices* property as if cogl_primitive_set_n_vertices() were called. This property defines the number of vertices to read when drawing.

Note The primitive API doesn't support drawing with high-level meta texture types such as CoglTexture2DSliced or CoglAtlasTexture so you need to ensure that only low-level textures that can be directly sampled by a GPU such as CoglTexture2D, CoglTextureRectangle or CoglTexture3D are associated with the layers of any pipeline used while drawing a primitive.

Parameters

context	A CoglContext	
mode	A CoglVerticesMode defining how to draw the vertices	

n_vertices	The number of vertices to read from `data` and also the number of vertices to read when later drawing.	
data	(type Cogl.VertexP2T2): An array of CoglVertexP2T2 vertices.	*[array length=n_vertices]*

Returns

A newly allocated CoglPrimitive with a reference of 1. This can be freed using cogl_object_unref().

[transfer full]

Since 1.6

Stability Level: Unstable

cogl_primitive_new_p3t2 ()

```
CoglPrimitive~*
cogl_primitive_new_p3t2 (CoglContext *context,
                         CoglVerticesMode mode,
                         int n_vertices,
                         const CoglVertexP3T2 *data);
```

Provides a convenient way to describe a primitive, such as a single triangle strip or a triangle fan, that will internally allocate the necessary CoglAttributeBuffer storage, describe the position and texture coordinate attributes with CoglAttributes and upload your data.

For example to draw a convex polygon with texture mapping you can do:

```
CoglVertexP3T2 triangle[] =
{
  { 0,    300, 0,   0.0, 1.0},
  { 150, 0,    0,   0.5, 0.0},
  { 300, 300, 0,   1.0, 1.0}
};
prim = cogl_primitive_new_p3t2 (COGL_VERTICES_MODE_TRIANGLE_FAN,
                                3, triangle);
cogl_primitive_draw (prim);
```

The value passed as *n_vertices* is initially used to determine how much can be read from *data* but it will also be used to update the CoglPrimitive *n_vertices* property as if cogl_primitive_set_n_vertices() were called. This property defines the number of vertices to read when drawing.

Note The primitive API doesn't support drawing with high-level meta texture types such as CoglTexture2DSliced or CoglAtlasTexture so you need to ensure that only low-level textures that can be directly sampled by a GPU such as CoglTexture2D, CoglTextureRectangle or CoglTexture3D are associated with the layers of any pipeline used while drawing a primitive.

Parameters

context	A CoglContext	
mode	A CoglVerticesMode defining how to draw the vertices	

n_vertices	The number of vertices to read from *data* and also the number of vertices to read when later drawing.	
data	(type Cogl.VertexP3T2): An array of CoglVertexP3T2 vertices.	*[array length=n_vertices]*

Returns

A newly allocated CoglPrimitive with a reference of 1. This can be freed using cogl_object_unref().

[transfer full]

Since 1.6

Stability Level: Unstable

cogl_primitive_new_p2t2c4 ()

```
CoglPrimitive~*
cogl_primitive_new_p2t2c4 (CoglContext *context,
                          CoglVerticesMode mode,
                          int n_vertices,
                          const CoglVertexP2T2C4 *data);
```

Provides a convenient way to describe a primitive, such as a single triangle strip or a triangle fan, that will internally allocate the necessary CoglAttributeBuffer storage, describe the position, texture coordinate and color attributes with CoglAttributes and upload your data.

For example to draw a convex polygon with texture mapping and a linear gradient you can do:

```
CoglVertexP2T2C4 triangle[] =
{
  { 0,    300,  0.0, 1.0,  0xff, 0x00, 0x00, 0xff},
  { 150, 0,    0.5, 0.0,  0x00, 0xff, 0x00, 0xff},
  { 300, 300,  1.0, 1.0,  0xff, 0x00, 0x00, 0xff}
};
prim = cogl_primitive_new_p2t2c4 (COGL_VERTICES_MODE_TRIANGLE_FAN,
                                  3, triangle);
cogl_primitive_draw (prim);
```

The value passed as *n_vertices* is initially used to determine how much can be read from *data* but it will also be used to update the CoglPrimitive *n_vertices* property as if cogl_primitive_set_n_vertices() were called. This property defines the number of vertices to read when drawing.

Note The primitive API doesn't support drawing with high-level meta texture types such as CoglTexture2DSliced or CoglAtlasTexture so you need to ensure that only low-level textures that can be directly sampled by a GPU such as CoglTexture2D, CoglTextureRectangle or CoglTexture3D are associated with the layers of any pipeline used while drawing a primitive.

Parameters

context	A CoglContext	
mode	A CoglVerticesMode defining how to draw the vertices	

n_vertices	The number of vertices to read from *data* and also the number of vertices to read when later drawing.	
data	(type Cogl.VertexP2T2C4): An array of CoglVertexP2T2C4 vertices.	*[array length=n_vertices]*

Returns

A newly allocated CoglPrimitive with a reference of 1. This can be freed using cogl_object_unref().

[transfer full]

Since 1.6

Stability Level: Unstable

cogl_primitive_new_p3t2c4 ()

```
CoglPrimitive~*
cogl_primitive_new_p3t2c4 (CoglContext *context,
                          CoglVerticesMode mode,
                          int n_vertices,
                          const CoglVertexP3T2C4 *data);
```

Provides a convenient way to describe a primitive, such as a single triangle strip or a triangle fan, that will internally allocate the necessary CoglAttributeBuffer storage, describe the position, texture coordinate and color attributes with CoglAttributes and upload your data.

For example to draw a convex polygon with texture mapping and a linear gradient you can do:

```
CoglVertexP3T2C4 triangle[] =
{
  { 0,    300, 0,  0.0, 1.0,  0xff, 0x00, 0x00, 0xff},
  { 150, 0,    0,  0.5, 0.0,  0x00, 0xff, 0x00, 0xff},
  { 300, 300, 0,  1.0, 1.0,  0xff, 0x00, 0x00, 0xff}
};
prim = cogl_primitive_new_p3t2c4 (COGL_VERTICES_MODE_TRIANGLE_FAN,
                                  3, triangle);
cogl_primitive_draw (prim);
```

The value passed as *n_vertices* is initially used to determine how much can be read from *data* but it will also be used to update the CoglPrimitive *n_vertices* property as if cogl_primitive_set_n_vertices() were called. This property defines the number of vertices to read when drawing.

Note The primitive API doesn't support drawing with high-level meta texture types such as CoglTexture2DSliced or CoglAtlasTexture so you need to ensure that only low-level textures that can be directly sampled by a GPU such as CoglTexture2D, CoglTextureRectangle or CoglTexture3D are associated with the layers of any pipeline used while drawing a primitive.

Parameters

context	A CoglContext	
mode	A CoglVerticesMode defining how to draw the vertices	

n_vertices	The number of vertices to read from *data* and also the number of vertices to read when later drawing.	
data	(type Cogl.VertexP3T2C4): An array of CoglVertexP3T2C4 vertices.	*[array length=n_vertices]*

Returns

A newly allocated CoglPrimitive with a reference of 1. This can be freed using cogl_object_unref().

[transfer full]

Since 1.6

Stability Level: Unstable

cogl_is_primitive ()

```
CoglBool
cogl_is_primitive (void *object);
```

Gets whether the given object references a CoglPrimitive.

Parameters

object	A CoglObject	

Returns

TRUE if the *object* references a CoglPrimitive, FALSE otherwise

Since 1.6

Stability Level: Unstable

cogl_primitive_get_first_vertex ()

```
int
cogl_primitive_get_first_vertex (CoglPrimitive *primitive);
```

cogl_primitive_set_first_vertex ()

```
void
cogl_primitive_set_first_vertex (CoglPrimitive *primitive,
                                 int first_vertex);
```

cogl_primitive_get_n_vertices ()

```
int
cogl_primitive_get_n_vertices (CoglPrimitive *primitive);
```

Queries the number of vertices to read when drawing the given *primitive*. Usually this value is implicitly set when associating vertex data or indices with a CoglPrimitive.

If cogl_primitive_set_indices() has been used to associate a sequence of CoglIndices with the given *primitive* then the number of vertices to read can also be phrased as the number of indices to read.

Note To be clear; it doesn't refer to the number of vertices - in terms of data - associated with the primitive it's just the number of vertices to read and draw.

Parameters

primitive	A CoglPrimitive object	

Returns

The number of vertices to read when drawing.

Since 1.8

Stability Level: Unstable

cogl_primitive_set_n_vertices ()

```
void
cogl_primitive_set_n_vertices (CoglPrimitive *primitive,
                               int n_vertices);
```

Specifies how many vertices should be read when drawing the given *primitive*.

Usually this value is set implicitly when associating vertex data or indices with a CoglPrimitive.

Note To be clear; it doesn't refer to the number of vertices - in terms of data - associated with the primitive it's just the number of vertices to read and draw.

Parameters

primitive	A CoglPrimitive object	
n_vertices	The number of vertices to read when drawing.	

Since 1.8

Stability Level: Unstable

cogl_primitive_get_mode ()

```
CoglVerticesMode
cogl_primitive_get_mode (CoglPrimitive *primitive);
```

cogl_primitive_set_mode ()

```
void
cogl_primitive_set_mode (CoglPrimitive *primitive,
                         CoglVerticesMode mode);
```

cogl_primitive_set_attributes ()

```
void
cogl_primitive_set_attributes (CoglPrimitive *primitive,
                               CoglAttribute **attributes,
                               int n_attributes);
```

Replaces all the attributes of the given CoglPrimitive object.

Parameters

primitive	A CoglPrimitive object	
attributes	an array of CoglAttribute pointers	
n_attributes	the number of elements in *attributes*	

Since 1.6

Stability Level: Unstable

cogl_primitive_get_indices ()

```
CoglIndices~*
cogl_primitive_get_indices (CoglPrimitive *primitive);
```

Parameters

primitive	A CoglPrimitive	

Returns

the indices that were set with cogl_primitive_set_indices() or NULL if no indices were set.

[transfer none]

Since 1.10

Stability Level: Unstable

cogl_primitive_set_indices ()

```
void
cogl_primitive_set_indices (CoglPrimitive *primitive,
                            CoglIndices *indices,
                            int n_indices);
```

Associates a sequence of CoglIndices with the given *primitive*.

CoglIndices provide a way to virtualize your real vertex data by providing a sequence of indices that index into your real vertex data. The GPU will walk though the index values to indirectly lookup the data for each vertex instead of sequentially walking through the data directly. This lets you save memory by indexing shared data multiple times instead of duplicating the data.

The value passed as *n_indices* will simply update the CoglPrimitive *n_vertices* property as if cogl_primitive_set_n_vertices() were called. This property defines the number of vertices to draw or, put another way, how many indices should be read from *indices* when drawing.

Note The CoglPrimitive *first_vertex* property also affects drawing with indices by defining the first entry of the indices to start drawing from.

Parameters

primitive	A CoglPrimitive	
indices	A CoglIndices array	
n_indices	The number of indices to reference when drawing	

Since 1.10

Stability Level: Unstable

cogl_primitive_copy ()

```
CoglPrimitive~*
cogl_primitive_copy (CoglPrimitive *primitive);
```

Makes a copy of an existing CoglPrimitive. Note that the primitive is a shallow copy which means it will use the same attributes and attribute buffers as the original primitive.

Parameters

primitive	A primitive copy	

Returns

the new primitive.

[transfer full]

Since 1.10

Stability Level: Unstable

CoglPrimitiveAttributeCallback ()

```
CoglBool
(*CoglPrimitiveAttributeCallback) (CoglPrimitive *primitive,
                                   CoglAttribute *attribute,
                                   void *user_data);
```

The callback prototype used with cogl_primitive_foreach_attribute() for iterating all the attributes of a CoglPrimitive.

The function should return TRUE to continue iteration or FALSE to stop.

Parameters

primitive	The CoglPrimitive whose attributes are being iterated	
attribute	The CoglAttribute	
user_data	The private data passed to cogl_primitive_foreach_attribute()	

Since 1.10

Stability Level: Unstable

cogl_primitive_foreach_attribute ()

```
void
cogl_primitive_foreach_attribute (CoglPrimitive *primitive,
                                  CoglPrimitiveAttributeCallback callback,
                                  void *user_data);
```

Iterates all the attributes of the given CoglPrimitive.

Parameters

primitive	A CoglPrimitive object	
callback	A CoglPrimitiveAttributeCallback to be called for each attribute.	*[scope call]*
user_data	Private data that will be passed to the callback.	*[closure]*

Since 1.10

Stability Level: Unstable

cogl_primitive_draw ()

```
void
cogl_primitive_draw (CoglPrimitive *primitive,
                     CoglFramebuffer *framebuffer,
                     CoglPipeline *pipeline);
```

Draws the given *primitive* geometry to the specified destination *framebuffer* using the graphics processing state described by *pipeline*.

This drawing api doesn't support high-level meta texture types such as CoglTexture2DSliced so it is the user's responsibility to ensure that only low-level textures that can be directly sampled by a GPU such as CoglTexture2D, CoglTextureRectangle or CoglTexture3D are associated with layers of the given *pipeline*.

Parameters

primitive	A CoglPrimitive geometry object	
framebuffer	A destination CoglFramebuffer	
pipeline	A CoglPipeline state object	

Since 1.16

Stability Level: Unstable

Types and Values

CoglPrimitive

```
typedef struct _CoglPrimitive CoglPrimitive;
```

1.7.2 Path Primitives

Path Primitives —

Description

Functions

Types and Values

1.8 Textures

1.8.1 Bitmap

Bitmap — Functions for loading images

Functions

CoglBool	cogl_is_bitmap ()
CoglBitmap *	cogl_bitmap_new_from_file ()
CoglBitmap *	cogl_bitmap_new_from_buffer ()
CoglBitmap *	cogl_bitmap_new_with_size ()
CoglBitmap *	cogl_bitmap_new_for_data ()
CoglPixelFormat	cogl_bitmap_get_format ()
int	cogl_bitmap_get_width ()
int	cogl_bitmap_get_height ()
int	cogl_bitmap_get_rowstride ()
CoglPixelBuffer *	cogl_bitmap_get_buffer ()
CoglBool	cogl_bitmap_get_size_from_file ()
#define	COGL_BITMAP_ERROR

Types and Values

	CoglBitmap
enum	CoglBitmapError

Description

Cogl allows loading image data into memory as CoglBitmaps without loading them immediately into GPU textures.

CoglBitmap is available since Cogl 1.0

Functions

cogl_is_bitmap ()

```
CoglBool
cogl_is_bitmap (void *object);
```

Checks whether *object* is a CoglBitmap

Parameters

object	a CoglObject pointer	

Returns

TRUE if the passed *object* represents a bitmap, and FALSE otherwise

Since 1.0

cogl_bitmap_new_from_file ()

```
CoglBitmap~*
cogl_bitmap_new_from_file (CoglContext *context,
                           const char *filename,
                           CoglError **error);
```

Loads an image file from disk. This function can be safely called from within a thread.

Parameters

context	A CoglContext	
filename	the file to load.	
error	a CoglError or NULL.	

Returns

a CoglBitmap to the new loaded image data, or NULL if loading the image failed.

[transfer full]

Since 1.0

cogl_bitmap_new_from_buffer ()

```
CoglBitmap~*
cogl_bitmap_new_from_buffer (CoglBuffer *buffer,
                             CoglPixelFormat format,
                             int width,
                             int height,
                             int rowstride,
                             int offset);
```

Wraps some image data that has been uploaded into a CoglBuffer as a CoglBitmap. The data is not copied in this process.

Parameters

buffer	A CoglBuffer containing image data	
format	The CoglPixelFormat defining the format of the image data in the given *buffer*.	
width	The width of the image data in the given *buffer*.	
height	The height of the image data in the given *buffer*.	
rowstride	The rowstride in bytes of the image data in the given *buffer*.	
offset	The offset into the given *buffer* to the first pixel that should be considered part of the CoglBitmap.	

Returns

a CoglBitmap encapsulating the given *buffer*.

[transfer full]

Since 1.8

Stability Level: Unstable

cogl_bitmap_new_with_size ()

```
CoglBitmap~*
cogl_bitmap_new_with_size (CoglContext *context,
                           unsigned int width,
                           unsigned int height,
                           CoglPixelFormat format);
```

Creates a new CoglBitmap with the given width, height and format. The initial contents of the bitmap are undefined.

The data for the bitmap will be stored in a newly created CoglPixelBuffer. You can get a pointer to the pixel buffer using cogl_bitmap_get_buffer(). The CoglBuffer API can then be used to fill the bitmap with data.

Note Cogl will try its best to provide a hardware array you can map, write into and effectively do a zero copy upload when creating a texture from it with cogl_texture_new_from_bitmap(). For various reasons, such arrays are likely to have a stride larger than width * bytes_per_pixel. The user must take the stride into account when writing into it. The stride can be retrieved with cogl_bitmap_get_rowstride().

Parameters

context	A CoglContext	
width	width of the bitmap in pixels	
height	height of the bitmap in pixels	
format	the format of the pixels the array will store	

Returns

a CoglPixelBuffer representing the newly created array or NULL on failure.

[transfer full]

Since 1.10

Stability Level: Unstable

cogl_bitmap_new_for_data ()

```
CoglBitmap~*
cogl_bitmap_new_for_data (CoglContext *context,
                          int width,
                          int height,
                          CoglPixelFormat format,
                          int rowstride,
                          uint8_t *data);
```

Creates a bitmap using some existing data. The data is not copied so the application must keep the buffer alive for the lifetime of the CoglBitmap. This can be used for example with cogl_framebuffer_read_pixels_into_bitmap() to read data directly into an application buffer with the specified rowstride.

Parameters

context	A CoglContext	
width	The width of the bitmap.	
height	The height of the bitmap.	
format	The format of the pixel data.	
rowstride	The rowstride of the bitmap (the number of bytes from the start of one row of the bitmap to the next).	
data	A pointer to the data. The bitmap will take ownership of this data.	

Returns

A new CoglBitmap.

[transfer full]

Since 1.10

Stability Level: Unstable

cogl_bitmap_get_format ()

```
CoglPixelFormat
cogl_bitmap_get_format (CoglBitmap *bitmap);
```

Parameters

bitmap	A CoglBitmap	

Returns

the CoglPixelFormat that the data for the bitmap is in.

Since 1.10

Stability Level: Unstable

cogl_bitmap_get_width ()

```
int
cogl_bitmap_get_width (CoglBitmap *bitmap);
```

Parameters

bitmap	A CoglBitmap	

Returns

the width of the bitmap

Since 1.10

Stability Level: Unstable

cogl_bitmap_get_height ()

```
int
cogl_bitmap_get_height (CoglBitmap *bitmap);
```

Parameters

bitmap	A CoglBitmap	

Returns

the height of the bitmap

Since 1.10

Stability Level: Unstable

cogl_bitmap_get_rowstride ()

```
int
cogl_bitmap_get_rowstride (CoglBitmap *bitmap);
```

Parameters

bitmap	A CoglBitmap	

Returns

the rowstride of the bitmap. This is the number of bytes between the address of start of one row to the address of the next row in the image.

Since 1.10

Stability Level: Unstable

cogl_bitmap_get_buffer ()

```
CoglPixelBuffer~*
cogl_bitmap_get_buffer (CoglBitmap *bitmap);
```

Parameters

bitmap	A CoglBitmap	

Returns

the CoglPixelBuffer that this buffer uses for storage. Note that if the bitmap was created with cogl_bitmap_new_from_file() then it will not actually be using a pixel buffer and this function will return NULL.

[transfer none]

Since 1.10

Stability Level: Unstable

cogl_bitmap_get_size_from_file ()

```
CoglBool
cogl_bitmap_get_size_from_file (const char *filename,
                                int *width,
                                int *height);
```

Parses an image file enough to extract the width and height of the bitmap.

Parameters

filename	the file to check	
width	return location for the bitmap width, or NULL.	*[out]*
height	return location for the bitmap height, or NULL.	*[out]*

Returns

TRUE if the image was successfully parsed

Since 1.0

COGL_BITMAP_ERROR

```
#define COGL_BITMAP_ERROR (cogl_bitmap_error_domain ())
```

CoglError domain for bitmap errors.

Since 1.4

Types and Values

CoglBitmap

```
typedef struct _CoglBitmap CoglBitmap;
```

enum CoglBitmapError

Error codes that can be thrown when performing bitmap operations. Note that gdk_pixbuf_new_from_file() can also throw errors directly from the underlying image loading library. For example, if GdkPixbuf is used then errors GdkPixbufErrors will be used directly.

Members

COGL_BITMAP_ERROR_FAILED	Generic failure code, something went wrong.
COGL_BITMAP_ERROR_UNKNOWN_TYPE	Unknown image type.
COGL_BITMAP_ERROR_CORRUPT_IMAGE	An image file was broken somehow.

Since 1.4

1.8.2 The Texture Interface

The Texture Interface — Common interface for manipulating textures

Functions

CoglBool	cogl_is_texture ()
#define	COGL_TEXTURE_ERROR
CoglBool	cogl_texture_allocate ()
int	cogl_texture_get_width ()

int	cogl_texture_get_height ()
CoglBool	cogl_texture_is_sliced ()
int	cogl_texture_get_data ()
CoglBool	cogl_texture_set_data ()
CoglBool	cogl_texture_set_region ()
void	cogl_texture_set_components ()
CoglTextureComponents	cogl_texture_get_components ()
void	cogl_texture_set_premultiplied ()
CoglBool	cogl_texture_get_premultiplied ()

Types and Values

typedef	CoglTexture
enum	CoglTextureError
enum	CoglTextureType
enum	CoglTextureComponents

Description

Cogl provides several different types of textures such as CoglTexture2D, CoglTexture3D, CoglTextureRectangle, CoglTexture2DSliced, CoglAtlasTexture, CoglSubTexture and CoglTexturePixmapX11 that each have specific apis for creating and manipulating them, but there are a number of common operations that can be applied to any of these texture types which are handled via this CoglTexture interface.

Functions

cogl_is_texture ()

```
CoglBool
cogl_is_texture (void *object);
```

Gets whether the given object references a texture object.

Parameters

object	A CoglObject pointer	

Returns

TRUE if the *object* references a texture, and FALSE otherwise

COGL_TEXTURE_ERROR

```
#define COGL_TEXTURE_ERROR (cogl_texture_error_domain ())
```

CoglError domain for texture errors.

Since 1.8

Stability Level: Unstable

cogl_texture_allocate ()

```
CoglBool
cogl_texture_allocate (CoglTexture *texture,
                       CoglError **error);
```

Explicitly allocates the storage for the given *texture* which allows you to be sure that there is enough memory for the texture and if not then the error can be handled gracefully.

Note Normally applications don't need to use this api directly since the texture will be implicitly allocated when data is set on the texture, or if the texture is attached to a CoglOffscreen framebuffer and rendered too.

Parameters

texture	A CoglTexture	
error	A CoglError to return exceptional errors or NULL	

Returns

TRUE if the texture was successfully allocated, otherwise FALSE and *error* will be updated if it wasn't NULL.

cogl_texture_get_width ()

```
int
cogl_texture_get_width (CoglTexture *texture);
```

Queries the width of a cogl texture.

Parameters

texture	a CoglTexture pointer.	

Returns

the width of the GPU side texture in pixels

cogl_texture_get_height ()

```
int
cogl_texture_get_height (CoglTexture *texture);
```

Queries the height of a cogl texture.

Parameters

texture	a CoglTexture pointer.	

Returns

the height of the GPU side texture in pixels

cogl_texture_is_sliced ()

```
CoglBool
cogl_texture_is_sliced (CoglTexture *texture);
```

Queries if a texture is sliced (stored as multiple GPU side tecture objects).

Parameters

texture	a CoglTexture pointer.

Returns

TRUE if the texture is sliced, FALSE if the texture is stored as a single GPU texture

cogl_texture_get_data ()

```
int
cogl_texture_get_data (CoglTexture *texture,
                       CoglPixelFormat format,
                       unsigned int rowstride,
                       uint8_t *data);
```

Copies the pixel data from a cogl texture to system memory.

Note The rowstride should be the rowstride you want for the destination *data* buffer you don't need to try and calculate the rowstride of the source texture

---

Parameters

texture	a CoglTexture pointer.	
format	the CoglPixelFormat to store the texture as.	
rowstride	the rowstride of *data* in bytes or pass 0 to calculate from the bytes-per-pixel of *format* multiplied by the *texture* width.	
data	memory location to write the *texture*'s contents, or NULL to only query the data size through the return value.	

Returns

the size of the texture data in bytes

cogl_texture_set_data ()

```
CoglBool
cogl_texture_set_data (CoglTexture *texture,
```

```
CoglPixelFormat format,
int rowstride,
const uint8_t *data,
int level,
CoglError **error);
```

Sets all the pixels for a given mipmap *level* by copying the pixel data pointed to by the *data* argument into the given *texture* .

data should point to the first pixel to copy corresponding to the top left of the mipmap *level* being set.

If *rowstride* equals 0 then it will be automatically calculated from the width of the mipmap level and the bytes-per-pixel for the given *format* .

A mipmap *level* of 0 corresponds to the largest, base image of a texture and *level* 1 is half the width and height of level 0. If dividing any dimension of the previous level by two results in a fraction then round the number down (floor()), but clamp to 1 something like this:

```
next_width = MAX (1, floor (prev_width));
```

You can determine the number of mipmap levels for a given texture like this:

```
n_levels = 1 + floor (log2 (max_dimension));
```

Where max_dimension is the larger of cogl_texture_get_width() and cogl_texture_get_height().

It is an error to pass a *level* number >= the number of levels that *texture* can have according to the above calculation.

Note Since the storage for a CoglTexture is allocated lazily then if the given *texture* has not previously been allocated then this api can return FALSE and throw an exceptional *error* if there is not enough memory to allocate storage for *texture*.

Parameters

format	the CoglPixelFormat used in the source *data* buffer.	
rowstride	rowstride of the source *data* buffer (computed from the texture width and *format* if it equals 0)	
data	the source data, pointing to the first top-left pixel to set	
level	The mipmap level to update (Normally 0 for the largest, base texture)	
error	A CoglError to return exceptional errors	

Returns

TRUE if the data upload was successful, and FALSE otherwise

cogl_texture_set_region ()

```
CoglBool
cogl_texture_set_region (CoglTexture *texture,
                         int width,
```

```
int height,
CoglPixelFormat format,
int rowstride,
const uint8_t *data,
int dst_x,
int dst_y,
int level,
CoglError **error);
```

Sets the pixels in a rectangular subregion of *texture* from an in-memory buffer containing pixel *data* .

data should point to the first pixel to copy corresponding to the top left of the region being set.

The rowstride determines how many bytes between the first pixel of a row of *data* and the first pixel of the next row. If *rowstride* equals 0 then it will be automatically calculated from *width* and the bytes-per-pixel for the given *format* .

A mipmap *level* of 0 corresponds to the largest, base image of a texture and *level* 1 is half the width and height of level 0. The size of any level can be calculated from the size of the base level as follows:

```
width = MAX (1, floor (base_width / 2 ^ level));
height = MAX (1, floor (base_height / 2 ^ level));
```

Or more succinctly put using C:

```
width = MAX (1, base_width >> level);
height = MAX (1, base_height >> level);
```

You can get the size of the base level using cogl_texture_get_width() and cogl_texture_get_height().

You can determine the number of mipmap levels for a given texture like this:

```
n_levels = 1 + floor (log2 (max_dimension));
```

Or more succinctly in C using the fls() - "Find Last Set" - function:

```
n_levels = fls (max_dimension);
```

Where max_dimension is the larger of cogl_texture_get_width() and cogl_texture_get_height().

It is an error to pass a *level* number >= the number of levels that *texture* can have according to the above calculation.

Note Since the storage for a CoglTexture is allocated lazily then if the given *texture* has not previously been allocated then this api can return FALSE and throw an exceptional *error* if there is not enough memory to allocate storage for *texture*.

Parameters

texture	a CoglTexture.	
width	width of the region to set.	
height	height of the region to set.	
format	the CoglPixelFormat used in the source *data* buffer.	
rowstride	rowstride in bytes of the source *data* buffer (computed from *width* and *format* if it equals 0)	
data	the source data, pointing to the first top-left pixel to set	
dst_x	upper left destination x coordinate.	

dst_y	upper left destination y coordinate.	
level	The mipmap level to update (Normally 0 for the largest, base image)	
error	A CoglError to return exceptional errors	

Returns

TRUE if the subregion upload was successful, and FALSE otherwise

cogl_texture_set_components ()

```
void
cogl_texture_set_components (CoglTexture *texture,
                             CoglTextureComponents components);
```

Affects the internal storage format for this texture by specifying what components will be required for sampling later.

This api affects how data is uploaded to the GPU since unused components can potentially be discarded from source data.

For textures created by the '_with_size' constructors the default is COGL_TEXTURE_COMPONENTS_RGBA. The other constructors which take a CoglBitmap or a data pointer default to the same components as the pixel format of the data.

Note that the COGL_TEXTURE_COMPONENTS_RG format is not available on all drivers. The availability can be determined by checking for the COGL_FEATURE_ID_TEXTURE_RG feature. If this format is used on a driver where it is not available then COGL_TEXTURE_ERROR_FORMAT will be raised when the texture is allocated. Even if the feature is not available then COGL_PIXEL_FORMAT_RG_88 can still be used as an image format as long as COGL_TEXTURE_COMPONENTS_RG isn't used as the texture's components.

Parameters

texture	a CoglTexture pointer.	

Since 1.18

cogl_texture_get_components ()

```
CoglTextureComponents
cogl_texture_get_components (CoglTexture *texture);
```

Queries what components the given *texture* stores internally as set via cogl_texture_set_components().

For textures created by the '_with_size' constructors the default is COGL_TEXTURE_COMPONENTS_RGBA. The other constructors which take a CoglBitmap or a data pointer default to the same components as the pixel format of the data.

Parameters

texture	a CoglTexture pointer.	

Since 1.18

cogl_texture_set_premultiplied ()

```
void
cogl_texture_set_premultiplied (CoglTexture *texture,
                                CoglBool premultiplied);
```

Affects the internal storage format for this texture by specifying whether red, green and blue color components should be stored as pre-multiplied alpha values.

This api affects how data is uploaded to the GPU since Cogl will convert source data to have premultiplied or unpremultiplied components according to this state.

For example if you create a texture via cogl_texture_2d_new_with_size() and then upload data via cogl_texture_set_data() passing a source format of COGL_PIXEL_FORMAT_RGBA_8888 then Cogl will internally multiply the red, green and blue components of the source data by the alpha component, for each pixel so that the internally stored data has pre-multiplied alpha components. If you instead upload data that already has pre-multiplied components by passing COGL_PIXEL_FORMAT_RGBA_8888_PRE as the source format to cogl_texture_set_data() then the data can be uploaded without being converted.

By default the *premultiplied* state is *TRUE* .

Parameters

texture	a CoglTexture pointer.	
premultiplied	Whether any internally stored red, green or blue components are pre-multiplied by an alpha component.	

Since 1.18

cogl_texture_get_premultiplied ()

```
CoglBool
cogl_texture_get_premultiplied (CoglTexture *texture);
```

Queries the pre-multiplied alpha status for internally stored red, green and blue components for the given texture as set by cogl_texture_set_premultiplied().

By default the pre-multipled state is *TRUE* .

Parameters

texture	a CoglTexture pointer.	

Returns

TRUE if red, green and blue components are internally stored pre-multiplied by the alpha value or FALSE if not.

Since 1.18

Types and Values

CoglTexture

```
typedef void CoglTexture;
```

enum CoglTextureError

Error codes that can be thrown when allocating textures.

Members

COGL_TEXTURE_ERROR_SIZE	Unsupported size
COGL_TEXTURE_ERROR_FORMAT	Unsupported format
COGL_TEXTURE_ERROR_BAD_PARAMETER	
COGL_TEXTURE_ERROR_TYPE	A primitive texture type that is unsupported by the driver was used

Since 1.8

Stability Level: Unstable

enum CoglTextureType

Constants representing the underlying hardware texture type of a CoglTexture.

Members

COGL_TEXTURE_TYPE_2D	A CoglTexture2D
COGL_TEXTURE_TYPE_3D	A CoglTexture3D
COGL_TEXTURE_TYPE_RECTANGLE	A CoglTextureRectangle

Since 1.10

Stability Level: Unstable

enum CoglTextureComponents

See cogl_texture_set_components().

Members

COGL_TEXTURE_COMPONENTS_A	Only the alpha component
COGL_TEXTURE_COMPONENTS_RG	Red and green components. Note that this can only be used if the COGL_FEATURE_ID_TEXTURE_RG feature is advertised.
COGL_TEXTURE_COMPONENTS_RGB	Red, green and blue components
COGL_TEXTURE_COMPONENTS_RGBA	Red, green, blue and alpha components

COGL_TEXTURE_COMPONENTS_DEPTH	Only a depth component

Since 1.18

1.9 Meta Textures

1.9.1 High Level Meta Textures

High Level Meta Textures — Interface for high-level textures built from low-level textures like CoglTexture2D and CoglTexture3D.

Functions

void	(*CoglMetaTextureCallback) ()
void	cogl_meta_texture_foreach_in_region ()

Types and Values

typedef	CoglMetaTexture

Description

Cogl helps to make it easy to deal with high level textures such as CoglAtlasTextures, CoglSubTextures, CoglTexturePixmapX11 textures and CoglTexture2DSliced textures consistently.

A CoglMetaTexture is a texture that might internally be represented by one or more low-level CoglTextures such as CoglTexture2D or CoglTexture3D. These low-level textures are the only ones that a GPU really understands but because applications often want more high-level texture abstractions (such as storing multiple textures inside one larger "atlas" texture) it's desirable to be able to deal with these using a common interface.

For example the GPU is not able to automatically handle repeating a texture that is part of a larger atlas texture but if you use COGL_PIPELINE_WRAP_MODE_REPEAT with an atlas texture when drawing with cogl_framebuffer_draw_rectangle() you should see that it "Just Works™" - at least if you don't use multi-texturing. The reason this works is because cogl_framebuffer_draw_rectangle() internally understands the CoglMetaTexture interface and is able to manually resolve the low-level textures using this interface and by making multiple draw calls it can emulate the texture repeat modes.

Cogl doesn't aim to pretend that meta-textures are just like real textures because it would get extremely complex to try and emulate low-level GPU semantics transparently for these textures. The low level drawing APIs of Cogl, such as cogl_primitive_draw() don't actually know anything about the CoglMetaTexture interface and its the developer's responsibility to resolve all textures referenced by a CoglPipeline to low-level textures before drawing.

If you want to develop custom primitive APIs like cogl_framebuffer_draw_rectangle() and you want to support drawing with CoglAtlasTextures or CoglSubTextures for example, then you will need to use this CoglMetaTexture interface to be able to resolve high-level textures into low-level textures before drawing with Cogl's low-level drawing APIs such as cogl_primitive_draw().

Note Most developers won't need to use this interface directly but still it is worth understanding the distinction between low-level and meta textures because you may find other references in the documentation that detail limitations of using meta-textures.

Functions

CoglMetaTextureCallback ()

```
void
(*CoglMetaTextureCallback) (CoglTexture *sub_texture,
                            const float *sub_texture_coords,
                            const float *meta_coords,
                            void *user_data);
```

A callback used with cogl_meta_texture_foreach_in_region() to retrieve details of all the low-level CoglTextures that make up a given CoglMetaTexture.

Parameters

sub_texture	A low-level CoglTexture making up part of a CoglMetaTexture.	
sub_texture_coords	A float 4-tuple ordered like (tx1,ty1,tx2,ty2) defining what region of the current *sub_texture* maps to a sub-region of a CoglMetaTexture. (tx1,ty1) is the top-left sub-region coordinate and (tx2,ty2) is the bottom-right. These are low-level texture coordinates.	
meta_coords	A float 4-tuple ordered like (tx1,ty1,tx2,ty2) defining what sub-region of a CoglMetaTexture this low-level *sub_texture* maps too. (tx1,ty1) is the top-left sub-region coordinate and (tx2,ty2) is the bottom-right. These are high-level meta-texture coordinates.	
user_data	A private pointer passed to cogl_meta_texture_foreach_in_region().	

Since 1.10

Stability Level: Unstable

cogl_meta_texture_foreach_in_region ()

```
void
cogl_meta_texture_foreach_in_region (CoglMetaTexture *meta_texture,
                                     float tx_1,
                                     float ty_1,
                                     float tx_2,
                                     float ty_2,
                                     CoglPipelineWrapMode wrap_s,
```

```
CoglPipelineWrapMode wrap_t,
CoglMetaTextureCallback callback,
void *user_data);
```

Allows you to manually iterate the low-level textures that define a given region of a high-level CoglMetaTexture.

For example cogl_texture_2d_sliced_new_with_size() can be used to create a meta texture that may slice a large image into multiple, smaller power-of-two sized textures. These high level textures are not directly understood by a GPU and so this API must be used to manually resolve the underlying textures for drawing.

All high level textures (CoglAtlasTexture, CoglSubTexture, CoglTexturePixmapX11, and CoglTexture2DSliced) can be handled consistently using this interface which greately simplifies implementing primitives that support all texture types.

For example if you use the cogl_framebuffer_draw_rectangle() API then Cogl will internally use this API to resolve the low level textures of any meta textures you have associated with CoglPipeline layers.

Note The low level drawing APIs such as cogl_primitive_draw() don't understand the CoglMetaTexture interface and so it is your responsibility to use this API to resolve all CoglPipeline textures into low-level textures before drawing.

For each low-level texture that makes up part of the given region of the *meta_texture*, *callback* is called specifying how the low-level texture maps to the original region.

Parameters

meta_texture	An object implementing the CoglMetaTexture interface.	
tx_1	The top-left x coordinate of the region to iterate	
ty_1	The top-left y coordinate of the region to iterate	
tx_2	The bottom-right x coordinate of the region to iterate	
ty_2	The bottom-right y coordinate of the region to iterate	
wrap_s	The wrap mode for the x-axis	
wrap_t	The wrap mode for the y-axis	
callback	A CoglMetaTextureCallback pointer to be called for each low-level texture within the specified region.	
user_data	A private pointer that is passed to *callback*.	

Since 1.10

Stability Level: Unstable

Types and Values

CoglMetaTexture

```
typedef void CoglMetaTexture;
```

1.9.2 Sub Textures

Sub Textures — Functions for creating and manipulating sub-textures.

Functions

CoglSubTexture *	cogl_sub_texture_new ()
CoglBool	cogl_is_sub_texture ()

Types and Values

	CoglSubTexture

Description

These functions allow high-level textures to be created that represent a sub-region of another texture. For example these can be used to implement custom texture atlasing schemes.

Functions

cogl_sub_texture_new ()

```
CoglSubTexture~*
cogl_sub_texture_new (CoglContext *ctx,
                      CoglTexture *parent_texture,
                      int sub_x,
                      int sub_y,
                      int sub_width,
                      int sub_height);
```

Creates a high-level CoglSubTexture representing a sub-region of any other CoglTexture. The sub-region must strictly lye within the bounds of the *parent_texture* . The returned texture implements the CoglMetaTexture interface because it's not a low level texture that hardware can understand natively.

Note Remember: Unless you are using high level drawing APIs such as cogl_framebuffer_draw_rectangle() or other APIs documented to understand the CoglMetaTexture interface then you need to use the CoglMetaTexture interface to resolve a CoglSubTexture into a low-level texture before drawing.

Parameters

ctx	A CoglContext pointer	
parent_texture	The full texture containing a sub-region you want to make a CoglSubTexture from.	
sub_x	The top-left x coordinate of the parent region to make a texture from.	

sub_y	The top-left y coordinate of the parent region to make a texture from.	
sub_width	The width of the parent region to make a texture from.	
sub_height	The height of the parent region to make a texture from.	

Returns

A newly allocated CoglSubTexture representing a sub-region of *parent_texture*.

[transfer full]

Since 1.10

Stability Level: Unstable

cogl_is_sub_texture ()

```
CoglBool
cogl_is_sub_texture (void *object);
```

Checks whether *object* is a CoglSubTexture.

Parameters

object	a CoglObject	

Returns

TRUE if the passed *object* represents a CoglSubTexture and FALSE otherwise.

Since 1.10

Stability Level: Unstable

Types and Values

CoglSubTexture

```
typedef struct _CoglSubTexture CoglSubTexture;
```

1.9.3   Sliced Textures

Sliced Textures — Functions for creating and manipulating 2D meta textures that may internally be comprised of multiple 2D textures with power-of-two sizes.

Functions

CoglTexture2DSliced *	cogl_texture_2d_sliced_new_with_size ()

CoglTexture2DSliced *	cogl_texture_2d_sliced_new_from_file ()
CoglTexture2DSliced *	cogl_texture_2d_sliced_new_from_data ()
CoglTexture2DSliced *	cogl_texture_2d_sliced_new_from_bitmap ()
CoglBool	cogl_is_texture_2d_sliced ()

Types and Values

	CoglTexture2DSliced

Description

These functions allow high-level meta textures (See the CoglMetaTexture interface) to be allocated that may internally be comprised of multiple 2D texture "slices" with power-of-two sizes.

This API can be useful when working with GPUs that don't have native support for non-power-of-two textures or if you want to load a texture that is larger than the GPUs maximum texture size limits.

The algorithm for slicing works by first trying to map a virtual size to the next larger power-of-two size and then seeing how many wasted pixels that would result in. For example if you have a virtual texture that's 259 texels wide, the next pot size = 512 and the amount of waste would be 253 texels. If the amount of waste is above a max-waste threshold then we would next slice that texture into one that's 256 texels and then looking at how many more texels remain unallocated after that we choose the next power-of-two size. For the example of a 259 texel image that would mean having a 256 texel wide texture, leaving 3 texels unallocated so we'd then create a 4 texel wide texture - now there is only one texel of waste. The algorithm continues to slice the right most textures until the amount of waste is less than or equal to a specfied max-waste threshold. The same logic for slicing from left to right is also applied from top to bottom.

Functions

cogl_texture_2d_sliced_new_with_size ()

```
CoglTexture2DSliced~*
cogl_texture_2d_sliced_new_with_size (CoglContext *ctx,
                                      int width,
                                      int height,
                                      int max_waste);
```

Creates a CoglTexture2DSliced that may internally be comprised of 1 or more CoglTexture2D textures depending on GPU limitations. For example if the GPU only supports power-of-two sized textures then a sliced texture will turn a non-power-of-two size into a combination of smaller power-of-two sized textures. If the requested texture size is larger than is supported by the hardware then the texture will be sliced into smaller textures that can be accessed by the hardware.

max_waste is used as a threshold for recursively slicing the right-most or bottom-most slices into smaller sizes until the wasted padding at the bottom and right of the textures is less than specified. A negative *max_waste* will disable slicing.

The storage for the texture is not allocated before this function returns. You can call cogl_texture_allocate() to explicitly allocate the underlying storage or let Cogl automatically allocate storage lazily.

Note It's possible for the allocation of a sliced texture to fail later due to impossible slicing constraints if a negative *max_waste* value is given. If the given virtual texture size size is larger than is supported by the hardware but slicing is disabled the texture size would be too large to handle.

Parameters

ctx	A CoglContext	

width	The virtual width of your sliced texture.	
height	The virtual height of your sliced texture.	
max_waste	The threshold of how wide a strip of wasted texels are allowed along the right and bottom textures before they must be sliced to reduce the amount of waste. A negative can be passed to disable slicing.	

Returns

A new CoglTexture2DSliced object with no storage allocated yet.

[transfer full]

Since 1.10

Stability Level: Unstable

cogl_texture_2d_sliced_new_from_file ()

```
CoglTexture2DSliced~*
cogl_texture_2d_sliced_new_from_file (CoglContext *ctx,
                                      const char *filename,
                                      int max_waste,
                                      CoglError **error);
```

Creates a CoglTexture2DSliced from an image file.

A CoglTexture2DSliced may internally be comprised of 1 or more CoglTexture2D textures depending on GPU limitations. For example if the GPU only supports power-of-two sized textures then a sliced texture will turn a non-power-of-two size into a combination of smaller power-of-two sized textures. If the requested texture size is larger than is supported by the hardware then the texture will be sliced into smaller textures that can be accessed by the hardware.

max_waste is used as a threshold for recursively slicing the right-most or bottom-most slices into smaller sizes until the wasted padding at the bottom and right of the textures is less than specified. A negative max_waste will disable slicing.

The storage for the texture is not allocated before this function returns. You can call cogl_texture_allocate() to explicitly allocate the underlying storage or let Cogl automatically allocate storage lazily.

Note It's possible for the allocation of a sliced texture to fail later due to impossible slicing constraints if a negative max_waste value is given. If the given virtual texture size is larger than is supported by the hardware but slicing is disabled the texture size would be too large to handle.

Parameters

ctx	A CoglContext	
filename	the file to load	
max_waste	The threshold of how wide a strip of wasted texels are allowed along the right and bottom textures before they must be sliced to reduce the amount of waste. A negative can be passed to disable slicing.	

error	A CoglError to catch exceptional errors or NULL	

Returns

A newly created CoglTexture2DSliced or NULL on failure and *error* will be updated.

[transfer full]

Since 1.16

cogl_texture_2d_sliced_new_from_data ()

```
CoglTexture2DSliced~*
cogl_texture_2d_sliced_new_from_data (CoglContext *ctx,
                                      int width,
                                      int height,
                                      int max_waste,
                                      CoglPixelFormat format,
                                      int rowstride,
                                      const uint8_t *data,
                                      CoglError **error);
```

Creates a new CoglTexture2DSliced texture based on data residing in memory.

A CoglTexture2DSliced may internally be comprised of 1 or more CoglTexture2D textures depending on GPU limitations. For example if the GPU only supports power-of-two sized textures then a sliced texture will turn a non-power-of-two size into a combination of smaller power-of-two sized textures. If the requested texture size is larger than is supported by the hardware then the texture will be sliced into smaller textures that can be accessed by the hardware.

max_waste is used as a threshold for recursively slicing the right-most or bottom-most slices into smaller sizes until the wasted padding at the bottom and right of the textures is less than specified. A negative *max_waste* will disable slicing.

Note This api will always immediately allocate GPU memory for all the required texture slices and upload the given data so that the *data* pointer does not need to remain valid once this function returns. This means it is not possible to configure the texture before it is allocated. If you do need to configure the texture before allocation (to specify constraints on the internal format for example) then you can instead create a CoglBitmap for your data and use cogl_texture_2d_sliced_new_from_bitmap() or use cogl_texture_2d_sliced_new_with_size() and then upload data using cogl_texture_set_data()

Note It's possible for the allocation of a sliced texture to fail due to impossible slicing constraints if a negative *max_waste* value is given. If the given virtual texture size is larger than is supported by the hardware but slicing is disabled the texture size would be too large to handle.

Parameters

ctx	A CoglContext	
width	width of texture in pixels	
height	height of texture in pixels	
format	the CoglPixelFormat the buffer is stored in in RAM	

max_waste	The threshold of how wide a strip of wasted texels are allowed along the right and bottom textures before they must be sliced to reduce the amount of waste. A negative can be passed to disable slicing.	
rowstride	the memory offset in bytes between the start of each row in *data* . A value of 0 will make Cogl automatically calculate *rowstride* from *width* and *format* .	
data	pointer the memory region where the source buffer resides	
error	A CoglError to catch exceptional errors or NULL.	

Returns

A newly created CoglTexture2DSliced or NULL on failure and *error* will be updated.

[transfer full]

Since 1.16

cogl_texture_2d_sliced_new_from_bitmap ()

```
CoglTexture2DSliced~*
cogl_texture_2d_sliced_new_from_bitmap
                            (CoglBitmap *bmp,
                             int max_waste);
```

Creates a new CoglTexture2DSliced texture based on data residing in a bitmap.

A CoglTexture2DSliced may internally be comprised of 1 or more CoglTexture2D textures depending on GPU limitations. For example if the GPU only supports power-of-two sized textures then a sliced texture will turn a non-power-of-two size into a combination of smaller power-of-two sized textures. If the requested texture size is larger than is supported by the hardware then the texture will be sliced into smaller textures that can be accessed by the hardware.

max_waste is used as a threshold for recursively slicing the right-most or bottom-most slices into smaller sizes until the wasted padding at the bottom and right of the textures is less than specified. A negative *max_waste* will disable slicing.

The storage for the texture is not allocated before this function returns. You can call cogl_texture_allocate() to explicitly allocate the underlying storage or let Cogl automatically allocate storage lazily.

Note It's possible for the allocation of a sliced texture to fail later due to impossible slicing constraints if a negative *max_waste* value is given. If the given virtual texture size is larger than is supported by the hardware but slicing is disabled the texture size would be too large to handle.

Parameters

bmp	A CoglBitmap	

	The threshold of how wide a strip of wasted texels are allowed along the right and bottom textures before they must be sliced to reduce the amount of waste. A negative can be passed to disable slicing.
max_waste	

Returns

A newly created CoglTexture2DSliced or NULL on failure and *error* will be updated.

[transfer full]

Since 1.16

cogl_is_texture_2d_sliced ()

```
CoglBool
cogl_is_texture_2d_sliced (void *object);
```

Gets whether the given object references a CoglTexture2DSliced.

Parameters

object	A CoglObject pointer

Returns

TRUE if the object references a CoglTexture2DSliced and FALSE otherwise.

Since 1.10

Stability Level: Unstable

Types and Values

CoglTexture2DSliced

```
typedef struct _CoglTexture2DSliced CoglTexture2DSliced;
```

1.9.4 X11 Texture From Pixmap

X11 Texture From Pixmap — Functions for creating and manipulating 2D meta textures derived from X11 pixmaps.

Functions

CoglBool	cogl_is_texture_pixmap_x11 ()
CoglTexturePixmapX11 *	cogl_texture_pixmap_x11_new ()
void	cogl_texture_pixmap_x11_update_area ()
CoglBool	cogl_texture_pixmap_x11_is_using_tfp_extension ()
void	cogl_texture_pixmap_x11_set_damage_object ()

Types and Values

enum	CoglTexturePixmapX11
	CoglTexturePixmapX11ReportLevel

Description

These functions allow high-level meta textures (See the CoglMetaTexture interface) that derive their contents from an X11 pixmap.

Functions

cogl_is_texture_pixmap_x11 ()

```
CoglBool
cogl_is_texture_pixmap_x11 (void *object);
```

Checks whether *object* points to a CoglTexturePixmapX11 instance.

Parameters

object	A pointer to a CoglObject	

Returns

TRUE if the object is a CoglTexturePixmapX11, and FALSE otherwise

Since 1.4

Stability Level: Unstable

cogl_texture_pixmap_x11_new ()

```
CoglTexturePixmapX11~*
cogl_texture_pixmap_x11_new (CoglContext *context,
                             uint32_t pixmap,
                             CoglBool automatic_updates,
                             CoglError **error);
```

Creates a texture that contains the contents of *pixmap*. If *automatic_updates* is TRUE then Cogl will attempt to listen for damage events on the pixmap and automatically update the texture when it changes.

Parameters

context	A CoglContext	
pixmap	A X11 pixmap ID	
automatic_updates	Whether to automatically copy the contents of the pixmap to the texture.	
error	A CoglError for exceptions	

Returns

a new CoglTexturePixmapX11 instance

Since 1.10

Stability Level: Unstable

cogl_texture_pixmap_x11_update_area ()

```
void
cogl_texture_pixmap_x11_update_area (CoglTexturePixmapX11 *texture,
                                     int x,
                                     int y,
                                     int width,
                                     int height);
```

Forces an update of the given `texture` so that it is refreshed with the contents of the pixmap that was given to cogl_texture_pixmap_x11_

Parameters

texture	A CoglTexturePixmapX11 instance	
x	x coordinate of the area to update	
y	y coordinate of the area to update	
width	width of the area to update	
height	height of the area to update	

Since 1.4

Stability Level: Unstable

cogl_texture_pixmap_x11_is_using_tfp_extension ()

```
CoglBool
cogl_texture_pixmap_x11_is_using_tfp_extension
                         (CoglTexturePixmapX11 *texture);
```

Checks whether the given `texture` is using the GLX_EXT_texture_from_pixmap or similar extension to copy the contents of the pixmap to the texture. This extension is usually implemented as zero-copy operation so it implies the updates are working efficiently.

Parameters

texture	A CoglTexturePixmapX11 instance	

Returns

TRUE if the texture is using an efficient extension and FALSE otherwise

Since 1.4

Stability Level: Unstable

cogl_texture_pixmap_x11_set_damage_object ()

```
void
cogl_texture_pixmap_x11_set_damage_object
                              (CoglTexturePixmapX11 *texture,
                               uint32_t damage,
                               CoglTexturePixmapX11ReportLevel report_level);
```

Sets the damage object that will be used to track automatic updates to the *texture* . Damage tracking can be disabled by passing 0 for *damage* . Otherwise this damage will replace the one used if TRUE was passed for automatic_updates to cogl_texture_pixmap_x11_new().

Note that Cogl will subtract from the damage region as it processes damage events.

Parameters

texture	A CoglTexturePixmapX11 instance	
damage	A X11 Damage object or 0	
report_level	The report level which describes how to interpret the damage events. This should match the level that the damage object was created with.	

Since 1.4

Stability Level: Unstable

Types and Values

CoglTexturePixmapX11

```
typedef struct _CoglTexturePixmapX11 CoglTexturePixmapX11;
```

enum CoglTexturePixmapX11ReportLevel

Members

COGL_TEXTURE_PIXMAP_X11_DAMAGE_RAW_RECTANGLES	
COGL_TEXTURE_PIXMAP_X11_DAMAGE_DELTA_RECTANGLES	
COGL_TEXTURE_PIXMAP_X11_DAMAGE_BOUNDING_BOX	
COGL_TEXTURE_PIXMAP_X11_DAMAGE_NON_EMPTY	

1.10 Primitive Textures

1.10.1 Low-level primitive textures

Low-level primitive textures — Interface for low-level textures like CoglTexture2D and CoglTexture3D.

Functions

CoglBool	cogl_is_primitive_texture ()
void	cogl_primitive_texture_set_auto_mipmap ()

Types and Values

typedef	CoglPrimitiveTexture

Description

A CoglPrimitiveTexture is a texture that is directly represented by a single texture on the GPU. For example these could be a CoglTexture2D, CoglTexture3D or CoglTextureRectangle. This is opposed to high level meta textures which may be composed of multiple primitive textures or a sub-region of another texture such as CoglAtlasTexture and CoglTexture2DSliced.

A texture that implements this interface can be directly used with the low level cogl_primitive_draw() API. Other types of textures need to be first resolved to primitive textures using the CoglMetaTexture interface.

Note Most developers won't need to use this interface directly but still it is worth understanding the distinction between high-level and primitive textures because you may find other references in the documentation that detail limitations of using primitive textures.

Functions

cogl_is_primitive_texture ()

```
CoglBool
cogl_is_primitive_texture (void *object);
```

Gets whether the given object references a primitive texture object.

Parameters

object	A CoglObject pointer	

Returns

TRUE if the pointer references a primitive texture, and FALSE otherwise

Since 2.0

Stability Level: Unstable

cogl_primitive_texture_set_auto_mipmap ()

```
void
cogl_primitive_texture_set_auto_mipmap
                        (CoglPrimitiveTexture *primitive_texture,
                         CoglBool value);
```

Sets whether the texture will automatically update the smaller mipmap levels after any part of level 0 is updated. The update will only occur whenever the texture is used for drawing with a texture filter that requires the lower mipmap levels. An application should disable this if it wants to upload its own data for the other levels. By default auto mipmapping is enabled.

Parameters

| primitive_texture | A CoglPrimitiveTexture | |
| value | The new value for whether to auto mipmap | |

Since 2.0

Stability Level: Unstable

Types and Values

CoglPrimitiveTexture

```
typedef void CoglPrimitiveTexture;
```

1.10.2   2D textures

2D textures — Functions for creating and manipulating 2D textures

Functions

CoglBool	cogl_is_texture_2d ()
CoglTexture2D *	cogl_texture_2d_new_with_size ()
CoglTexture2D *	cogl_texture_2d_new_from_file ()
CoglTexture2D *	cogl_texture_2d_new_from_bitmap ()
CoglTexture2D *	cogl_texture_2d_new_from_data ()
CoglTexture2D *	cogl_texture_2d_gl_new_from_foreign ()

Types and Values

| CoglTexture2D

Description

These functions allow low-level 2D textures to be allocated. These differ from sliced textures for example which may internally be made up of multiple 2D textures, or atlas textures where Cogl must internally modify user texture coordinates before they can be used by the GPU.

You should be aware that many GPUs only support power of two sizes for CoglTexture2D textures. You can check support for non power of two textures by checking for the COGL_FEATURE_ID_TEXTURE_NPOT feature via cogl_has_feature().

Functions

cogl_is_texture_2d ()

```
CoglBool
cogl_is_texture_2d (void *object);
```

Gets whether the given object references an existing CoglTexture2D object.

Parameters

| object | A CoglObject | |

Returns

TRUE if the object references a CoglTexture2D, FALSE otherwise

cogl_texture_2d_new_with_size ()

```
CoglTexture2D~*
cogl_texture_2d_new_with_size (CoglContext *ctx,
                               int width,
                               int height);
```

Creates a low-level CoglTexture2D texture with a given *width* and *height* that your GPU can texture from directly.

The storage for the texture is not allocated before this function returns. You can call cogl_texture_allocate() to explicitly allocate the underlying storage or preferably let Cogl automatically allocate storage lazily when it may know more about how the texture is being used and can optimize how it is allocated.

The texture is still configurable until it has been allocated so for example you can influence the internal format of the texture using cogl_texture_set_components() and cogl_texture_set_premultiplied().

Note Many GPUs only support power of two sizes for CoglTexture2D textures. You can check support for non power of two textures by checking for the COGL_FEATURE_ID_TEXTURE_NPOT feature via cogl_has_feature().

Parameters

ctx	A CoglContext	
width	Width of the texture to allocate	
height	Height of the texture to allocate	

Returns

A new CoglTexture2D object with no storage yet allocated.

[transfer full]

Since 2.0

cogl_texture_2d_new_from_file ()

```
CoglTexture2D~*
cogl_texture_2d_new_from_file (CoglContext *ctx,
                               const char *filename,
                               CoglError **error);
```

Creates a low-level CoglTexture2D texture from an image file.

The storage for the texture is not allocated before this function returns. You can call cogl_texture_allocate() to explicitly allocate the underlying storage or preferably let Cogl automatically allocate storage lazily when it may know more about how the texture is being used and can optimize how it is allocated.

The texture is still configurable until it has been allocated so for example you can influence the internal format of the texture using cogl_texture_set_components() and cogl_texture_set_premultiplied().

> **Note** Many GPUs only support power of two sizes for CoglTexture2D textures. You can check support for non power of two textures by checking for the COGL_FEATURE_ID_TEXTURE_NPOT feature via cogl_has_feature().

Parameters

ctx	A CoglContext	
filename	the file to load	
error	A CoglError to catch exceptional errors or NULL	

Returns

A newly created CoglTexture2D or NULL on failure and *error* will be updated.

[transfer full]

Since 1.16

cogl_texture_2d_new_from_bitmap ()

```
CoglTexture2D~*
cogl_texture_2d_new_from_bitmap (CoglBitmap *bitmap);
```

Creates a low-level CoglTexture2D texture based on data residing in a CoglBitmap.

The storage for the texture is not allocated before this function returns. You can call cogl_texture_allocate() to explicitly allocate the underlying storage or preferably let Cogl automatically allocate storage lazily when it may know more about how the texture is being used and can optimize how it is allocated.

The texture is still configurable until it has been allocated so for example you can influence the internal format of the texture using cogl_texture_set_components() and cogl_texture_set_premultiplied().

> **Note** Many GPUs only support power of two sizes for CoglTexture2D textures. You can check support for non power of two textures by checking for the COGL_FEATURE_ID_TEXTURE_NPOT feature via cogl_has_feature().

Parameters

bitmap	A CoglBitmap	

Returns

A newly allocated CoglTexture2D.

[transfer full]

Since 2.0

Stability Level: Unstable

cogl_texture_2d_new_from_data ()

```
CoglTexture2D~*
cogl_texture_2d_new_from_data (CoglContext *ctx,
                               int width,
```

```
                                int height,
                                CoglPixelFormat format,
                                int rowstride,
                                const uint8_t *data,
                                CoglError **error);
```

Creates a low-level CoglTexture2D texture based on data residing in memory.

Note This api will always immediately allocate GPU memory for the texture and upload the given data so that the *data* pointer does not need to remain valid once this function returns. This means it is not possible to configure the texture before it is allocated. If you do need to configure the texture before allocation (to specify constraints on the internal format for example) then you can instead create a CoglBitmap for your data and use cogl_texture_2d_new_from_bitmap() or use cogl_texture_2d_new_with_size() and then upload data using cogl_texture_set_data()

Note Many GPUs only support power of two sizes for CoglTexture2D textures. You can check support for non power of two textures by checking for the COGL_FEATURE_ID_TEXTURE_NPOT feature via cogl_has_feature().

Parameters

ctx	A CoglContext	
width	width of texture in pixels	
height	height of texture in pixels	
format	the CoglPixelFormat the buffer is stored in in RAM	
rowstride	the memory offset in bytes between the starts of scanlines in *data* . A value of 0 will make Cogl automatically calculate *rowstride* from *width* and *format* .	
data	pointer the memory region where the source buffer resides	
error	A CoglError for exceptions	

Returns

A newly allocated CoglTexture2D, or if the size is not supported (because it is too large or a non-power-of-two size that the hardware doesn't support) it will return NULL and set *error* .

[transfer full]

Since 2.0

cogl_texture_2d_gl_new_from_foreign ()

```
CoglTexture2D~*
cogl_texture_2d_gl_new_from_foreign (CoglContext *ctx,
                                     unsigned int gl_handle,
                                     int width,
                                     int height,
                                     CoglPixelFormat format);
```

Wraps an existing GL_TEXTURE_2D texture object as a CoglTexture2D. This can be used for integrating Cogl with software using OpenGL directly.

The texture is still configurable until it has been allocated so for example you can declare whether the texture is premultiplied with cogl_texture_set_premultiplied().

Note The results are undefined for passing an invalid `gl_handle` or if `width` or `height` don't have the correct texture geometry.

Parameters

ctx	A CoglContext	
gl_handle	A GL handle for a GL_TEXTURE_2D texture object	
width	Width of the foreign GL texture	
height	Height of the foreign GL texture	
format	The format of the texture	

Returns

A newly allocated CoglTexture2D.

[transfer full]

Since 2.0

Types and Values

CoglTexture2D

```
typedef struct _CoglTexture2D CoglTexture2D;
```

1.10.3 3D textures

3D textures — Functions for creating and manipulating 3D textures

Functions

CoglTexture3D *	cogl_texture_3d_new_with_size ()
CoglTexture3D *	cogl_texture_3d_new_from_bitmap ()
CoglTexture3D *	cogl_texture_3d_new_from_data ()
CoglBool	cogl_is_texture_3d ()

Types and Values

	CoglTexture3D

Description

These functions allow 3D textures to be used. 3D textures can be thought of as layers of 2D images arranged into a cuboid shape. When choosing a texel from the texture, Cogl will take into account the 'r' texture coordinate to select one of the images.

Functions

cogl_texture_3d_new_with_size ()

```
CoglTexture3D~*
cogl_texture_3d_new_with_size (CoglContext *context,
                               int width,
                               int height,
                               int depth);
```

Creates a low-level CoglTexture3D texture with the specified dimensions and pixel format.

The storage for the texture is not allocated before this function returns. You can call cogl_texture_allocate() to explicitly allocate the underlying storage or preferably let Cogl automatically allocate storage lazily when it may know more about how the texture is going to be used and can optimize how it is allocated.

The texture is still configurable until it has been allocated so for example you can influence the internal format of the texture using cogl_texture_set_components() and cogl_texture_set_premultiplied().

> **Note** This texture will fail to allocate later if COGL_FEATURE_ID_TEXTURE_3D is not advertised. Allocation can also fail if the requested dimensions are not supported by the GPU.

Parameters

context	a CoglContext	
width	width of the texture in pixels.	
height	height of the texture in pixels.	
depth	depth of the texture in pixels.	

Returns

A new CoglTexture3D object with no storage yet allocated.

[transfer full]

Since 1.10

Stability Level: Unstable

cogl_texture_3d_new_from_bitmap ()

```
CoglTexture3D~*
cogl_texture_3d_new_from_bitmap (CoglBitmap *bitmap,
                                 int height,
                                 int depth);
```

Creates a low-level 3D texture and initializes it with the images in `bitmap`. The images are assumed to be packed together after one another in the increasing y axis. The height of individual image is given as `height` and the number of images is given in *depth* . The actual height of the bitmap can be larger than *height* × *depth* . In this case it assumes there is padding between the images.

The storage for the texture is not allocated before this function returns. You can call cogl_texture_allocate() to explicitly allocate the underlying storage or preferably let Cogl automatically allocate storage lazily when it may know more about how the texture is going to be used and can optimize how it is allocated.

The texture is still configurable until it has been allocated so for example you can influence the internal format of the texture using cogl_texture_set_components() and cogl_texture_set_premultiplied().

Note This texture will fail to allocate later if COGL_FEATURE_ID_TEXTURE_3D is not advertised. Allocation can also fail if the requested dimensions are not supported by the GPU.

Parameters

bitmap	A CoglBitmap object.	
height	height of the texture in pixels.	
depth	depth of the texture in pixels.	

Returns

a newly created CoglTexture3D.

[transfer full]

Since 2.0

Stability Level: Unstable

---

cogl_texture_3d_new_from_data ()

```
CoglTexture3D~*
cogl_texture_3d_new_from_data (CoglContext *context,
                               int width,
                               int height,
                               int depth,
                               CoglPixelFormat format,
                               int rowstride,
                               int image_stride,
                               const uint8_t *data,
                               CoglError **error);
```

Creates a low-level 3D texture and initializes it with *data* . The data is assumed to be packed array of *depth* images. There can be padding between the images using *image_stride* .

Note This api will always immediately allocate GPU memory for the texture and upload the given data so that the *data* pointer does not need to remain valid once this function returns. This means it is not possible to configure the texture before it is allocated. If you do need to configure the texture before allocation (to specify constraints on the internal format for example) then you can instead create a CoglBitmap for your data and use cogl_texture_3d_new_from_bitmap().

Parameters

context	a CoglContext	
width	width of the texture in pixels.	
height	height of the texture in pixels.	
depth	depth of the texture in pixels.	
format	the CoglPixelFormat the buffer is stored in in RAM	
rowstride	the memory offset in bytes between the starts of scanlines in data or 0 to infer it from the width and format	
image_stride	the number of bytes from one image to the next. This can be used to add padding between the images in a similar way that the rowstride can be used to add padding between rows. Alternatively 0 can be passed to infer the image_stride from the height.	
data	pointer the memory region where the source buffer resides	
error	A CoglError return location.	

Returns

the newly created CoglTexture3D or NULL if there was an error and an exception will be returned through error.

[transfer full]

Since 1.10

Stability Level: Unstable

cogl_is_texture_3d ()

```
CoglBool
cogl_is_texture_3d (void *object);
```

Checks whether the given object references a CoglTexture3D

Parameters

object	a CoglObject	

Returns

TRUE if the passed object represents a 3D texture and FALSE otherwise

Since 1.4

Stability Level: Unstable

Types and Values

CoglTexture3D

```
typedef struct _CoglTexture3D CoglTexture3D;
```

1.10.4   Rectangle textures (non-normalized coordinates)

Rectangle textures (non-normalized coordinates) — Functions for creating and manipulating rectangle textures for use with non-normalized coordinates.

Functions

CoglTextureRectangle *	cogl_texture_rectangle_new_with_size ()
CoglTextureRectangle *	cogl_texture_rectangle_new_from_bitmap ()
CoglBool	cogl_is_texture_rectangle ()

Types and Values

	CoglTextureRectangle

Description

These functions allow low-level "rectangle" textures to be allocated. These textures are never constrained to power-of-two sizes but they also don't support having a mipmap and can only be wrapped with COGL_PIPELINE_WRAP_MODE_CLAMP_TO_EDGE.

The most notable difference between rectangle textures and 2D textures is that rectangle textures are sampled using un-normalized texture coordinates, so instead of using coordinates (0,0) and (1,1) to map to the top-left and bottom right corners of the texture you would instead use (0,0) and (width,height).

The use of non-normalized coordinates can be particularly convenient when writing glsl shaders that use a texture as a lookup table since you don't need to upload separate uniforms to map normalized coordinates to texels.

If you want to sample from a rectangle texture from GLSL you should use the sampler2DRect sampler type.

Applications wanting to use CoglTextureRectangle should first check for the COGL_FEATURE_ID_TEXTURE_RECTANGLE feature using cogl_has_feature().

Functions

cogl_texture_rectangle_new_with_size ()

```
CoglTextureRectangle *
cogl_texture_rectangle_new_with_size (CoglContext *ctx,
                                      int width,
                                      int height);
```

Creates a new CoglTextureRectangle texture with a given *width* , and *height* . This texture is a low-level texture that the GPU can sample from directly unlike high-level textures such as CoglTexture2DSliced and CoglAtlasTexture.

Note Unlike for CoglTexture2D textures, coordinates for CoglTextureRectangle textures should not be normalized. So instead of using the coordinate (1, 1) to sample the bottom right corner of a rectangle texture you would use (`width`, `height`) where `width` and `height` are the width and height of the texture.

Note If you want to sample from a rectangle texture from GLSL you should use the sampler2DRect sampler type.

Note Applications wanting to use CoglTextureRectangle should first check for the COGL_FEATURE_ID_TEXTURE_RECTANGLE feature using cogl_has_feature().

The storage for the texture is not allocated before this function returns. You can call cogl_texture_allocate() to explicitly allocate the underlying storage or preferably let Cogl automatically allocate storage lazily when it may know more about how the texture is going to be used and can optimize how it is allocated.

Parameters

ctx	A CoglContext pointer	
width	The texture width to allocate	
height	The texture height to allocate	

Returns

A pointer to a new CoglTextureRectangle object with no storage allocated yet.

Since 1.10

Stability Level: Unstable

cogl_texture_rectangle_new_from_bitmap ()

```
CoglTextureRectangle~*
cogl_texture_rectangle_new_from_bitmap
                          (CoglBitmap *bitmap);
```

Allocates a new CoglTextureRectangle texture which will be initialized with the pixel data from `bitmap` . This texture is a low-level texture that the GPU can sample from directly unlike high-level textures such as CoglTexture2DSliced and CoglAtlasTexture.

Note Unlike for CoglTexture2D textures, coordinates for CoglTextureRectangle textures should not be normalized. So instead of using the coordinate (1, 1) to sample the bottom right corner of a rectangle texture you would use (`width`, `height`) where `width` and `height` are the width and height of the texture.

Note If you want to sample from a rectangle texture from GLSL you should use the sampler2DRect sampler type.

Note Applications wanting to use CoglTextureRectangle should first check for the COGL_FEATURE_ID_TEXTURE_RECTANGLE feature using cogl_has_feature().

The storage for the texture is not allocated before this function returns. You can call cogl_texture_allocate() to explicitly allocate the underlying storage or preferably let Cogl automatically allocate storage lazily when it may know more about how the texture is going to be used and can optimize how it is allocated.

Parameters

| bitmap | A CoglBitmap | |

Returns

A pointer to a new CoglTextureRectangle texture.

Since 2.0

Stability Level: Unstable

cogl_is_texture_rectangle ()

```
CoglBool
cogl_is_texture_rectangle (void *object);
```

Gets whether the given object references an existing CoglTextureRectangle object.

Parameters

| object | A CoglObject | |

Returns

TRUE if the object references a CoglTextureRectangle, FALSE otherwise.

Types and Values

CoglTextureRectangle

```
typedef struct _CoglTextureRectangle CoglTextureRectangle;
```

1.11 Framebuffers

1.11.1 CoglFramebuffer: The Framebuffer Interface

CoglFramebuffer: The Framebuffer Interface — A common interface for manipulating framebuffers

Functions

#define	COGL_FRAMEBUFFER()
CoglBool	cogl_framebuffer_allocate ()
int	cogl_framebuffer_get_width ()
int	cogl_framebuffer_get_height ()
void	cogl_framebuffer_set_viewport ()

float	cogl_framebuffer_get_viewport_x ()
float	cogl_framebuffer_get_viewport_y ()
float	cogl_framebuffer_get_viewport_width ()
float	cogl_framebuffer_get_viewport_height ()
void	cogl_framebuffer_get_viewport4fv ()
int	cogl_framebuffer_get_red_bits ()
int	cogl_framebuffer_get_green_bits ()
int	cogl_framebuffer_get_blue_bits ()
int	cogl_framebuffer_get_alpha_bits ()
int	cogl_framebuffer_get_depth_bits ()
CoglColorMask	cogl_framebuffer_get_color_mask ()
void	cogl_framebuffer_set_color_mask ()
int	cogl_framebuffer_get_samples_per_pixel ()
void	cogl_framebuffer_set_samples_per_pixel ()
void	cogl_framebuffer_resolve_samples ()
void	cogl_framebuffer_resolve_samples_region ()
CoglContext *	cogl_framebuffer_get_context ()
void	cogl_framebuffer_clear ()
void	cogl_framebuffer_clear4f ()
CoglBool	cogl_framebuffer_read_pixels_into_bitmap ()
CoglBool	cogl_framebuffer_read_pixels ()
void	cogl_framebuffer_set_dither_enabled ()
CoglBool	cogl_framebuffer_get_dither_enabled ()
void	cogl_framebuffer_draw_rectangle ()
void	cogl_framebuffer_draw_textured_rectangle ()
void	cogl_framebuffer_draw_multitextured_rectangle ()
void	cogl_framebuffer_draw_rectangles ()
void	cogl_framebuffer_draw_textured_rectangles ()
void	cogl_framebuffer_discard_buffers ()
void	cogl_framebuffer_finish ()
void	cogl_framebuffer_push_matrix ()
void	cogl_framebuffer_pop_matrix ()
void	cogl_framebuffer_identity_matrix ()
void	cogl_framebuffer_scale ()
void	cogl_framebuffer_translate ()
void	cogl_framebuffer_rotate ()
void	cogl_framebuffer_rotate_euler ()
void	cogl_framebuffer_rotate_quaternion ()
void	cogl_framebuffer_transform ()
void	cogl_framebuffer_get_modelview_matrix ()
void	cogl_framebuffer_set_modelview_matrix ()
void	cogl_framebuffer_perspective ()
void	cogl_framebuffer_frustum ()
void	cogl_framebuffer_orthographic ()
void	cogl_framebuffer_get_projection_matrix ()
void	cogl_framebuffer_set_projection_matrix ()
void	cogl_framebuffer_push_scissor_clip ()
void	cogl_framebuffer_push_rectangle_clip ()
void	cogl_framebuffer_push_primitive_clip ()
void	cogl_framebuffer_pop_clip ()

Types and Values

typedef	CoglFramebuffer

Description

Framebuffers are a collection of buffers that can be rendered too. A framebuffer may be comprised of one or more color buffers, an optional depth buffer and an optional stencil buffer. Other configuration parameters are associated with framebuffers too such as whether the framebuffer supports multi-sampling (an anti-aliasing technique) or dithering.

There are two kinds of framebuffer in Cogl, CoglOnscreen framebuffers and CoglOffscreen framebuffers. As the names imply offscreen framebuffers are for rendering something offscreen (perhaps to a texture which is bound as one of the color buffers). The exact semantics of onscreen framebuffers depends on the window system backend that you are using, but typically you can expect rendering to a CoglOnscreen framebuffer will be immediately visible to the user.

If you want to create a new framebuffer then you should start by looking at the CoglOnscreen and CoglOffscreen constructor functions, such as cogl_offscreen_new_with_texture() or cogl_onscreen_new(). The CoglFramebuffer interface deals with all aspects that are common between those two types of framebuffer.

Setup of a new CoglFramebuffer happens in two stages. There is a configuration stage where you specify all the options and ancillary buffers you want associated with your framebuffer and then when you are happy with the configuration you can "allocate" the framebuffer using cogl_framebuffer_allocate(). Technically explicitly calling cogl_framebuffer_allocate() is optional for convenience and the framebuffer will automatically be allocated when you first try to draw to it, but if you do the allocation manually then you can also catch any possible errors that may arise from your configuration.

Functions

COGL_FRAMEBUFFER()

```
#define COGL_FRAMEBUFFER(X) ((CoglFramebuffer *)(X))
```

cogl_framebuffer_allocate ()

```
CoglBool
cogl_framebuffer_allocate (CoglFramebuffer *framebuffer,
                           CoglError **error);
```

Explicitly allocates a configured CoglFramebuffer allowing developers to check and handle any errors that might arise from an unsupported configuration so that fallback configurations may be tried.

Note Many applications don't support any fallback options at least when they are initially developed and in that case the don't need to use this API since Cogl will automatically allocate a framebuffer when it first gets used. The disadvantage of relying on automatic allocation is that the program will abort with an error message if there is an error during automatic allocation.

Parameters

framebuffer	A CoglFramebuffer	
error	A pointer to a CoglError for returning exceptions.	

Returns

TRUE if there were no error allocating the framebuffer, else FALSE.

Since 1.8

Stability Level: Unstable

cogl_framebuffer_get_width ()

```
int
cogl_framebuffer_get_width (CoglFramebuffer *framebuffer);
```

Queries the current width of the given *framebuffer*.

Parameters

framebuffer	A CoglFramebuffer

Returns

The width of *framebuffer*.

Since 1.8

Stability Level: Unstable

cogl_framebuffer_get_height ()

```
int
cogl_framebuffer_get_height (CoglFramebuffer *framebuffer);
```

Queries the current height of the given *framebuffer*.

Parameters

framebuffer	A CoglFramebuffer

Returns

The height of *framebuffer*.

Since 1.8

Stability Level: Unstable

cogl_framebuffer_set_viewport ()

```
void
cogl_framebuffer_set_viewport (CoglFramebuffer *framebuffer,
                               float x,
                               float y,
                               float width,
                               float height);
```

Defines a scale and offset for everything rendered relative to the top-left of the destination framebuffer.

By default the viewport has an origin of (0,0) and width and height that match the framebuffer's size. Assuming a default projection and modelview matrix then you could translate the contents of a window down and right by leaving the viewport size unchanged by moving the offset to (10,10). The viewport coordinates are measured in pixels. If you left the x and y origin as (0,0) you could scale the windows contents down by specify and width and height that's half the real size of the framebuffer.

Note Although the function takes floating point arguments, existing drivers only allow the use of integer values. In the future floating point values will be exposed via a checkable feature.

Parameters

framebuffer	A CoglFramebuffer	
x	The top-left x coordinate of the viewport origin (only integers supported currently)	
y	The top-left y coordinate of the viewport origin (only integers supported currently)	
width	The width of the viewport (only integers supported currently)	
height	The height of the viewport (only integers supported currently)	

Since 1.8

Stability Level: Unstable

cogl_framebuffer_get_viewport_x ()

```
float
cogl_framebuffer_get_viewport_x (CoglFramebuffer *framebuffer);
```

Queries the x coordinate of the viewport origin as set using cogl_framebuffer_set_viewport() or the default value which is 0.

Parameters

framebuffer	A CoglFramebuffer	

Returns

The x coordinate of the viewport origin.

Since 1.8

Stability Level: Unstable

cogl_framebuffer_get_viewport_y ()

```
float
cogl_framebuffer_get_viewport_y (CoglFramebuffer *framebuffer);
```

Queries the y coordinate of the viewport origin as set using cogl_framebuffer_set_viewport() or the default value which is 0.

Parameters

framebuffer	A CoglFramebuffer	

Returns

The y coordinate of the viewport origin.

Since 1.8

Stability Level: Unstable

cogl_framebuffer_get_viewport_width ()

```
float
cogl_framebuffer_get_viewport_width (CoglFramebuffer *framebuffer);
```

Queries the width of the viewport as set using cogl_framebuffer_set_viewport() or the default value which is the width of the framebuffer.

Parameters

framebuffer	A CoglFramebuffer	

Returns

The width of the viewport.

Since 1.8

Stability Level: Unstable

cogl_framebuffer_get_viewport_height ()

```
float
cogl_framebuffer_get_viewport_height (CoglFramebuffer *framebuffer);
```

Queries the height of the viewport as set using cogl_framebuffer_set_viewport() or the default value which is the height of the framebuffer.

Parameters

framebuffer	A CoglFramebuffer	

Returns

The height of the viewport.

Since 1.8

Stability Level: Unstable

cogl_framebuffer_get_viewport4fv ()

```
void
cogl_framebuffer_get_viewport4fv (CoglFramebuffer *framebuffer,
                                  float *viewport);
```

Queries the x, y, width and height components of the current viewport as set using cogl_framebuffer_set_viewport() or the default values which are 0, 0, framebuffer_width and framebuffer_height. The values are written into the given *viewport* array.

Parameters

framebuffer	A CoglFramebuffer	
viewport	A pointer to an array of 4 floats to receive the (x, y, width, height) components of the current viewport.	*[out caller-allocates][array fixed-size=4]*

Since 1.8

Stability Level: Unstable

cogl_framebuffer_get_red_bits ()

```
int
cogl_framebuffer_get_red_bits (CoglFramebuffer *framebuffer);
```

Retrieves the number of red bits of *framebuffer*

Parameters

framebuffer	a pointer to a CoglFramebuffer	

Returns

the number of bits

Since 1.8

Stability Level: Unstable

cogl_framebuffer_get_green_bits ()

```
int
cogl_framebuffer_get_green_bits (CoglFramebuffer *framebuffer);
```

Retrieves the number of green bits of *framebuffer*

Parameters

framebuffer	a pointer to a CoglFramebuffer	

Returns

the number of bits

Since 1.8

Stability Level: Unstable

cogl_framebuffer_get_blue_bits ()

```
int
cogl_framebuffer_get_blue_bits (CoglFramebuffer *framebuffer);
```

Retrieves the number of blue bits of *framebuffer*

Parameters

| framebuffer | a pointer to a CoglFramebuffer | |

Returns

the number of bits

Since 1.8

Stability Level: Unstable

cogl_framebuffer_get_alpha_bits ()

```
int
cogl_framebuffer_get_alpha_bits (CoglFramebuffer *framebuffer);
```

Retrieves the number of alpha bits of *framebuffer*

Parameters

| framebuffer | a pointer to a CoglFramebuffer | |

Returns

the number of bits

Since 1.8

Stability Level: Unstable

cogl_framebuffer_get_depth_bits ()

```
int
cogl_framebuffer_get_depth_bits (CoglFramebuffer *framebuffer);
```

Retrieves the number of depth bits of *framebuffer*

Parameters

| framebuffer | a pointer to a CoglFramebuffer | |

Returns

the number of bits

Since 2.0

Stability Level: Unstable

cogl_framebuffer_get_color_mask ()

```
CoglColorMask
cogl_framebuffer_get_color_mask (CoglFramebuffer *framebuffer);
```

Gets the current CoglColorMask of which channels would be written to the current framebuffer. Each bit set in the mask means that the corresponding color would be written.

Parameters

framebuffer	a pointer to a CoglFramebuffer

Returns

A CoglColorMask

Since 1.8

Stability Level: Unstable

cogl_framebuffer_set_color_mask ()

```
void
cogl_framebuffer_set_color_mask (CoglFramebuffer *framebuffer,
                                 CoglColorMask color_mask);
```

Defines a bit mask of which color channels should be written to the given *framebuffer* . If a bit is set in *color_mask* that means that color will be written.

Parameters

framebuffer	a pointer to a CoglFramebuffer
color_mask	A CoglColorMask of which color channels to write to the current framebuffer.

Since 1.8

Stability Level: Unstable

cogl_framebuffer_get_samples_per_pixel ()

```
int
cogl_framebuffer_get_samples_per_pixel
                             (CoglFramebuffer *framebuffer);
```

Gets the number of points that are sampled per-pixel when rasterizing geometry. Usually by default this will return 0 which means that single-sample not multisample rendering has been chosen. When using a GPU supporting multisample rendering it's possible to increase the number of samples per pixel using cogl_framebuffer_set_samples_per_pixel().

Calling cogl_framebuffer_get_samples_per_pixel() before the framebuffer has been allocated will simply return the value set using cogl_framebuffer_set_samples_per_pixel(). After the framebuffer has been allocated the value will reflect the actual number of samples that will be made by the GPU.

Parameters

framebuffer	A CoglFramebuffer framebuffer	

Returns

The number of point samples made per pixel when rasterizing geometry or 0 if single-sample rendering has been chosen.

Since 1.10

Stability Level: Unstable

cogl_framebuffer_set_samples_per_pixel ()

```
void
cogl_framebuffer_set_samples_per_pixel
                      (CoglFramebuffer *framebuffer,
                       int samples_per_pixel);
```

Requires that when rendering to *framebuffer* then *n* point samples should be made per pixel which will all contribute to the final resolved color for that pixel. The idea is that the hardware aims to get quality similar to what you would get if you rendered everything twice as big (for 4 samples per pixel) and then scaled that image back down with filtering. It can effectively remove the jagged edges of polygons and should be more efficient than if you were to manually render at a higher resolution and downscale because the hardware is often able to take some shortcuts. For example the GPU may only calculate a single texture sample for all points of a single pixel, and for tile based architectures all the extra sample data (such as depth and stencil samples) may be handled on-chip and so avoid increased demand on system memory bandwidth.

By default this value is usually set to 0 and that is referred to as "single-sample" rendering. A value of 1 or greater is referred to as "multisample" rendering.

Note There are some semantic differences between single-sample rendering and multisampling with just 1 point sample such as it being redundant to use the cogl_framebuffer_resolve_samples() and cogl_framebuffer_resolve_samples_region() apis with single-sample rendering.

Note It's recommended that cogl_framebuffer_resolve_samples_region() be explicitly used at the end of rendering to a point sample buffer to minimize the number of samples that get resolved. By default Cogl will implicitly resolve all framebuffer samples but if only a small region of a framebuffer has changed this can lead to redundant work being done.

Parameters

framebuffer	A CoglFramebuffer framebuffer	
samples_per_pixel	The minimum number of samples per pixel	

Since 1.8

Stability Level: Unstable

cogl_framebuffer_resolve_samples ()

```
void
cogl_framebuffer_resolve_samples (CoglFramebuffer *framebuffer);
```

When point sample rendering (also known as multisample rendering) has been enabled via cogl_framebuffer_set_samples_per_pixel() then you can optionally call this function (or cogl_framebuffer_resolve_samples_region()) to explicitly resolve the point samples into values for the final color buffer.

Some GPUs will implicitly resolve the point samples during rendering and so this function is effectively a nop, but with other architectures it is desirable to defer the resolve step until the end of the frame.

Since Cogl will automatically ensure samples are resolved if the target color buffer is used as a source this API only needs to be used if explicit control is desired - perhaps because you want to ensure that the resolve is completed in advance to avoid later having to wait for the resolve to complete.

If you are performing incremental updates to a framebuffer you should consider using cogl_framebuffer_resolve_samples_region() instead to avoid resolving redundant pixels.

Parameters

framebuffer	A CoglFramebuffer framebuffer	

Since 1.8

Stability Level: Unstable

cogl_framebuffer_resolve_samples_region ()

```
void
cogl_framebuffer_resolve_samples_region
                        (CoglFramebuffer *framebuffer,
                         int x,
                         int y,
                         int width,
                         int height);
```

When point sample rendering (also known as multisample rendering) has been enabled via cogl_framebuffer_set_samples_per_pixel() then you can optionally call this function (or cogl_framebuffer_resolve_samples()) to explicitly resolve the point samples into values for the final color buffer.

Some GPUs will implicitly resolve the point samples during rendering and so this function is effectively a nop, but with other architectures it is desirable to defer the resolve step until the end of the frame.

Use of this API is recommended if incremental, small updates to a framebuffer are being made because by default Cogl will implicitly resolve all the point samples of the framebuffer which can result in redundant work if only a small number of samples have changed.

Because some GPUs implicitly resolve point samples this function only guarantees that at-least the region specified will be resolved and if you have rendered to a larger region then it's possible that other samples may be implicitly resolved.

Parameters

framebuffer	A CoglFramebuffer framebuffer	
x	top-left x coordinate of region to resolve	

y	top-left y coordinate of region to resolve	
width	width of region to resolve	
height	height of region to resolve	

Since 1.8

Stability Level: Unstable

cogl_framebuffer_get_context ()

```
CoglContext~*
cogl_framebuffer_get_context (CoglFramebuffer *framebuffer);
```

Can be used to query the CoglContext a given *framebuffer* was instantiated within. This is the CoglContext that was passed to cogl_onscreen_new() for example.

Parameters

framebuffer	A CoglFramebuffer	

Returns

The CoglContext that the given *framebuffer* was instantiated within.

[transfer none]

Since 1.8

Stability Level: Unstable

cogl_framebuffer_clear ()

```
void
cogl_framebuffer_clear (CoglFramebuffer *framebuffer,
                        CoglBufferBit buffers,
                        const CoglColor *color);
```

Clears all the auxiliary buffers identified in the *buffers* mask, and if that includes the color buffer then the specified *color* is used.

Parameters

framebuffer	A CoglFramebuffer	
buffers	A mask of CoglBufferBit's identifying which auxiliary buffers to clear	
color	The color to clear the color buffer too if specified in *buffers*.	

Since 1.8

Stability Level: Unstable

cogl_framebuffer_clear4f ()

```
void
cogl_framebuffer_clear4f (CoglFramebuffer *framebuffer,
                          CoglBufferBit buffers,
                          float red,
                          float green,
                          float blue,
                          float alpha);
```

Clears all the auxiliary buffers identified in the *buffers* mask, and if that includes the color buffer then the specified *color* is used.

Parameters

framebuffer	A CoglFramebuffer	
buffers	A mask of CoglBufferBit's identifying which auxiliary buffers to clear	
red	The red component of color to clear the color buffer too if specified in *buffers*.	
green	The green component of color to clear the color buffer too if specified in *buffers*.	
blue	The blue component of color to clear the color buffer too if specified in *buffers*.	
alpha	The alpha component of color to clear the color buffer too if specified in *buffers*.	

Since 1.8

Stability Level: Unstable

cogl_framebuffer_read_pixels_into_bitmap ()

```
CoglBool
cogl_framebuffer_read_pixels_into_bitmap
                          (CoglFramebuffer *framebuffer,
                           int x,
                           int y,
                           CoglReadPixelsFlags source,
                           CoglBitmap *bitmap,
                           CoglError **error);
```

This reads a rectangle of pixels from the given framebuffer where position (0, 0) is the top left. The pixel at (x, y) is the first read, and a rectangle of pixels with the same size as the bitmap is read right and downwards from that point.

Currently Cogl assumes that the framebuffer is in a premultiplied format so if the format of *bitmap* is non-premultiplied it will convert it. To read the pixel values without any conversion you should either specify a format that doesn't use an alpha channel or use one of the formats ending in PRE.

Parameters

framebuffer	A CoglFramebuffer	
x	The x position to read from	
y	The y position to read from	
source	Identifies which auxillary buffer you want to read (only COGL_READ_PIXELS_COLOR_BUFFER supported currently)	
bitmap	The bitmap to store the results in.	
error	A CoglError to catch exceptional errors	

Returns

TRUE if the read succeeded or FALSE otherwise. The function is only likely to fail if the bitmap points to a pixel buffer and it could not be mapped.

Since 1.10

Stability Level: Unstable

cogl_framebuffer_read_pixels ()

```
CoglBool
cogl_framebuffer_read_pixels (CoglFramebuffer *framebuffer,
                              int x,
                              int y,
                              int width,
                              int height,
                              CoglPixelFormat format,
                              uint8_t *pixels);
```

This is a convenience wrapper around cogl_framebuffer_read_pixels_into_bitmap() which allocates a temporary CoglBitmap to read pixel data directly into the given buffer. The rowstride of the buffer is assumed to be the width of the region times the bytes per pixel of the format. The source for the data is always taken from the color buffer. If you want to use any other rowstride or source, please use the cogl_framebuffer_read_pixels_into_bitmap() function directly.

The implementation of the function looks like this:

```
bitmap = cogl_bitmap_new_for_data (context,
                                   width, height,
                                   format,
                                   /<!-- -->* rowstride *<!-- -->/
                                   bpp * width,
                                   pixels);
cogl_framebuffer_read_pixels_into_bitmap (framebuffer,
                                          x, y,
                                          COGL_READ_PIXELS_COLOR_BUFFER,
                                          bitmap);
cogl_object_unref (bitmap);
```

Parameters

framebuffer	A CoglFramebuffer	

x	The x position to read from	
y	The y position to read from	
width	The width of the region of rectangles to read	
height	The height of the region of rectangles to read	
format	The pixel format to store the data in	
pixels	The address of the buffer to store the data in	

Returns

TRUE if the read succeeded or FALSE otherwise.

Since 1.10

Stability Level: Unstable

cogl_framebuffer_set_dither_enabled ()

```
void
cogl_framebuffer_set_dither_enabled (CoglFramebuffer *framebuffer,
                                     CoglBool dither_enabled);
```

Enables or disabled dithering if supported by the hardware.

Dithering is a hardware dependent technique to increase the visible color resolution beyond what the underlying hardware supports by playing tricks with the colors placed into the framebuffer to give the illusion of other colors. (For example this can be compared to half-toning used by some news papers to show varying levels of grey even though their may only be black and white are available).

If the current display pipeline for *framebuffer* does not support dithering then this has no affect.

Dithering is enabled by default.

Parameters

framebuffer	a pointer to a CoglFramebuffer	
dither_enabled	TRUE to enable dithering or FALSE to disable	

Since 1.8

Stability Level: Unstable

cogl_framebuffer_get_dither_enabled ()

```
CoglBool
cogl_framebuffer_get_dither_enabled (CoglFramebuffer *framebuffer);
```

Returns whether dithering has been requested for the given *framebuffer* . See cogl_framebuffer_set_dither_enabled() for more details about dithering.

Note This may return TRUE even when the underlying *framebuffer* display pipeline does not support dithering. This value only represents the user's request for dithering.

Parameters

framebuffer	a pointer to a CoglFramebuffer	

Returns

TRUE if dithering has been requested or FALSE if not.

Since 1.8

Stability Level: Unstable

cogl_framebuffer_draw_rectangle ()

```
void
cogl_framebuffer_draw_rectangle (CoglFramebuffer *framebuffer,
                                 CoglPipeline *pipeline,
                                 float x_1,
                                 float y_1,
                                 float x_2,
                                 float y_2);
```

Draws a rectangle to *framebuffer* with the given *pipeline* state and with the top left corner positioned at (x_1, y_1) and the bottom right corner positioned at (x_2, y_2).

Note The position is the position before the rectangle has been transformed by the model-view matrix and the projection matrix.

Note If you want to describe a rectangle with a texture mapped on it then you can use cogl_framebuffer_draw_textured_rectangle().

Parameters

framebuffer	A destination CoglFramebuffer	
pipeline	A CoglPipeline state object	
x_1	X coordinate of the top-left corner	
y_1	Y coordinate of the top-left corner	
x_2	X coordinate of the bottom-right corner	
y_2	Y coordinate of the bottom-right corner	

Since 1.10

Stability Level: Unstable

cogl_framebuffer_draw_textured_rectangle ()

```
void
cogl_framebuffer_draw_textured_rectangle
                                (CoglFramebuffer *framebuffer,
                                CoglPipeline *pipeline,
                                float x_1,
                                float y_1,
                                float x_2,
                                float y_2,
                                float s_1,
                                float t_1,
                                float s_2,
                                float t_2);
```

Draws a textured rectangle to $framebuffer$ using the given $pipeline$ state with the top left corner positioned at (x_1, y_1) and the bottom right corner positioned at (x_2, y_2). The top left corner will have texture coordinates of (s_1, t_1) and the bottom right corner will have texture coordinates of (s_2, t_2).

Note The position is the position before the rectangle has been transformed by the model-view matrix and the projection matrix.

This is a high level drawing api that can handle any kind of CoglMetaTexture texture such as CoglTexture2DSliced textures which may internally be comprised of multiple low-level textures. This is unlike low-level drawing apis such as cogl_primitive_draw() which only support low level texture types that are directly supported by GPUs such as CoglTexture2D.

Note The given texture coordinates will only be used for the first texture layer of the pipeline and if your pipeline has more than one layer then all other layers will have default texture coordinates of s_1=0.0 t_1=0.0 s_2=1.0 t_2=1.0

The given texture coordinates should always be normalized such that (0, 0) corresponds to the top left and (1, 1) corresponds to the bottom right. To map an entire texture across the rectangle pass in s_1=0, t_1=0, s_2=1, t_2=1.

Note Even if you have associated a CoglTextureRectangle texture with one of your $pipeline$ layers which normally implies working with non-normalized texture coordinates this api should still be passed normalized texture coordinates.

Parameters

framebuffer	A destination CoglFramebuffer	
pipeline	A CoglPipeline state object	
x_1	x coordinate upper left on screen.	
y_1	y coordinate upper left on screen.	
x_2	x coordinate lower right on screen.	
y_2	y coordinate lower right on screen.	
s_1	S texture coordinate of the top-left coorner	
t_1	T texture coordinate of the top-left coorner	
s_2	S texture coordinate of the bottom-right coorner	
t_2	T texture coordinate of the bottom-right coorner	

Since 1.10

Stability Level: Unstable

cogl_framebuffer_draw_multitextured_rectangle ()

```
void
cogl_framebuffer_draw_multitextured_rectangle
                            (CoglFramebuffer *framebuffer,
                             CoglPipeline *pipeline,
                             float x_1,
                             float y_1,
                             float x_2,
                             float y_2,
                             const float *tex_coords,
                             int tex_coords_len);
```

Draws a textured rectangle to $framebuffer$ with the given $pipeline$ state with the top left corner positioned at (x_1, y_1) and the bottom right corner positioned at (x_2, y_2). As a pipeline may contain multiple texture layers this interface lets you supply texture coordinates for each layer of the pipeline.

Note The position is the position before the rectangle has been transformed by the model-view matrix and the projection matrix.

This is a high level drawing api that can handle any kind of CoglMetaTexture texture for the first layer such as CoglTexture2DSliced textures which may internally be comprised of multiple low-level textures. This is unlike low-level drawing apis such as cogl_primitive_draw() which only support low level texture types that are directly supported by GPUs such as CoglTexture2D.

Note This api can not currently handle multiple high-level meta texture layers. The first layer may be a high level meta texture such as CoglTexture2DSliced but all other layers much be low level textures such as CoglTexture2D and additionally they should be textures that can be sampled using normalized coordinates (so not CoglTextureRectangle textures).

The top left texture coordinate for layer 0 of any pipeline will be (tex_coords[0], tex_coords[1]) and the bottom right coordinate will be (tex_coords[2], tex_coords[3]). The coordinates for layer 1 would be (tex_coords[4], tex_coords[5]) (tex_coords[6], tex_coords[7]) and so on...

The given texture coordinates should always be normalized such that (0, 0) corresponds to the top left and (1, 1) corresponds to the bottom right. To map an entire texture across the rectangle pass in tex_coords[0]=0, tex_coords[1]=0, tex_coords[2]=1, tex_coords[3]=1.

Note Even if you have associated a CoglTextureRectangle texture which normally implies working with non-normalized texture coordinates this api should still be passed normalized texture coordinates.

The first pair of coordinates are for the first layer (with the smallest layer index) and if you supply less texture coordinates than there are layers in the current source material then default texture coordinates (0.0, 0.0, 1.0, 1.0) are generated.

Parameters

framebuffer	A destination CoglFramebuffer	
pipeline	A CoglPipeline state object	

x_1	x coordinate upper left on screen.	
y_1	y coordinate upper left on screen.	
x_2	x coordinate lower right on screen.	
y_2	y coordinate lower right on screen.	
tex_coords	An array containing groups of 4 float values: [s_1, t_1, s_2, t_2] that are interpreted as two texture coordinates; one for the top left texel, and one for the bottom right texel. Each value should be between 0.0 and 1.0, where the coordinate (0.0, 0.0) represents the top left of the texture, and (1.0, 1.0) the bottom right.	*[in][array][transfer none]*
tex_coords_len	The length of the `tex_coords` array. (For one layer and one group of texture coordinates, this would be 4)	

Since 1.10

Stability Level: Unstable

cogl_framebuffer_draw_rectangles ()

```
void
cogl_framebuffer_draw_rectangles (CoglFramebuffer *framebuffer,
                                  CoglPipeline *pipeline,
                                  const float *coordinates,
                                  unsigned int n_rectangles);
```

Draws a series of rectangles to *framebuffer* with the given *pipeline* state in the same way that cogl_framebuffer_draw_rectangle() does.

The top left corner of the first rectangle is positioned at (coordinates[0], coordinates[1]) and the bottom right corner is positioned at (coordinates[2], coordinates[3]). The positions for the second rectangle are (coordinates[4], coordinates[5]) and (coordinates[6], coordinates[7]) and so on...

Note The position is the position before the rectangle has been transformed by the model-view matrix and the projection matrix.

As a general rule for better performance its recommended to use this this API instead of calling cogl_framebuffer_draw_textured_rectang separately for multiple rectangles if all of the rectangles will be drawn together with the same *pipeline* state.

Parameters

framebuffer	A destination CoglFramebuffer	

pipeline	A CoglPipeline state object	
coordinates	an array of coordinates containing groups of 4 float values: [x_1, y_1, x_2, y_2] that are interpreted as two position coordinates; one for the top left of the rectangle (x1, y1), and one for the bottom right of the rectangle (x2, y2).	*[in][array][transfer none]*
n_rectangles	number of rectangles defined in *coordinates*.	

Since 1.10

Stability Level: Unstable

cogl_framebuffer_draw_textured_rectangles ()

```
void
cogl_framebuffer_draw_textured_rectangles
                          (CoglFramebuffer *framebuffer,
                           CoglPipeline *pipeline,
                           const float *coordinates,
                           unsigned int n_rectangles);
```

Draws a series of rectangles to *framebuffer* with the given *pipeline* state in the same way that cogl_framebuffer_draw_textured_rectangle() does.

Note The position is the position before the rectangle has been transformed by the model-view matrix and the projection matrix.

This is a high level drawing api that can handle any kind of CoglMetaTexture texture such as CoglTexture2DSliced textures which may internally be comprised of multiple low-level textures. This is unlike low-level drawing apis such as cogl_primitive_draw() which only support low level texture types that are directly supported by GPUs such as CoglTexture2D.

The top left corner of the first rectangle is positioned at (coordinates[0], coordinates[1]) and the bottom right corner is positioned at (coordinates[2], coordinates[3]). The top left texture coordinate is (coordinates[4], coordinates[5]) and the bottom right texture coordinate is (coordinates[6], coordinates[7]). The coordinates for subsequent rectangles are defined similarly by the subsequent coordinates.

As a general rule for better performance its recommended to use this this API instead of calling cogl_framebuffer_draw_textured_rectangle() separately for multiple rectangles if all of the rectangles will be drawn together with the same *pipeline* state.

The given texture coordinates should always be normalized such that (0, 0) corresponds to the top left and (1, 1) corresponds to the bottom right. To map an entire texture across the rectangle pass in tex_coords[0]=0, tex_coords[1]=0, tex_coords[2]=1, tex_coords[3]=1.

Note Even if you have associated a CoglTextureRectangle texture which normally implies working with non-normalized texture coordinates this api should still be passed normalized texture coordinates.

Parameters

framebuffer	A destination CoglFramebuffer	
pipeline	A CoglPipeline state object	
coordinates	an array containing groups of 8 float values: [x_1, y_1, x_2, y_2, s_1, t_1, s_2, t_2] that have the same meaning as the arguments for cogl_framebuffer_draw_textured_rectangle().	*[in][array][transfer none]*
n_rectangles	number of rectangles to *coordinates* to draw	

Since 1.10

Stability Level: Unstable

cogl_framebuffer_discard_buffers ()

```
void
cogl_framebuffer_discard_buffers (CoglFramebuffer *framebuffer,
                                  CoglBufferBit buffers);
```

Declares that the specified *buffers* no longer need to be referenced by any further rendering commands. This can be an important optimization to avoid subsequent frames of rendering depending on the results of a previous frame.

For example; some tile-based rendering GPUs are able to avoid allocating and accessing system memory for the depth and stencil buffer so long as these buffers are not required as input for subsequent frames and that can save a significant amount of memory bandwidth used to save and restore their contents to system memory between frames.

It is currently considered an error to try and explicitly discard the color buffer by passing COGL_BUFFER_BIT_COLOR. This is because the color buffer is already implicitly discard when you finish rendering to a CoglOnscreen framebuffer, and it's not meaningful to try and discard the color buffer of a CoglOffscreen framebuffer since they are single-buffered.

Parameters

| framebuffer | A CoglFramebuffer | |
| buffers | A CoglBufferBit mask of which ancillary buffers you want to discard. | |

Since 1.8

Stability Level: Unstable

cogl_framebuffer_finish ()

```
void
cogl_framebuffer_finish (CoglFramebuffer *framebuffer);
```

This blocks the CPU until all pending rendering associated with the specified framebuffer has completed. It's very rare that developers should ever need this level of synchronization with the GPU and should never be used unless you clearly understand why you need to explicitly force synchronization.

One example might be for benchmarking purposes to be sure timing measurements reflect the time that the GPU is busy for not just the time it takes to queue rendering commands.

Parameters

framebuffer	A CoglFramebuffer pointer

Since 1.10

Stability Level: Unstable

cogl_framebuffer_push_matrix ()

```
void
cogl_framebuffer_push_matrix (CoglFramebuffer *framebuffer);
```

Copies the current model-view matrix onto the matrix stack. The matrix can later be restored with cogl_framebuffer_pop_matrix().

Parameters

framebuffer	A CoglFramebuffer pointer

Since 1.10

cogl_framebuffer_pop_matrix ()

```
void
cogl_framebuffer_pop_matrix (CoglFramebuffer *framebuffer);
```

Restores the model-view matrix on the top of the matrix stack.

Parameters

framebuffer	A CoglFramebuffer pointer

Since 1.10

cogl_framebuffer_identity_matrix ()

```
void
cogl_framebuffer_identity_matrix (CoglFramebuffer *framebuffer);
```

Resets the current model-view matrix to the identity matrix.

Parameters

framebuffer	A CoglFramebuffer pointer

Since 1.10

Stability Level: Unstable

cogl_framebuffer_scale ()

```
void
cogl_framebuffer_scale (CoglFramebuffer *framebuffer,
                        float x,
                        float y,
                        float z);
```

Multiplies the current model-view matrix by one that scales the x, y and z axes by the given values.

Parameters

framebuffer	A CoglFramebuffer pointer	
x	Amount to scale along the x-axis	
y	Amount to scale along the y-axis	
z	Amount to scale along the z-axis	

Since 1.10

Stability Level: Unstable

cogl_framebuffer_translate ()

```
void
cogl_framebuffer_translate (CoglFramebuffer *framebuffer,
                            float x,
                            float y,
                            float z);
```

Multiplies the current model-view matrix by one that translates the model along all three axes according to the given values.

Parameters

framebuffer	A CoglFramebuffer pointer	
x	Distance to translate along the x-axis	
y	Distance to translate along the y-axis	
z	Distance to translate along the z-axis	

Since 1.10

Stability Level: Unstable

cogl_framebuffer_rotate ()

```
void
cogl_framebuffer_rotate (CoglFramebuffer *framebuffer,
                         float angle,
                         float x,
                         float y,
                         float z);
```

Multiplies the current model-view matrix by one that rotates the model around the axis-vector specified by x, y and z. The rotation follows the right-hand thumb rule so for example rotating by 10 degrees about the axis-vector (0, 0, 1) causes a small counter-clockwise rotation.

Parameters

framebuffer	A CoglFramebuffer pointer	
angle	Angle in degrees to rotate.	
x	X-component of vertex to rotate around.	
y	Y-component of vertex to rotate around.	
z	Z-component of vertex to rotate around.	

Since 1.10

Stability Level: Unstable

cogl_framebuffer_rotate_euler ()

```
void
cogl_framebuffer_rotate_euler (CoglFramebuffer *framebuffer,
                               const CoglEuler *euler);
```

Multiplies the current model-view matrix by one that rotates according to the rotation described by *euler*.

Parameters

framebuffer	A CoglFramebuffer pointer	
euler	A CoglEuler	

Since 2.0

Stability Level: Unstable

cogl_framebuffer_rotate_quaternion ()

```
void
cogl_framebuffer_rotate_quaternion (CoglFramebuffer *framebuffer,
                                    const CoglQuaternion *quaternion);
```

Multiplies the current model-view matrix by one that rotates according to the rotation described by *quaternion*.

Parameters

framebuffer	A CoglFramebuffer pointer	
quaternion	A CoglQuaternion	

Since 2.0

Stability Level: Unstable

cogl_framebuffer_transform ()

```
void
cogl_framebuffer_transform (CoglFramebuffer *framebuffer,
                            const CoglMatrix *matrix);
```

Multiplies the current model-view matrix by the given matrix.

Parameters

framebuffer	A CoglFramebuffer pointer	
matrix	the matrix to multiply with the current model-view	

Since 1.10

Stability Level: Unstable

cogl_framebuffer_get_modelview_matrix ()

```
void
cogl_framebuffer_get_modelview_matrix (CoglFramebuffer *framebuffer,
                                       CoglMatrix *matrix);
```

Stores the current model-view matrix in `matrix` .

Parameters

framebuffer	A CoglFramebuffer pointer	
matrix	return location for the model-view matrix.	[out]

Since 1.10

Stability Level: Unstable

cogl_framebuffer_set_modelview_matrix ()

```
void
cogl_framebuffer_set_modelview_matrix (CoglFramebuffer *framebuffer,
                                       const CoglMatrix *matrix);
```

Sets `matrix` as the new model-view matrix.

Parameters

framebuffer	A CoglFramebuffer pointer	
matrix	the new model-view matrix	

Since 1.10

Stability Level: Unstable

cogl_framebuffer_perspective ()

```
void
cogl_framebuffer_perspective (CoglFramebuffer *framebuffer,
                              float fov_y,
                              float aspect,
                              float z_near,
                              float z_far);
```

Replaces the current projection matrix with a perspective matrix based on the provided values.

Note You should be careful not to have to great a z_far / z_near ratio since that will reduce the effectiveness of depth testing since there wont be enough precision to identify the depth of objects near to each other.

Parameters

framebuffer	A CoglFramebuffer pointer	
fov_y	Vertical field of view angle in degrees.	
aspect	The (width over height) aspect ratio for display	
z_near	The distance to the near clipping plane (Must be positive, and must not be 0)	
z_far	The distance to the far clipping plane (Must be positive)	

Since 1.10

Stability Level: Unstable

cogl_framebuffer_frustum ()

```
void
cogl_framebuffer_frustum (CoglFramebuffer *framebuffer,
                          float left,
                          float right,
                          float bottom,
                          float top,
                          float z_near,
                          float z_far);
```

Replaces the current projection matrix with a perspective matrix for a given viewing frustum defined by 4 side clip planes that all cross through the origin and 2 near and far clip planes.

Parameters

framebuffer	A CoglFramebuffer pointer	
left	X position of the left clipping plane where it intersects the near clipping plane	

right	X position of the right clipping plane where it intersects the near clipping plane	
bottom	Y position of the bottom clipping plane where it intersects the near clipping plane	
top	Y position of the top clipping plane where it intersects the near clipping plane	
z_near	The distance to the near clipping plane (Must be positive)	
z_far	The distance to the far clipping plane (Must be positive)	

Since 1.10

Stability Level: Unstable

cogl_framebuffer_orthographic ()

```
void
cogl_framebuffer_orthographic (CoglFramebuffer *framebuffer,
                               float x_1,
                               float y_1,
                               float x_2,
                               float y_2,
                               float near,
                               float far);
```

Replaces the current projection matrix with an orthographic projection matrix.

Parameters

framebuffer	A CoglFramebuffer pointer	
x_1	The x coordinate for the first vertical clipping plane	
y_1	The y coordinate for the first horizontal clipping plane	
x_2	The x coordinate for the second vertical clipping plane	
y_2	The y coordinate for the second horizontal clipping plane	
near	The *distance* to the near clipping plane (will be *negative* if the plane is behind the viewer)	
far	The *distance* to the far clipping plane (will be *negative* if the plane is behind the viewer)	

Since 1.10

Stability Level: Unstable

cogl_framebuffer_get_projection_matrix ()

```
void
cogl_framebuffer_get_projection_matrix
                            (CoglFramebuffer *framebuffer,
                             CoglMatrix *matrix);
```

Stores the current projection matrix in *matrix* .

Parameters

framebuffer	A CoglFramebuffer pointer	
matrix	return location for the projection matrix.	*[out]*

Since 1.10

Stability Level: Unstable

cogl_framebuffer_set_projection_matrix ()

```
void
cogl_framebuffer_set_projection_matrix
                            (CoglFramebuffer *framebuffer,
                             const CoglMatrix *matrix);
```

Sets *matrix* as the new projection matrix.

Parameters

framebuffer	A CoglFramebuffer pointer
matrix	the new projection matrix

Since 1.10

Stability Level: Unstable

cogl_framebuffer_push_scissor_clip ()

```
void
cogl_framebuffer_push_scissor_clip (CoglFramebuffer *framebuffer,
                                    int x,
                                    int y,
                                    int width,
                                    int height);
```

Specifies a rectangular clipping area for all subsequent drawing operations. Any drawing commands that extend outside the rectangle will be clipped so that only the portion inside the rectangle will be displayed. The rectangle dimensions are not transformed by the current model-view matrix.

The rectangle is intersected with the current clip region. To undo the effect of this function, call cogl_framebuffer_pop_clip().

Parameters

framebuffer	A CoglFramebuffer pointer	
x	left edge of the clip rectangle in window coordinates	
y	top edge of the clip rectangle in window coordinates	
width	width of the clip rectangle	
height	height of the clip rectangle	

Since 1.10

Stability Level: Unstable

cogl_framebuffer_push_rectangle_clip ()

```
void
cogl_framebuffer_push_rectangle_clip (CoglFramebuffer *framebuffer,
                                      float x_1,
                                      float y_1,
                                      float x_2,
                                      float y_2);
```

Specifies a modelview transformed rectangular clipping area for all subsequent drawing operations. Any drawing commands that extend outside the rectangle will be clipped so that only the portion inside the rectangle will be displayed. The rectangle dimensions are transformed by the current model-view matrix.

The rectangle is intersected with the current clip region. To undo the effect of this function, call cogl_framebuffer_pop_clip().

Parameters

framebuffer	A CoglFramebuffer pointer	
x_1	x coordinate for top left corner of the clip rectangle	
y_1	y coordinate for top left corner of the clip rectangle	
x_2	x coordinate for bottom right corner of the clip rectangle	
y_2	y coordinate for bottom right corner of the clip rectangle	

Since 1.10

Stability Level: Unstable

cogl_framebuffer_push_primitive_clip ()

```
void
cogl_framebuffer_push_primitive_clip (CoglFramebuffer *framebuffer,
                                      CoglPrimitive *primitive,
                                      float bounds_x1,
                                      float bounds_y1,
```

```
                          float bounds_x2,
                          float bounds_y2);
```

Sets a new clipping area using a 2D shaped described with a CoglPrimitive. The shape must not contain self overlapping geometry and must lie on a single 2D plane. A bounding box of the 2D shape in local coordinates (the same coordinates used to describe the shape) must be given. It is acceptable for the bounds to be larger than the true bounds but behaviour is undefined if the bounds are smaller than the true bounds.

The primitive is transformed by the current model-view matrix and the silhouette is intersected with the previous clipping area. To restore the previous clipping area, call cogl_framebuffer_pop_clip().

Parameters

framebuffer	A CoglFramebuffer pointer	
primitive	A CoglPrimitive describing a flat 2D shape	
bounds_x1	x coordinate for the top-left corner of the primitives bounds	
bounds_y1	y coordinate for the top-left corner of the primitives bounds	
bounds_x2	x coordinate for the bottom-right corner of the primitives bounds.	
bounds_y2	y coordinate for the bottom-right corner of the primitives bounds.	

Since 1.10

Stability Level: Unstable

cogl_framebuffer_pop_clip ()

```
void
cogl_framebuffer_pop_clip (CoglFramebuffer *framebuffer);
```

Reverts the clipping region to the state before the last call to cogl_framebuffer_push_scissor_clip(), cogl_framebuffer_push_rectangle_clip() cogl_framebuffer_push_path_clip(), or cogl_framebuffer_push_primitive_clip().

Parameters

framebuffer	A CoglFramebuffer pointer	

Since 1.10

Stability Level: Unstable

Types and Values

CoglFramebuffer

```
typedef void CoglFramebuffer;
```

1.11.2 CoglOnscreen: The Onscreen Framebuffer Interface

CoglOnscreen: The Onscreen Framebuffer Interface —

Functions

CoglBool	cogl_is_onscreen ()
#define	COGL_ONSCREEN()
CoglOnscreen *	cogl_onscreen_new ()
void	(*CoglOnscreenX11MaskCallback) ()
void	cogl_x11_onscreen_set_foreign_window_xid ()
uint32_t	cogl_x11_onscreen_get_window_xid ()
uint32_t	cogl_x11_onscreen_get_visual_xid ()
void	cogl_win32_onscreen_set_foreign_window ()
HWND	cogl_win32_onscreen_get_window ()
void	cogl_onscreen_show ()
void	cogl_onscreen_hide ()
void	(*CoglFrameCallback) ()
CoglFrameClosure *	cogl_onscreen_add_frame_callback ()
void	cogl_onscreen_remove_frame_callback ()
void	(*CoglOnscreenDirtyCallback) ()
CoglOnscreenDirtyClosure *	cogl_onscreen_add_dirty_callback ()
void	cogl_onscreen_remove_dirty_callback ()
void	(*CoglOnscreenResizeCallback) ()
CoglOnscreenResizeClosure *	cogl_onscreen_add_resize_callback ()
void	cogl_onscreen_remove_resize_callback ()
void	cogl_onscreen_swap_buffers ()
void	cogl_onscreen_swap_buffers_with_damage ()
void	cogl_onscreen_swap_region ()
void	cogl_onscreen_set_swap_throttled ()

Types and Values

	CoglOnscreen
typedef	CoglFrameClosure
struct	CoglOnscreenDirtyInfo
typedef	CoglOnscreenDirtyClosure
typedef	CoglOnscreenResizeClosure

Description

Functions

cogl_is_onscreen ()

```
CoglBool
cogl_is_onscreen (void *object);
```

Gets whether the given object references a CoglOnscreen.

Parameters

object	A CoglObject pointer	

Returns

TRUE if the object references a CoglOnscreen and FALSE otherwise.

Since 1.10

Stability Level: Unstable

COGL_ONSCREEN()

```
#define COGL_ONSCREEN(X) ((CoglOnscreen *)(X))
```

cogl_onscreen_new ()

```
CoglOnscreen~*
cogl_onscreen_new (CoglContext *context,
                   int width,
                   int height);
```

Instantiates an "unallocated" CoglOnscreen framebuffer that may be configured before later being allocated, either implicitly when it is first used or explicitly via cogl_framebuffer_allocate().

Parameters

context	A CoglContext	
width	The desired framebuffer width	
height	The desired framebuffer height	

Returns

A newly instantiated CoglOnscreen framebuffer.

[transfer full]

Since 1.8

Stability Level: Unstable

CoglOnscreenX11MaskCallback ()

```
void
(*CoglOnscreenX11MaskCallback) (CoglOnscreen *onscreen,
                                uint32_t event_mask,
                                void *user_data);
```

cogl_x11_onscreen_set_foreign_window_xid ()

```
void
cogl_x11_onscreen_set_foreign_window_xid
                                (CoglOnscreen *onscreen,
                                uint32_t xid,
                                CoglOnscreenX11MaskCallback update,
                                void *user_data);
```

Ideally we would recommend that you let Cogl be responsible for creating any X window required to back an onscreen frame-buffer but if you really need to target a window created manually this function can be called before *onscreen* has been allocated to set a foreign XID for your existing X window.

Since Cogl needs, for example, to track changes to the size of an X window it requires that certain events be selected for via the core X protocol. This requirement may also be changed asynchronously so you must pass in an *update* callback to inform you of Cogl's required event mask.

For example if you are using Xlib you could use this API roughly as follows: [{ static void my_update_cogl_x11_event_mask (CoglOnscreen *onscreen, uint32_t event_mask, void *user_data) { XSetWindowAttributes attrs; MyData *data = user_data; attrs.event_mask = event_mask | data->my_event_mask; XChangeWindowAttributes (data->xdpy, data->xwin, CWEventMask, &attrs); }

{ *snip* cogl_x11_onscreen_set_foreign_window_xid (onscreen, data->xwin, my_update_cogl_x11_event_mask, data); *snip* } }]

Parameters

onscreen	The unallocated framebuffer to associated with an X window.	
xid	The XID of an existing X window	
update	A callback that notifies of updates to what Cogl requires to be in the core X protocol event mask.	
user_data	user data passed to *update*	

Since 2.0

Stability Level: Unstable

cogl_x11_onscreen_get_window_xid ()

```
uint32_t
cogl_x11_onscreen_get_window_xid (CoglOnscreen *onscreen);
```

Assuming you know the given *onscreen* framebuffer is based on an x11 window this queries the XID of that window. If cogl_x11_onscreen_set_foreign_window_xid() was previously called then it will return that same XID otherwise it will be the XID of a window Cogl created internally. If the window has not been allocated yet and a foreign xid has not been set then it's undefined what value will be returned.

It's undefined what this function does if called when not using an x11 based renderer.

Parameters

onscreen	A CoglOnscreen framebuffer	

Since 1.10

Stability Level: Unstable

cogl_x11_onscreen_get_visual_xid ()

```
uint32_t
cogl_x11_onscreen_get_visual_xid (CoglOnscreen *onscreen);
```

cogl_win32_onscreen_set_foreign_window ()

```
void
cogl_win32_onscreen_set_foreign_window
                              (CoglOnscreen *onscreen,
                               HWND hwnd);
```

Ideally we would recommend that you let Cogl be responsible for creating any window required to back an onscreen framebuffer but if you really need to target a window created manually this function can be called before *onscreen* has been allocated to set a foreign XID for your existing X window.

Parameters

onscreen	A CoglOnscreen framebuffer	
hwnd	A win32 window handle	

Since 1.10

Stability Level: Unstable

cogl_win32_onscreen_get_window ()

```
HWND
cogl_win32_onscreen_get_window (CoglOnscreen *onscreen);
```

Queries the internally created window HWND backing the given *onscreen* framebuffer. If cogl_win32_onscreen_set_foreign_window() has been used then it will return the same handle set with that API.

Parameters

onscreen	A CoglOnscreen framebuffer	

Since 1.10

Stability Level: Unstable

cogl_onscreen_show ()

```
void
cogl_onscreen_show (CoglOnscreen *onscreen);
```

This requests to make *onscreen* visible to the user.

Actually the precise semantics of this function depend on the window system currently in use, and if you don't have a multi-windowining system this function may in-fact do nothing.

This function will implicitly allocate the given *onscreen* framebuffer before showing it if it hasn't already been allocated.

When using the Wayland winsys calling this will set the surface to a toplevel type which will make it appear. If the application wants to set a different type for the surface, it can avoid calling cogl_onscreen_show() and set its own type directly with the Wayland client API via cogl_wayland_onscreen_get_surface().

Note Since Cogl doesn't explicitly track the visibility status of onscreen framebuffers it wont try to avoid redundant window system requests e.g. to show an already visible window. This also means that it's acceptable to alternatively use native APIs to show and hide windows without confusing Cogl.

Parameters

onscreen	The onscreen framebuffer to make visible

Since 2.0

Stability Level: Unstable

cogl_onscreen_hide ()

```
void
cogl_onscreen_hide (CoglOnscreen *onscreen);
```

This requests to make *onscreen* invisible to the user.

Actually the precise semantics of this function depend on the window system currently in use, and if you don't have a multi-windowining system this function may in-fact do nothing.

This function does not implicitly allocate the given *onscreen* framebuffer before hiding it.

Note Since Cogl doesn't explicitly track the visibility status of onscreen framebuffers it wont try to avoid redundant window system requests e.g. to show an already visible window. This also means that it's acceptable to alternatively use native APIs to show and hide windows without confusing Cogl.

Parameters

onscreen	The onscreen framebuffer to make invisible

Since 2.0

Stability Level: Unstable

CoglFrameCallback ()

```
void
(*CoglFrameCallback) (CoglOnscreen *onscreen,
                      CoglFrameEvent event,
                      CoglFrameInfo *info,
                      void *user_data);
```

Is a callback that can be registered via cogl_onscreen_add_frame_callback() to be called when a frame progresses in some notable way.

Please see the documentation for CoglFrameEvent and cogl_onscreen_add_frame_callback() for more details about what events can be notified.

Parameters

onscreen	The onscreen that the frame is associated with	
event	A CoglFrameEvent notifying how the frame has progressed	
info	The meta information, such as timing information, about the frame that has progressed.	
user_data	The user pointer passed to cogl_onscreen_add_frame_callback()	

Since 1.14

Stability Level: Unstable

cogl_onscreen_add_frame_callback ()

```
CoglFrameClosure~*
cogl_onscreen_add_frame_callback (CoglOnscreen *onscreen,
                                  CoglFrameCallback callback,
                                  void *user_data,
                                  CoglUserDataDestroyCallback destroy);
```

Installs a `callback` function that will be called for significant events relating to the given `onscreen` framebuffer.

The `callback` will be used to notify when the system compositor is ready for this application to render a new frame. In this case COGL_FRAME_EVENT_SYNC will be passed as the event argument to the given `callback` in addition to the CoglFrameInfo corresponding to the frame beeing acknowledged by the compositor.

The `callback` will also be called to notify when the frame has ended. In this case COGL_FRAME_EVENT_COMPLETE will be passed as the event argument to the given `callback` in addition to the CoglFrameInfo corresponding to the newly presented frame. The meaning of "ended" here simply means that no more timing information will be collected within the corresponding CoglFrameInfo and so this is a good opportunity to analyse the given info. It does not necessarily mean that the GPU has finished rendering the corresponding frame.

We highly recommend throttling your application according to COGL_FRAME_EVENT_SYNC events so that your application can avoid wasting resources, drawing more frames than your system compositor can display.

Parameters

onscreen	A CoglOnscreen framebuffer	
callback	A callback function to call for frame events	
user_data	A private pointer to be passed to `callback`	
destroy	An optional callback to destroy `user_data` when the `callback` is removed or `onscreen` is freed.	

Returns

a CoglFrameClosure pointer that can be used to remove the callback and associated *user_data* later.

Since 1.14

Stability Level: Unstable

cogl_onscreen_remove_frame_callback ()

```
void
cogl_onscreen_remove_frame_callback (CoglOnscreen *onscreen,
                                     CoglFrameClosure *closure);
```

Removes a callback and associated user data that were previously registered using cogl_onscreen_add_frame_callback().

If a destroy callback was passed to cogl_onscreen_add_frame_callback() to destroy the user data then this will get called.

Parameters

onscreen	A CoglOnscreen	
closure	A CoglFrameClosure returned from cogl_onscreen_add_frame_callback()	

Since 1.14

Stability Level: Unstable

CoglOnscreenDirtyCallback ()

```
void
(*CoglOnscreenDirtyCallback) (CoglOnscreen *onscreen,
                              const CoglOnscreenDirtyInfo *info,
                              void *user_data);
```

Is a callback that can be registered via cogl_onscreen_add_dirty_callback() to be called when the windowing system determines that a region of the onscreen window has been lost and the application should redraw it.

Parameters

onscreen	The onscreen that the frame is associated with	
info	A CoglOnscreenDirtyInfo struct containing the details of the dirty area	
user_data	The user pointer passed to cogl_onscreen_add_frame_callback()	

Since 1.16

Stability Level: Unstable

cogl_onscreen_add_dirty_callback ()

```
CoglOnscreenDirtyClosure~*
cogl_onscreen_add_dirty_callback (CoglOnscreen *onscreen,
                                  CoglOnscreenDirtyCallback callback,
                                  void *user_data,
                                  CoglUserDataDestroyCallback destroy);
```

Installs a *callback* function that will be called whenever the window system has lost the contents of a region of the onscreen buffer and the application should redraw it to repair the buffer. For example this may happen in a window system without a compositor if a window that was previously covering up the onscreen window has been moved causing a region of the onscreen to be exposed.

The *callback* will be passed a CoglOnscreenDirtyInfo struct which decribes a rectangle containing the newly dirtied region. Note that this may be called multiple times to describe a non-rectangular region composed of multiple smaller rectangles.

The dirty events are separate from COGL_FRAME_EVENT_SYNC events so the application should also listen for this event before rendering the dirty region to ensure that the framebuffer is actually ready for rendering.

Parameters

onscreen	A CoglOnscreen framebuffer	
callback	A callback function to call for dirty events	
user_data	A private pointer to be passed to *callback*	
destroy	An optional callback to destroy *user_data* when the *callback* is removed or *onscreen* is freed.	

Returns

a CoglOnscreenDirtyClosure pointer that can be used to remove the callback and associated *user_data* later.

Since 1.16

Stability Level: Unstable

cogl_onscreen_remove_dirty_callback ()

```
void
cogl_onscreen_remove_dirty_callback (CoglOnscreen *onscreen,
                                     CoglOnscreenDirtyClosure *closure);
```

Removes a callback and associated user data that were previously registered using cogl_onscreen_add_dirty_callback().

If a destroy callback was passed to cogl_onscreen_add_dirty_callback() to destroy the user data then this will also get called.

Parameters

onscreen	A CoglOnscreen	
closure	A CoglOnscreenDirtyClosure returned from cogl_onscreen_add_dirty_callback()	

Since 1.16

Stability Level: Unstable

CoglOnscreenResizeCallback ()

```
void
(*CoglOnscreenResizeCallback) (CoglOnscreen *onscreen,
                               int width,
                               int height,
                               void *user_data);
```

Is a callback type used with the cogl_onscreen_add_resize_callback() allowing applications to be notified whenever an *onscreen* framebuffer is resized.

Note Cogl automatically updates the viewport of an *onscreen* framebuffer that is resized so this callback is also an indication that the viewport has been modified too

---

Note A resize callback will only ever be called while dispatching Cogl events from the system mainloop; so for example during cogl_poll_renderer_dispatch(). This is so that callbacks shouldn't occur while an application might have arbitrary locks held for example.

Parameters

onscreen	A CoglOnscreen framebuffer that was resized	
width	The new width of *onscreen*	
height	The new height of *onscreen*	
user_data	The private passed to cogl_onscreen_add_resize_callback()	

Since 2.0

cogl_onscreen_add_resize_callback ()

```
CoglOnscreenResizeClosure~*
cogl_onscreen_add_resize_callback (CoglOnscreen *onscreen,
                                   CoglOnscreenResizeCallback callback,
                                   void *user_data,
                                   CoglUserDataDestroyCallback destroy);
```

Registers a *callback* with *onscreen* that will be called whenever the *onscreen* framebuffer changes size.

The *callback* can be removed using cogl_onscreen_remove_resize_callback() passing the returned closure pointer.

Note Since Cogl automatically updates the viewport of an *onscreen* framebuffer that is resized, a resize callback can also be used to track when the viewport has been changed automatically by Cogl in case your application needs more specialized control over the viewport.

Note A resize callback will only ever be called while dispatching Cogl events from the system mainloop; so for example during cogl_poll_renderer_dispatch(). This is so that callbacks shouldn't occur while an application might have arbitrary locks held for example.

Parameters

onscreen	A CoglOnscreen framebuffer	
callback	A CoglOnscreenResize-Callback to call when the onscreen changes size.	
user_data	Private data to be passed to callback.	
destroy	An optional callback to destroy user_data when the callback is removed or onscreen is freed.	

Returns

a CoglOnscreenResizeClosure pointer that can be used to remove the callback and associated user_data later.

Since 2.0

cogl_onscreen_remove_resize_callback ()

```
void
cogl_onscreen_remove_resize_callback (CoglOnscreen *onscreen,
                                      CoglOnscreenResizeClosure *closure);
```

Removes a resize callback and user_data pair that were previously associated with onscreen via cogl_onscreen_add_resize_callback().

Parameters

onscreen	A CoglOnscreen framebuffer	
closure	An identifier returned from cogl_onscreen_add_resize_callback()	

Since 2.0

cogl_onscreen_swap_buffers ()

```
void
cogl_onscreen_swap_buffers (CoglOnscreen *onscreen);
```

Swaps the current back buffer being rendered too, to the front for display.

This function also implicitly discards the contents of the color, depth and stencil buffers as if cogl_framebuffer_discard_buffers() were used. The significance of the discard is that you should not expect to be able to start a new frame that incrementally builds on the contents of the previous frame.

> **Note** It is highly recommended that applications use cogl_onscreen_swap_buffers_with_damage() instead whenever possible and also use the cogl_onscreen_get_buffer_age() api so they can perform incremental updates to older buffers instead of having to render a full buffer for every frame.

Parameters

onscreen	A CoglOnscreen framebuffer	

Since 1.10

Stability Level: Unstable

cogl_onscreen_swap_buffers_with_damage ()

```
void
cogl_onscreen_swap_buffers_with_damage
                          (CoglOnscreen *onscreen,
                           const int *rectangles,
                           int n_rectangles);
```

Swaps the current back buffer being rendered too, to the front for display and provides information to any system compositor about what regions of the buffer have changed (damage) with respect to the last swapped buffer.

This function has the same semantics as cogl_framebuffer_swap_buffers() except that it additionally allows applications to pass a list of damaged rectangles which may be passed on to a compositor so that it can minimize how much of the screen is redrawn in response to this applications newly swapped front buffer.

For example if your application is only animating a small object in the corner of the screen and everything else is remaining static then it can help the compositor to know that only the bottom right corner of your newly swapped buffer has really changed with respect to your previously swapped front buffer.

If $n\_rectangles$ is 0 then the whole buffer will implicitly be reported as damaged as if cogl_onscreen_swap_buffers() had been called.

This function also implicitly discards the contents of the color, depth and stencil buffers as if cogl_framebuffer_discard_buffers() were used. The significance of the discard is that you should not expect to be able to start a new frame that incrementally builds on the contents of the previous frame. If you want to perform incremental updates to older back buffers then please refer to the cogl_onscreen_get_buffer_age() api.

Whenever possible it is recommended that applications use this function instead of cogl_onscreen_swap_buffers() to improve performance when running under a compositor.

> **Note** It is highly recommended to use this API in conjunction with the cogl_onscreen_get_buffer_age() api so that your application can perform incremental rendering based on old back buffers.

Parameters

onscreen	A CoglOnscreen framebuffer	
rectangles	An array of integer 4-tuples representing damaged rectangles as (x, y, width, height) tuples.	
n_rectangles	The number of 4-tuples to be read from $rectangles$	

Since 1.16

Stability Level: Unstable

cogl_onscreen_swap_region ()

```
void
cogl_onscreen_swap_region (CoglOnscreen *onscreen,
                           const int *rectangles,
                           int n_rectangles);
```

Swaps a region of the back buffer being rendered too, to the front for display. `rectangles` represents the region as array of `n_rectangles` each defined by 4 sequential (x, y, width, height) integers.

This function also implicitly discards the contents of the color, depth and stencil buffers as if cogl_framebuffer_discard_buffers() were used. The significance of the discard is that you should not expect to be able to start a new frame that incrementally builds on the contents of the previous frame.

Parameters

onscreen	A CoglOnscreen framebuffer	
rectangles	An array of integer 4-tuples representing rectangles as (x, y, width, height) tuples.	
n_rectangles	The number of 4-tuples to be read from `rectangles`	

Since 1.10

Stability Level: Unstable

cogl_onscreen_set_swap_throttled ()

```
void
cogl_onscreen_set_swap_throttled (CoglOnscreen *onscreen,
                                  CoglBool throttled);
```

Requests that the given `onscreen` framebuffer should have swap buffer requests (made using cogl_onscreen_swap_buffers()) throttled either by a displays vblank period or perhaps some other mechanism in a composited environment.

Parameters

onscreen	A CoglOnscreen framebuffer	
throttled	Whether swap throttling is wanted or not.	

Since 1.8

Stability Level: Unstable

Types and Values

CoglOnscreen

```
typedef struct _CoglOnscreen CoglOnscreen;
```

CoglFrameClosure

```
typedef struct _CoglClosure CoglFrameClosure;
```

An opaque type that tracks a CoglFrameCallback and associated user data. A CoglFrameClosure pointer will be returned from cogl_onscreen_add_frame_callback() and it allows you to remove a callback later using cogl_onscreen_remove_frame_callback().

Since 1.14

Stability Level: Unstable

struct CoglOnscreenDirtyInfo

```
struct CoglOnscreenDirtyInfo {
  int x, y;
  int width, height;
};
```

A structure passed to callbacks registered using cogl_onscreen_add_dirty_callback(). The members describe a rectangle within the onscreen buffer that should be redrawn.

Members

int x;	Left edge of the dirty rectangle
int y;	Top edge of the dirty rectangle, measured from the top of the window

int *width*;	Width of the dirty rect- an- gle
int *height*;	Height of the dirty rect- an- gle

Since 1.16

Stability Level: Unstable

CoglOnscreenDirtyClosure

```
typedef struct _CoglClosure CoglOnscreenDirtyClosure;
```

An opaque type that tracks a CoglOnscreenDirtyCallback and associated user data. A CoglOnscreenDirtyClosure pointer will be returned from cogl_onscreen_add_dirty_callback() and it allows you to remove a callback later using cogl_onscreen_remove_dirty_callback().

Since 1.16

Stability Level: Unstable

CoglOnscreenResizeClosure

```
typedef struct _CoglClosure CoglOnscreenResizeClosure;
```

An opaque type that tracks a CoglOnscreenResizeCallback and associated user data. A CoglOnscreenResizeClosure pointer will be returned from cogl_onscreen_add_resize_callback() and it allows you to remove a callback later using cogl_onscreen_remove_resize_callbac

Since 2.0

Stability Level: Unstable

1.11.3 Offscreen Framebuffers

Offscreen Framebuffers — Functions for creating and manipulating offscreen framebuffers.

Functions

CoglBool	cogl_is_offscreen ()
CoglOffscreen *	cogl_offscreen_new_with_texture ()

Types and Values

	CoglOffscreen

Description

Cogl allows creating and operating on offscreen framebuffers.

Functions

cogl_is_offscreen ()

```
CoglBool
cogl_is_offscreen (void *object);
```

Determines whether the given CoglObject references an offscreen framebuffer object.

Parameters

object	A pointer to a CoglObject

Returns

TRUE if *object* is a CoglOffscreen framebuffer, FALSE otherwise

cogl_offscreen_new_with_texture ()

```
CoglOffscreen~*
cogl_offscreen_new_with_texture (CoglTexture *texture);
```

This creates an offscreen framebuffer object using the given *texture* as the primary color buffer. It doesn't just initialize the contents of the offscreen buffer with the *texture* ; they are tightly bound so that drawing to the offscreen buffer effectively updates the contents of the given texture. You don't need to destroy the offscreen buffer before you can use the *texture* again.

Note This api only works with low-level CoglTexture types such as CoglTexture2D, CoglTexture3D and CoglTextureRectangle, and not with meta-texture types such as CoglTexture2DSliced.

The storage for the framebuffer is actually allocated lazily so this function will never return NULL to indicate a runtime error. This means it is still possible to configure the framebuffer before it is really allocated.

Simple applications without full error handling can simply rely on Cogl to lazily allocate the storage of framebuffers but you should be aware that if Cogl encounters an error (such as running out of GPU memory) then your application will simply abort with an error message. If you need to be able to catch such exceptions at runtime then you can explicitly allocate your framebuffer when you have finished configuring it by calling cogl_framebuffer_allocate() and passing in a CoglError argument to catch any exceptions.

Parameters

texture	A CoglTexture pointer

Returns

a newly instantiated CoglOffscreen framebuffer.

[transfer full]

Types and Values

CoglOffscreen

```
typedef struct _CoglOffscreen CoglOffscreen;
```

1.12   Utilities

1.12.1   Color Type

Color Type — A generic color definition

Functions

CoglColor *	cogl_color_copy ()
void	cogl_color_free ()
void	cogl_color_init_from_4ub ()
void	cogl_color_init_from_4f ()
void	cogl_color_init_from_4fv ()
float	cogl_color_get_red ()
float	cogl_color_get_green ()
float	cogl_color_get_blue ()
float	cogl_color_get_alpha ()
uint8_t	cogl_color_get_red_byte ()
uint8_t	cogl_color_get_green_byte ()
uint8_t	cogl_color_get_blue_byte ()
uint8_t	cogl_color_get_alpha_byte ()
float	cogl_color_get_red_float ()
float	cogl_color_get_green_float ()
float	cogl_color_get_blue_float ()
float	cogl_color_get_alpha_float ()
void	cogl_color_set_red ()
void	cogl_color_set_green ()
void	cogl_color_set_blue ()
void	cogl_color_set_alpha ()
void	cogl_color_set_red_byte ()
void	cogl_color_set_green_byte ()
void	cogl_color_set_blue_byte ()
void	cogl_color_set_alpha_byte ()
void	cogl_color_set_red_float ()
void	cogl_color_set_green_float ()
void	cogl_color_set_blue_float ()
void	cogl_color_set_alpha_float ()
void	cogl_color_premultiply ()
void	cogl_color_unpremultiply ()
CoglBool	cogl_color_equal ()
void	cogl_color_init_from_hsl ()
void	cogl_color_to_hsl ()

Types and Values

| struct | CoglColor |

Description

CoglColor is a simple structure holding the definition of a color such that it can be efficiently used by GL

Functions

cogl_color_copy ()

```
CoglColor~*
cogl_color_copy (const CoglColor *color);
```

Creates a copy of color

Parameters

color	the color to copy	

Returns

a newly-allocated CoglColor. Use cogl_color_free() to free the allocate resources

Since 1.0

cogl_color_free ()

```
void
cogl_color_free (CoglColor *color);
```

Frees the resources allocated by cogl_color_copy().

Parameters

color	the color to free	

Since 1.0

cogl_color_init_from_4ub ()

```
void
cogl_color_init_from_4ub (CoglColor *color,
                          uint8_t red,
                          uint8_t green,
                          uint8_t blue,
                          uint8_t alpha);
```

Sets the values of the passed channels into a CoglColor.

Parameters

color	A pointer to a CoglColor to initialize	

red	value of the red channel, between 0 and 255	
green	value of the green channel, between 0 and 255	
blue	value of the blue channel, between 0 and 255	
alpha	value of the alpha channel, between 0 and 255	

Since 1.4

cogl_color_init_from_4f ()

```
void
cogl_color_init_from_4f (CoglColor *color,
                         float red,
                         float green,
                         float blue,
                         float alpha);
```

Sets the values of the passed channels into a CoglColor

Parameters

color	A pointer to a CoglColor to initialize	
red	value of the red channel, between 0 and 1.0	
green	value of the green channel, between 0 and 1.0	
blue	value of the blue channel, between 0 and 1.0	
alpha	value of the alpha channel, between 0 and 1.0	

Since 1.4

cogl_color_init_from_4fv ()

```
void
cogl_color_init_from_4fv (CoglColor *color,
                          const float *color_array);
```

Sets the values of the passed channels into a CoglColor

Parameters

color	A pointer to a CoglColor to initialize	
color_array	a pointer to an array of 4 float color components	

Since 1.4

cogl_color_get_red ()

```
float
cogl_color_get_red (const CoglColor *color);
```

Retrieves the red channel of *color* as a fixed point value between 0 and 1.0.

Parameters

| color | a CoglColor | |

Returns

the red channel of the passed color

Since 1.0

cogl_color_get_green ()

```
float
cogl_color_get_green (const CoglColor *color);
```

Retrieves the green channel of *color* as a fixed point value between 0 and 1.0.

Parameters

| color | a CoglColor | |

Returns

the green channel of the passed color

Since 1.0

cogl_color_get_blue ()

```
float
cogl_color_get_blue (const CoglColor *color);
```

Retrieves the blue channel of *color* as a fixed point value between 0 and 1.0.

Parameters

| color | a CoglColor | |

Returns

the blue channel of the passed color

Since 1.0

cogl_color_get_alpha ()

```
float
cogl_color_get_alpha (const CoglColor *color);
```

Retrieves the alpha channel of *color* as a fixed point value between 0 and 1.0.

Parameters

color	a CoglColor	

Returns

the alpha channel of the passed color

Since 1.0

cogl_color_get_red_byte ()

```
uint8_t
cogl_color_get_red_byte (const CoglColor *color);
```

Retrieves the red channel of *color* as a byte value between 0 and 255

Parameters

color	a CoglColor	

Returns

the red channel of the passed color

Since 1.0

cogl_color_get_green_byte ()

```
uint8_t
cogl_color_get_green_byte (const CoglColor *color);
```

Retrieves the green channel of *color* as a byte value between 0 and 255

Parameters

color	a CoglColor	

Returns

the green channel of the passed color

Since 1.0

cogl_color_get_blue_byte ()

```
uint8_t
cogl_color_get_blue_byte (const CoglColor *color);
```

Retrieves the blue channel of *color* as a byte value between 0 and 255

Parameters

| color | a CoglColor | |

Returns

the blue channel of the passed color

Since 1.0

cogl_color_get_alpha_byte ()

```
uint8_t
cogl_color_get_alpha_byte (const CoglColor *color);
```

Retrieves the alpha channel of *color* as a byte value between 0 and 255

Parameters

| color | a CoglColor | |

Returns

the alpha channel of the passed color

Since 1.0

cogl_color_get_red_float ()

```
float
cogl_color_get_red_float (const CoglColor *color);
```

Retrieves the red channel of *color* as a floating point value between 0.0 and 1.0

Parameters

| color | a CoglColor | |

Returns

the red channel of the passed color

Since 1.0

cogl_color_get_green_float ()

```
float
cogl_color_get_green_float (const CoglColor *color);
```

Retrieves the green channel of *color* as a floating point value between 0.0 and 1.0

Parameters

| color | a CoglColor | |

Returns

the green channel of the passed color

Since 1.0

cogl_color_get_blue_float ()

```
float
cogl_color_get_blue_float (const CoglColor *color);
```

Retrieves the blue channel of *color* as a floating point value between 0.0 and 1.0

Parameters

| color | a CoglColor | |

Returns

the blue channel of the passed color

Since 1.0

cogl_color_get_alpha_float ()

```
float
cogl_color_get_alpha_float (const CoglColor *color);
```

Retrieves the alpha channel of *color* as a floating point value between 0.0 and 1.0

Parameters

| color | a CoglColor | |

Returns

the alpha channel of the passed color

Since 1.0

cogl_color_set_red ()

```
void
cogl_color_set_red (CoglColor *color,
                    float red);
```

Sets the red channel of *color* to *red* .

Parameters

color	a CoglColor	
red	a float value between 0.0f and 1.0f	

Since 1.4

cogl_color_set_green ()

```
void
cogl_color_set_green (CoglColor *color,
                      float green);
```

Sets the green channel of *color* to *green* .

Parameters

color	a CoglColor	
green	a float value between 0.0f and 1.0f	

Since 1.4

cogl_color_set_blue ()

```
void
cogl_color_set_blue (CoglColor *color,
                     float blue);
```

Sets the blue channel of *color* to *blue* .

Parameters

color	a CoglColor	
blue	a float value between 0.0f and 1.0f	

Since 1.4

cogl_color_set_alpha ()

```
void
cogl_color_set_alpha (CoglColor *color,
```

```
                     float alpha);
```

Sets the alpha channel of *color* to *alpha* .

Parameters

color	a CoglColor	
alpha	a float value between 0.0f and 1.0f	

Since 1.4

cogl_color_set_red_byte ()

```
void
cogl_color_set_red_byte (CoglColor *color,
                         uint8_t red);
```

Sets the red channel of *color* to *red* .

Parameters

color	a CoglColor	
red	a byte value between 0 and 255	

Since 1.4

cogl_color_set_green_byte ()

```
void
cogl_color_set_green_byte (CoglColor *color,
                           uint8_t green);
```

Sets the green channel of *color* to *green* .

Parameters

color	a CoglColor	
green	a byte value between 0 and 255	

Since 1.4

cogl_color_set_blue_byte ()

```
void
cogl_color_set_blue_byte (CoglColor *color,
                          uint8_t blue);
```

Sets the blue channel of *color* to *blue* .

Parameters

color	a CoglColor	
blue	a byte value between 0 and 255	

Since 1.4

cogl_color_set_alpha_byte ()

```
void
cogl_color_set_alpha_byte (CoglColor *color,
                           uint8_t alpha);
```

Sets the alpha channel of *color* to *alpha* .

Parameters

color	a CoglColor	
alpha	a byte value between 0 and 255	

Since 1.4

cogl_color_set_red_float ()

```
void
cogl_color_set_red_float (CoglColor *color,
                          float red);
```

Sets the red channel of *color* to *red* .

Parameters

color	a CoglColor	
red	a float value between 0.0f and 1.0f	

Since 1.4

cogl_color_set_green_float ()

```
void
cogl_color_set_green_float (CoglColor *color,
                            float green);
```

Sets the green channel of *color* to *green* .

Parameters

color	a CoglColor	
green	a float value between 0.0f and 1.0f	

Since 1.4

cogl_color_set_blue_float ()

```
void
cogl_color_set_blue_float (CoglColor *color,
                           float blue);
```

Sets the blue channel of *color* to *blue* .

Parameters

color	a CoglColor	
blue	a float value between 0.0f and 1.0f	

Since 1.4

cogl_color_set_alpha_float ()

```
void
cogl_color_set_alpha_float (CoglColor *color,
                            float alpha);
```

Sets the alpha channel of *color* to *alpha* .

Parameters

color	a CoglColor	
alpha	a float value between 0.0f and 1.0f	

Since 1.4

cogl_color_premultiply ()

```
void
cogl_color_premultiply (CoglColor *color);
```

Converts a non-premultiplied color to a pre-multiplied color. For example, semi-transparent red is (1.0, 0, 0, 0.5) when non-premultiplied and (0.5, 0, 0, 0.5) when premultiplied.

Parameters

color	the color to premultiply	

Since 1.0

cogl_color_unpremultiply ()

```
void
cogl_color_unpremultiply (CoglColor *color);
```

Converts a pre-multiplied color to a non-premultiplied color. For example, semi-transparent red is (0.5, 0, 0, 0.5) when premultiplied and (1.0, 0, 0, 0.5) when non-premultiplied.

Parameters

color	the color to unpremultiply

Since 1.4

cogl_color_equal ()

```
CoglBool
cogl_color_equal (const void *v1,
                  const void *v2);
```

Compares two CoglColors and checks if they are the same.

This function can be passed to g_hash_table_new() as the *key_equal_func* parameter, when using CoglColors as keys in a GHashTable.

Parameters

v1	a CoglColor
v2	a CoglColor

Returns

TRUE if the two colors are the same.

Since 1.0

cogl_color_init_from_hsl ()

```
void
cogl_color_init_from_hsl (CoglColor *color,
                          float hue,
                          float saturation,
                          float luminance);
```

Converts a color expressed in HLS (hue, luminance and saturation) values into a CoglColor.

Parameters

color	return location for a CoglColor.	[out]

hue	hue value, in the 0 .. 360 range	
saturation	saturation value, in the 0 .. 1 range	
luminance	luminance value, in the 0 .. 1 range	

Since 1.16

cogl_color_to_hsl ()

```
void
cogl_color_to_hsl (const CoglColor *color,
                   float *hue,
                   float *saturation,
                   float *luminance);
```

Converts `color` to the HLS format.

The `hue` value is in the 0 .. 360 range. The `luminance` and `saturation` values are in the 0 .. 1 range.

Parameters

color	a CoglColor	
hue	return location for the hue value or NULL.	[out]
saturation	return location for the saturation value or NULL.	[out]
luminance	return location for the luminance value or NULL.	[out]

Since 1.16

Types and Values

struct CoglColor

```
struct CoglColor {
  float red;
  float green;
  float blue;
  float alpha;
};
```

A structure for holding a single color definition.

Members

| float red; | amount of red |
| float green; | amount of green |

| float *blue*; | amount of green |
| float *alpha*; | alpha |

Since 1.0

1.12.2 Matrices

Matrices — Functions for initializing and manipulating 4x4 matrices

Functions

void	cogl_matrix_init_identity ()
void	cogl_matrix_init_from_array ()
void	cogl_matrix_init_translation ()
void	cogl_matrix_init_from_quaternion ()
void	cogl_matrix_init_from_euler ()
CoglMatrix *	cogl_matrix_copy ()
CoglBool	cogl_matrix_equal ()
void	cogl_matrix_free ()
void	cogl_matrix_frustum ()
void	cogl_matrix_orthographic ()
void	cogl_matrix_perspective ()
void	cogl_matrix_look_at ()
void	cogl_matrix_multiply ()
void	cogl_matrix_rotate ()
void	cogl_matrix_rotate_quaternion ()
void	cogl_matrix_rotate_euler ()
void	cogl_matrix_translate ()
void	cogl_matrix_scale ()
void	cogl_matrix_transpose ()
const float *	cogl_matrix_get_array ()
CoglBool	cogl_matrix_get_inverse ()
void	cogl_matrix_transform_point ()
void	cogl_matrix_transform_points ()
void	cogl_matrix_project_points ()
CoglBool	cogl_matrix_is_identity ()

Types and Values

| | CoglMatrix |

Description

Matrices are used in Cogl to describe affine model-view transforms, texture transforms, and projective transforms. This exposes a utility API that can be used for direct manipulation of these matrices.

Functions

cogl_matrix_init_identity ()

```
void
cogl_matrix_init_identity (CoglMatrix *matrix);
```

Resets matrix to the identity matrix:

```
.xx=1;  .xy=0;  .xz=0;  .xw=0;
.yx=0;  .yy=1;  .yz=0;  .yw=0;
.zx=0;  .zy=0;  .zz=1;  .zw=0;
.wx=0;  .wy=0;  .wz=0;  .ww=1;
```

Parameters

matrix	A 4x4 transformation matrix	

cogl_matrix_init_from_array ()

```
void
cogl_matrix_init_from_array (CoglMatrix *matrix,
                             const float *array);
```

Initializes *matrix* with the contents of *array*

Parameters

matrix	A 4x4 transformation matrix	
array	A linear array of 16 floats (column-major order)	

cogl_matrix_init_translation ()

```
void
cogl_matrix_init_translation (CoglMatrix *matrix,
                              float tx,
                              float ty,
                              float tz);
```

Resets matrix to the (tx, ty, tz) translation matrix:

```
.xx=1;  .xy=0;  .xz=0;  .xw=tx;
.yx=0;  .yy=1;  .yz=0;  .yw=ty;
.zx=0;  .zy=0;  .zz=1;  .zw=tz;
.wx=0;  .wy=0;  .wz=0;  .ww=1;
```

Parameters

matrix	A 4x4 transformation matrix	
tx	x coordinate of the translation vector	
ty	y coordinate of the translation vector	

tz	z coordinate of the translation vector	

Since 2.0

cogl_matrix_init_from_quaternion ()

```
void
cogl_matrix_init_from_quaternion (CoglMatrix *matrix,
                                  const CoglQuaternion *quaternion);
```

Initializes *matrix* from a CoglQuaternion rotation.

Parameters

matrix	A 4x4 transformation matrix	
quaternion	A CoglQuaternion	

cogl_matrix_init_from_euler ()

```
void
cogl_matrix_init_from_euler (CoglMatrix *matrix,
                             const CoglEuler *euler);
```

Initializes *matrix* from a CoglEuler rotation.

Parameters

matrix	A 4x4 transformation matrix	
euler	A CoglEuler	

cogl_matrix_copy ()

```
CoglMatrix~*
cogl_matrix_copy (const CoglMatrix *matrix);
```

Allocates a new CoglMatrix on the heap and initializes it with the same values as *matrix* .

Parameters

matrix	A 4x4 transformation matrix you want to copy	

Returns

A newly allocated CoglMatrix which should be freed using cogl_matrix_free().

[transfer full]

Since 1.6

cogl_matrix_equal ()

```
CoglBool
cogl_matrix_equal (const void *v1,
                   const void *v2);
```

Compares two matrices to see if they represent the same transformation. Although internally the matrices may have different annotations associated with them and may potentially have a cached inverse matrix these are not considered in the comparison.

Parameters

v1	A 4x4 transformation matrix	
v2	A 4x4 transformation matrix	

Since 1.4

cogl_matrix_free ()

```
void
cogl_matrix_free (CoglMatrix *matrix);
```

Frees a CoglMatrix that was previously allocated via a call to cogl_matrix_copy().

Parameters

matrix	A 4x4 transformation matrix you want to free	

Since 1.6

cogl_matrix_frustum ()

```
void
cogl_matrix_frustum (CoglMatrix *matrix,
                     float left,
                     float right,
                     float bottom,
                     float top,
                     float z_near,
                     float z_far);
```

Multiplies *matrix* by the given frustum perspective matrix.

Parameters

matrix	A 4x4 transformation matrix	
left	X position of the left clipping plane where it intersects the near clipping plane	

right	X position of the right clipping plane where it intersects the near clipping plane	
bottom	Y position of the bottom clipping plane where it intersects the near clipping plane	
top	Y position of the top clipping plane where it intersects the near clipping plane	
z_near	The distance to the near clipping plane (Must be positive)	
z_far	The distance to the far clipping plane (Must be positive)	

cogl_matrix_orthographic ()

```
void
cogl_matrix_orthographic (CoglMatrix *matrix,
                          float x_1,
                          float y_1,
                          float x_2,
                          float y_2,
                          float near,
                          float far);
```

Multiplies `matrix` by a parallel projection matrix.

Parameters

matrix	A 4x4 transformation matrix	
x_1	The x coordinate for the first vertical clipping plane	
y_1	The y coordinate for the first horizontal clipping plane	
x_2	The x coordinate for the second vertical clipping plane	
y_2	The y coordinate for the second horizontal clipping plane	
near	The *distance* to the near clipping plane (will be *negative* if the plane is behind the viewer)	
far	The *distance* to the far clipping plane (will be *negative* if the plane is behind the viewer)	

Since 1.10

Stability Level: Unstable

cogl_matrix_perspective ()

```
void
cogl_matrix_perspective (CoglMatrix *matrix,
                         float fov_y,
                         float aspect,
                         float z_near,
                         float z_far);
```

Multiplies `matrix` by the described perspective matrix

Note You should be careful not to have to great a `z_far` / `z_near` ratio since that will reduce the effectiveness of depth testing since there wont be enough precision to identify the depth of objects near to each other.

Parameters

matrix	A 4x4 transformation matrix	
fov_y	Vertical field of view angle in degrees.	
aspect	The (width over height) aspect ratio for display	
z_near	The distance to the near clipping plane (Must be positive, and must not be 0)	
z_far	The distance to the far clipping plane (Must be positive)	

cogl_matrix_look_at ()

```
void
cogl_matrix_look_at (CoglMatrix *matrix,
                     float eye_position_x,
                     float eye_position_y,
                     float eye_position_z,
                     float object_x,
                     float object_y,
                     float object_z,
                     float world_up_x,
                     float world_up_y,
                     float world_up_z);
```

Applies a view transform `matrix` that positions the camera at the coordinate (`eye_position_x`, `eye_position_y`, `eye_position_z`) looking towards an object at the coordinate (`object_x`, `object_y`, `object_z`). The top of the camera is aligned to the given world up vector, which is normally simply (0, 1, 0) to map up to the positive direction of the y axis.

Because there is a lot of missleading documentation online for gluLookAt regarding the up vector we want to try and be a bit clearer here.

The up vector should simply be relative to your world coordinates and does not need to change as you move the eye and object positions. Many online sources may claim that the up vector needs to be perpendicular to the vector between the eye and object position (partly because the man page is somewhat missleading) but that is not necessary for this function.

Note You should never look directly along the world-up vector.

Note It is assumed you are using a typical projection matrix where your origin maps to the center of your viewport.

Note Almost always when you use this function it should be the first transform applied to a new modelview transform

Parameters

matrix	A 4x4 transformation matrix	
eye_position_x	The X coordinate to look from	
eye_position_y	The Y coordinate to look from	
eye_position_z	The Z coordinate to look from	
object_x	The X coordinate of the object to look at	
object_y	The Y coordinate of the object to look at	
object_z	The Z coordinate of the object to look at	
world_up_x	The X component of the world's up direction vector	
world_up_y	The Y component of the world's up direction vector	
world_up_z	The Z component of the world's up direction vector	

Since 1.8

Stability Level: Unstable

cogl_matrix_multiply ()

```
void
cogl_matrix_multiply (CoglMatrix *result,
                      const CoglMatrix *a,
                      const CoglMatrix *b);
```

Multiplies the two supplied matrices together and stores the resulting matrix inside *result* .

Note It is possible to multiply the *a* matrix in-place, so *result* can be equal to *a* but can't be equal to *b*.

Parameters

result	The address of a 4x4 matrix to store the result in	

a	A 4x4 transformation matrix	
b	A 4x4 transformation matrix	

cogl_matrix_rotate ()

```
void
cogl_matrix_rotate (CoglMatrix *matrix,
                    float angle,
                    float x,
                    float y,
                    float z);
```

Multiplies *matrix* with a rotation matrix that applies a rotation of *angle* degrees around the specified 3D vector.

Parameters

matrix	A 4x4 transformation matrix	
angle	The angle you want to rotate in degrees	
x	X component of your rotation vector	
y	Y component of your rotation vector	
z	Z component of your rotation vector	

cogl_matrix_rotate_quaternion ()

```
void
cogl_matrix_rotate_quaternion (CoglMatrix *matrix,
                               const CoglQuaternion *quaternion);
```

Multiplies *matrix* with a rotation transformation described by the given CoglQuaternion.

Parameters

matrix	A 4x4 transformation matrix	
quaternion	A quaternion describing a rotation	

Since 2.0

cogl_matrix_rotate_euler ()

```
void
cogl_matrix_rotate_euler (CoglMatrix *matrix,
                          const CoglEuler *euler);
```

Multiplies *matrix* with a rotation transformation described by the given CoglEuler.

Parameters

matrix	A 4x4 transformation matrix	
euler	A euler describing a rotation	

Since 2.0

cogl_matrix_translate ()

```
void
cogl_matrix_translate (CoglMatrix *matrix,
                       float x,
                       float y,
                       float z);
```

Multiplies *matrix* with a transform matrix that translates along the X, Y and Z axis.

Parameters

matrix	A 4x4 transformation matrix	
x	The X translation you want to apply	
y	The Y translation you want to apply	
z	The Z translation you want to apply	

cogl_matrix_scale ()

```
void
cogl_matrix_scale (CoglMatrix *matrix,
                   float sx,
                   float sy,
                   float sz);
```

Multiplies *matrix* with a transform matrix that scales along the X, Y and Z axis.

Parameters

matrix	A 4x4 transformation matrix	
sx	The X scale factor	
sy	The Y scale factor	
sz	The Z scale factor	

cogl_matrix_transpose ()

```
void
cogl_matrix_transpose (CoglMatrix *matrix);
```

Replaces *matrix* with its transpose. Ie, every element (i,j) in the new matrix is taken from element (j,i) in the old matrix.

Parameters

| matrix | A CoglMatrix | |

Since 1.10

cogl_matrix_get_array ()

```
const float~*
cogl_matrix_get_array (const CoglMatrix *matrix);
```

Casts *matrix* to a float array which can be directly passed to OpenGL.

Parameters

| matrix | A 4x4 transformation matrix | |

Returns

a pointer to the float array

cogl_matrix_get_inverse ()

```
CoglBool
cogl_matrix_get_inverse (const CoglMatrix *matrix,
                         CoglMatrix *inverse);
```

Gets the inverse transform of a given matrix and uses it to initialize a new CoglMatrix.

Note Although the first parameter is annotated as const to indicate that the transform it represents isn't modified this function may technically save a copy of the inverse transform within the given CoglMatrix so that subsequent requests for the inverse transform may avoid costly inversion calculations.

Parameters

| matrix | A 4x4 transformation matrix | |
| inverse | The destination for a 4x4 inverse transformation matrix. | [out] |

Returns

TRUE if the inverse was successfully calculated or FALSE for degenerate transformations that can't be inverted (in this case the *inverse* matrix will simply be initialized with the identity matrix)

Since 1.2

cogl_matrix_transform_point ()

```
void
cogl_matrix_transform_point (const CoglMatrix *matrix,
                             float *x,
                             float *y,
                             float *z,
                             float *w);
```

Transforms a point whos position is given and returned as four float components.

Parameters

matrix	A 4x4 transformation matrix	
x	The X component of your points position.	*[inout]*
y	The Y component of your points position.	*[inout]*
z	The Z component of your points position.	*[inout]*
w	The W component of your points position.	*[inout]*

cogl_matrix_transform_points ()

```
void
cogl_matrix_transform_points (const CoglMatrix *matrix,
                              int n_components,
                              size_t stride_in,
                              const void *points_in,
                              size_t stride_out,
                              void *points_out,
                              int n_points);
```

Transforms an array of input points and writes the result to another array of output points. The input points can either have 2 or 3 components each. The output points always have 3 components. The output array can simply point to the input array to do the transform in-place.

If you need to transform 4 component points see cogl_matrix_project_points().

Here's an example with differing input/output strides:

```
typedef struct {
  float x,y;
  uint8_t r,g,b,a;
  float s,t,p;
} MyInVertex;
typedef struct {
  uint8_t r,g,b,a;
  float x,y,z;
} MyOutVertex;
MyInVertex vertices[N_VERTICES];
MyOutVertex results[N_VERTICES];
CoglMatrix matrix;

my_load_vertices (vertices);
my_get_matrix (&matrix);
```

```
cogl_matrix_transform_points (&matrix,
                              2,
                              sizeof (MyInVertex),
                              &vertices[0].x,
                              sizeof (MyOutVertex),
                              &results[0].x,
                              N_VERTICES);
```

Parameters

matrix	A transformation matrix	
n_components	The number of position components for each input point. (either 2 or 3)	
stride_in	The stride in bytes between input points.	
points_in	A pointer to the first component of the first input point.	
stride_out	The stride in bytes between output points.	
points_out	A pointer to the first component of the first output point.	
n_points	The number of points to transform.	

Stability Level: Unstable

cogl_matrix_project_points ()

```
void
cogl_matrix_project_points (const CoglMatrix *matrix,
                            int n_components,
                            size_t stride_in,
                            const void *points_in,
                            size_t stride_out,
                            void *points_out,
                            int n_points);
```

Projects an array of input points and writes the result to another array of output points. The input points can either have 2, 3 or 4 components each. The output points always have 4 components (known as homogenous coordinates). The output array can simply point to the input array to do the transform in-place.

Here's an example with differing input/output strides:

```
typedef struct {
  float x,y;
  uint8_t r,g,b,a;
  float s,t,p;
} MyInVertex;
typedef struct {
  uint8_t r,g,b,a;
  float x,y,z;
} MyOutVertex;
MyInVertex vertices[N_VERTICES];
MyOutVertex results[N_VERTICES];
```

```
CoglMatrix matrix;

my_load_vertices (vertices);
my_get_matrix (&matrix);

cogl_matrix_project_points (&matrix,
                            2,
                            sizeof (MyInVertex),
                            &vertices[0].x,
                            sizeof (MyOutVertex),
                            &results[0].x,
                            N_VERTICES);
```

Parameters

matrix	A projection matrix	
n_components	The number of position components for each input point. (either 2, 3 or 4)	
stride_in	The stride in bytes between input points.	
points_in	A pointer to the first component of the first input point.	
stride_out	The stride in bytes between output points.	
points_out	A pointer to the first component of the first output point.	
n_points	The number of points to transform.	

Stability Level: Unstable

cogl_matrix_is_identity ()

```
CoglBool
cogl_matrix_is_identity (const CoglMatrix *matrix);
```

Determines if the given matrix is an identity matrix.

Parameters

matrix	A CoglMatrix

Returns

TRUE if matrix is an identity matrix else FALSE

Since 1.8

Types and Values

CoglMatrix

```
typedef struct {
  /* column 0 */
  float xx;
  float yx;
  float zx;
  float wx;

  /* column 1 */
  float xy;
  float yy;
  float zy;
  float wy;

  /* column 2 */
  float xz;
  float yz;
  float zz;
  float wz;

  /* column 3 */
  float xw;
  float yw;
  float zw;
  float ww;
} CoglMatrix;
```

A CoglMatrix holds a 4x4 transform matrix. This is a single precision, column-major matrix which means it is compatible with what OpenGL expects.

A CoglMatrix can represent transforms such as, rotations, scaling, translation, sheering, and linear projections. You can combine these transforms by multiplying multiple matrices in the order you want them applied.

The transformation of a vertex (x, y, z, w) by a CoglMatrix is given by:

```
x_new = xx * x + xy * y + xz * z + xw * w
y_new = yx * x + yy * y + yz * z + yw * w
z_new = zx * x + zy * y + zz * z + zw * w
w_new = wx * x + wy * y + wz * z + ww * w
```

Where w is normally 1

Note You must consider the members of the CoglMatrix structure read only, and all matrix modifications must be done via the cogl_matrix API. This allows Cogl to annotate the matrices internally. Violation of this will give undefined results. If you need to initialize a matrix with a constant other than the identity matrix you can use cogl_matrix_init_from_array().

1.12.3 Matrix Stacks

Matrix Stacks — Functions for efficiently tracking many related transformations

Functions

CoglMatrixStack *	cogl_matrix_stack_new ()
void	cogl_matrix_stack_push ()

void	cogl_matrix_stack_pop ()
void	cogl_matrix_stack_load_identity ()
void	cogl_matrix_stack_scale ()
void	cogl_matrix_stack_translate ()
void	cogl_matrix_stack_rotate ()
void	cogl_matrix_stack_rotate_quaternion ()
void	cogl_matrix_stack_rotate_euler ()
void	cogl_matrix_stack_multiply ()
void	cogl_matrix_stack_frustum ()
void	cogl_matrix_stack_perspective ()
void	cogl_matrix_stack_orthographic ()
CoglBool	cogl_matrix_stack_get_inverse ()
CoglMatrixEntry *	cogl_matrix_stack_get_entry ()
CoglMatrix *	cogl_matrix_stack_get ()
CoglMatrix *	cogl_matrix_entry_get ()
void	cogl_matrix_stack_set ()
CoglBool	cogl_matrix_entry_calculate_translation ()
CoglBool	cogl_matrix_entry_is_identity ()
CoglBool	cogl_matrix_entry_equal ()
CoglMatrixEntry *	cogl_matrix_entry_ref ()
void	cogl_matrix_entry_unref ()

Types and Values

	CoglMatrixStack
	CoglMatrixEntry

Description

Matrices can be used (for example) to describe the model-view transforms of objects, texture transforms, and projective transforms.

The CoglMatrix api provides a good way to manipulate individual matrices representing a single transformation but if you need to track many-many such transformations for many objects that are organized in a scenegraph for example then using a separate CoglMatrix for each object may not be the most efficient way.

A CoglMatrixStack enables applications to track lots of transformations that are related to each other in some kind of hierarchy. In a scenegraph for example if you want to know how to transform a particular node then you usually have to walk up through the ancestors and accumulate their transforms before finally applying the transform of the node itself. In this model things are grouped together spatially according to their ancestry and all siblings with the same parent share the same initial transformation. The CoglMatrixStack API is suited to tracking lots of transformations that fit this kind of model.

Compared to using the CoglMatrix api directly to track many related transforms, these can be some advantages to using a CoglMatrixStack:

- Faster equality comparisons of transformations

- Efficient comparisons of the differences between arbitrary transformations

- Avoid redundant arithmetic related to common transforms

- Can be more space efficient (not always though)

For reference (to give an idea of when a CoglMatrixStack can provide a space saving) a CoglMatrix can be expected to take 72 bytes whereas a single CoglMatrixEntry in a CoglMatrixStack is currently around 32 bytes on a 32bit CPU or 36 bytes on a 64bit CPU. An entry is needed for each individual operation applied to the stack (such as rotate, scale, translate) so if most of your leaf node transformations only need one or two simple operations relative to their parent then a matrix stack will likely take less space than having a CoglMatrix for each node.

Even without any space saving though the ability to perform fast comparisons and avoid redundant arithmetic (especially sine and cosine calculations for rotations) can make using a matrix stack worthwhile.

Functions

cogl_matrix_stack_new ()

```
CoglMatrixStack~*
cogl_matrix_stack_new (CoglContext *ctx);
```

Allocates a new CoglMatrixStack that can be used to build up transformations relating to objects in a scenegraph like hierarchy. (See the description of CoglMatrixStack and CoglMatrixEntry for more details of what a matrix stack is best suited for)

When a CoglMatrixStack is first allocated it is conceptually positioned at the root of your scenegraph hierarchy. As you traverse your scenegraph then you should call cogl_matrix_stack_push() whenever you move down a level and cogl_matrix_stack_pop() whenever you move back up a level towards the root.

Once you have allocated a CoglMatrixStack you can get a reference to the current transformation for the current position in the hierarchy by calling cogl_matrix_stack_get_entry().

Once you have allocated a CoglMatrixStack you can apply operations such as rotate, scale and translate to modify the current transform for the current position in the hierarchy by calling cogl_matrix_stack_rotate(), cogl_matrix_stack_scale() and cogl_matrix_stack_translate().

Parameters

ctx	A CoglContext	

Returns

A newly allocated CoglMatrixStack.

[transfer full]

cogl_matrix_stack_push ()

```
void
cogl_matrix_stack_push (CoglMatrixStack *stack);
```

Saves the current transform and starts a new transform that derives from the current transform.

This is usually called while traversing a scenegraph whenever you traverse one level deeper. cogl_matrix_stack_pop() can then be called when going back up one layer to restore the previous transform of an ancestor.

Parameters

stack	A CoglMatrixStack	

cogl_matrix_stack_pop ()

```
void
cogl_matrix_stack_pop (CoglMatrixStack *stack);
```

Restores the previous transform that was last saved by calling cogl_matrix_stack_push().

This is usually called while traversing a scenegraph whenever you return up one level in the graph towards the root node.

Parameters

stack	A CoglMatrixStack	

cogl_matrix_stack_load_identity ()

```
void
cogl_matrix_stack_load_identity (CoglMatrixStack *stack);
```

Resets the current matrix to the identity matrix.

Parameters

stack	A CoglMatrixStack	

cogl_matrix_stack_scale ()

```
void
cogl_matrix_stack_scale (CoglMatrixStack *stack,
                         float x,
                         float y,
                         float z);
```

Multiplies the current matrix by one that scales the x, y and z axes by the given values.

Parameters

stack	A CoglMatrixStack	
x	Amount to scale along the x-axis	
y	Amount to scale along the y-axis	
z	Amount to scale along the z-axis	

cogl_matrix_stack_translate ()

```
void
cogl_matrix_stack_translate (CoglMatrixStack *stack,
                             float x,
                             float y,
                             float z);
```

Multiplies the current matrix by one that translates along all three axes according to the given values.

Parameters

stack	A CoglMatrixStack	
x	Distance to translate along the x-axis	
y	Distance to translate along the y-axis	
z	Distance to translate along the z-axis	

cogl_matrix_stack_rotate ()

```
void
cogl_matrix_stack_rotate (CoglMatrixStack *stack,
                          float angle,
                          float x,
                          float y,
                          float z);
```

Multiplies the current matrix by one that rotates the around the axis-vector specified by x , y and z . The rotation follows the right-hand thumb rule so for example rotating by 10 degrees about the axis-vector (0, 0, 1) causes a small counter-clockwise rotation.

Parameters

stack	A CoglMatrixStack	
angle	Angle in degrees to rotate.	
x	X-component of vertex to rotate around.	
y	Y-component of vertex to rotate around.	
z	Z-component of vertex to rotate around.	

cogl_matrix_stack_rotate_quaternion ()

```
void
cogl_matrix_stack_rotate_quaternion (CoglMatrixStack *stack,
                                     const CoglQuaternion *quaternion);
```

Multiplies the current matrix by one that rotates according to the rotation described by $quaternion$.

Parameters

stack	A CoglMatrixStack	
quaternion	A CoglQuaternion	

cogl_matrix_stack_rotate_euler ()

```
void
cogl_matrix_stack_rotate_euler (CoglMatrixStack *stack,
                                const CoglEuler *euler);
```

Multiplies the current matrix by one that rotates according to the rotation described by $euler$.

Parameters

stack	A CoglMatrixStack	
euler	A CoglEuler	

cogl_matrix_stack_multiply ()

```
void
```

```
cogl_matrix_stack_multiply (CoglMatrixStack *stack,
                            const CoglMatrix *matrix);
```

Multiplies the current matrix by the given matrix.

Parameters

stack	A CoglMatrixStack	
matrix	the matrix to multiply with the current model-view	

cogl_matrix_stack_frustum ()

```
void
cogl_matrix_stack_frustum (CoglMatrixStack *stack,
                           float left,
                           float right,
                           float bottom,
                           float top,
                           float z_near,
                           float z_far);
```

Replaces the current matrix with a perspective matrix for a given viewing frustum defined by 4 side clip planes that all cross through the origin and 2 near and far clip planes.

Parameters

stack	A CoglMatrixStack	
left	X position of the left clipping plane where it intersects the near clipping plane	
right	X position of the right clipping plane where it intersects the near clipping plane	
bottom	Y position of the bottom clipping plane where it intersects the near clipping plane	
top	Y position of the top clipping plane where it intersects the near clipping plane	
z_near	The distance to the near clipping plane (Must be positive)	
z_far	The distance to the far clipping plane (Must be positive)	

cogl_matrix_stack_perspective ()

```
void
```

```
cogl_matrix_stack_perspective (CoglMatrixStack *stack,
                               float fov_y,
                               float aspect,
                               float z_near,
                               float z_far);
```

Replaces the current matrix with a perspective matrix based on the provided values.

Note You should be careful not to have too great a z_far / z_near ratio since that will reduce the effectiveness of depth testing since there wont be enough precision to identify the depth of objects near to each other.

Parameters

stack	A CoglMatrixStack	
fov_y	Vertical field of view angle in degrees.	
aspect	The (width over height) aspect ratio for display	
z_near	The distance to the near clipping plane (Must be positive, and must not be 0)	
z_far	The distance to the far clipping plane (Must be positive)	

cogl_matrix_stack_orthographic ()

```
void
cogl_matrix_stack_orthographic (CoglMatrixStack *stack,
                                float x_1,
                                float y_1,
                                float x_2,
                                float y_2,
                                float near,
                                float far);
```

Replaces the current matrix with an orthographic projection matrix.

Parameters

stack	A CoglMatrixStack	
x_1	The x coordinate for the first vertical clipping plane	
y_1	The y coordinate for the first horizontal clipping plane	
x_2	The x coordinate for the second vertical clipping plane	
y_2	The y coordinate for the second horizontal clipping plane	

near	The *distance* to the near clipping plane (will be *negative* if the plane is behind the viewer)	
far	The *distance* to the far clipping plane (will be *negative* if the plane is behind the viewer)	

cogl_matrix_stack_get_inverse ()

```
CoglBool
cogl_matrix_stack_get_inverse (CoglMatrixStack *stack,
                               CoglMatrix *inverse);
```

Gets the inverse transform of the current matrix and uses it to initialize a new CoglMatrix.

Parameters

stack	A CoglMatrixStack	
inverse	The destination for a 4x4 inverse transformation matrix.	*[out]*

Returns

TRUE if the inverse was successfully calculated or FALSE for degenerate transformations that can't be inverted (in this case the *inverse* matrix will simply be initialized with the identity matrix)

cogl_matrix_stack_get_entry ()

```
CoglMatrixEntry~*
cogl_matrix_stack_get_entry (CoglMatrixStack *stack);
```

Gets a reference to the current transform represented by a CoglMatrixEntry pointer.

Note The transform represented by a CoglMatrixEntry is immutable.

Note CoglMatrixEntrys are reference counted using cogl_matrix_entry_ref() and cogl_matrix_entry_unref() and you should call cogl_matrix_entry_unref() when you are finished with and entry you get via cogl_matrix_stack_get_entry().

Parameters

stack	A CoglMatrixStack	

Returns

A pointer to the CoglMatrixEntry representing the current matrix stack transform.

[transfer none]

cogl_matrix_stack_get ()

```
CoglMatrix~*
cogl_matrix_stack_get (CoglMatrixStack *stack,
                       CoglMatrix *matrix);
```

Resolves the current `stack` transform into a CoglMatrix by combining the operations that have been applied to build up the current transform.

There are two possible ways that this function may return its result depending on whether the stack is able to directly point to an internal CoglMatrix or whether the result needs to be composed of multiple operations.

If an internal matrix contains the required result then this function will directly return a pointer to that matrix, otherwise if the function returns NULL then `matrix` will be initialized to match the current transform of `stack` .

> **Note** `matrix` will be left untouched if a direct pointer is returned.

Parameters

stack	A CoglMatrixStack	
matrix	The potential destination for the current matrix.	*[out]*

Returns

A direct pointer to the current transform or NULL and in that case `matrix` will be initialized with the value of the current transform.

cogl_matrix_entry_get ()

```
CoglMatrix~*
cogl_matrix_entry_get (CoglMatrixEntry *entry,
                       CoglMatrix *matrix);
```

Resolves the current `entry` transform into a CoglMatrix by combining the sequence of operations that have been applied to build up the current transform.

There are two possible ways that this function may return its result depending on whether it's possible to directly point to an internal CoglMatrix or whether the result needs to be composed of multiple operations.

If an internal matrix contains the required result then this function will directly return a pointer to that matrix, otherwise if the function returns NULL then `matrix` will be initialized to match the transform of `entry` .

> **Note** `matrix` will be left untouched if a direct pointer is returned.

Parameters

entry	A CoglMatrixEntry	
matrix	The potential destination for the transform as a matrix.	*[out]*

Returns

A direct pointer to a CoglMatrix transform or NULL and in that case `matrix` will be initialized with the effective transform represented by `entry`.

cogl_matrix_stack_set ()

```
void
cogl_matrix_stack_set (CoglMatrixStack *stack,
                       const CoglMatrix *matrix);
```

Replaces the current `stack` matrix value with the value of `matrix`. This effectively discards any other operations that were applied since the last time cogl_matrix_stack_push() was called or since the stack was initialized.

Parameters

stack	A CoglMatrixStack	
matrix	A CoglMatrix replace the current matrix value with	

cogl_matrix_entry_calculate_translation ()

```
CoglBool
cogl_matrix_entry_calculate_translation
                        (CoglMatrixEntry *entry0,
                         CoglMatrixEntry *entry1,
                         float *x,
                         float *y,
                         float *z);
```

Determines if the only difference between two transforms is a translation and if so returns what the x, y, and z components of the translation are.

If the difference between the two translations involves anything other than a translation then the function returns FALSE.

Parameters

entry0	The first reference transform	
entry1	A second reference transform	
x	The destination for the x-component of the translation.	[out]
y	The destination for the y-component of the translation.	[out]
z	The destination for the z-component of the translation.	[out]

Returns

TRUE if the only difference between the transform of `entry0` and the transform of `entry1` is a translation, otherwise FALSE.

cogl_matrix_entry_is_identity ()

```
CoglBool
cogl_matrix_entry_is_identity (CoglMatrixEntry *entry);
```

Determines whether `entry` is known to represent an identity transform.

If this returns TRUE then the entry is definitely the identity matrix. If it returns FALSE it may or may not be the identity matrix but no expensive comparison is performed to verify it.

Parameters

entry	A CoglMatrixEntry

Returns

TRUE if `entry` is definitely an identity transform, otherwise FALSE.

cogl_matrix_entry_equal ()

```
CoglBool
cogl_matrix_entry_equal (CoglMatrixEntry *entry0,
                         CoglMatrixEntry *entry1);
```

Compares two arbitrary CoglMatrixEntry transforms for equality returning TRUE if they are equal or FALSE otherwise.

Note In many cases it is unnecessary to use this api and instead direct pointer comparisons of entries are good enough and much cheaper too.

Parameters

entry0	The first CoglMatrixEntry to compare	
entry1	A second CoglMatrixEntry to compare	

Returns

TRUE if `entry0` represents the same transform as `entry1`, otherwise FALSE.

cogl_matrix_entry_ref ()

```
CoglMatrixEntry~*
cogl_matrix_entry_ref (CoglMatrixEntry *entry);
```

Takes a reference on the given `entry` to ensure the `entry` stays alive and remains valid. When you are finished with the `entry` then you should call cogl_matrix_entry_unref().

It is an error to pass an `entry` pointer to cogl_object_ref() and cogl_object_unref()

Parameters

| entry | A CoglMatrixEntry | |

cogl_matrix_entry_unref ()

```
void
cogl_matrix_entry_unref (CoglMatrixEntry *entry);
```

Releases a reference on *entry* either taken by calling cogl_matrix_entry_unref() or to release the reference given when calling cogl_matrix_stack_get_entry().

Parameters

| entry | A CoglMatrixEntry | |

Types and Values

CoglMatrixStack

```
typedef struct _CoglMatrixStack CoglMatrixStack;
```

Tracks your current position within a hierarchy and lets you build up a graph of transformations as you traverse through a hierarchy such as a scenegraph.

A CoglMatrixStack always maintains a reference to a single transformation at any point in time, representing the transformation at the current position in the hierarchy. You can get a reference to the current transformation by calling cogl_matrix_stack_get_entry().

When a CoglMatrixStack is first created with cogl_matrix_stack_new() then it is conceptually positioned at the root of your hierarchy and the current transformation simply represents an identity transformation.

As you traverse your object hierarchy (your scenegraph) then you should call cogl_matrix_stack_push() whenever you move down one level and call cogl_matrix_stack_pop() whenever you move back up one level towards the root.

At any time you can apply a set of operations, such as "rotate", "scale", "translate" on top of the current transformation of a CoglMatrixStack using functions such as cogl_matrix_stack_rotate(), cogl_matrix_stack_scale() and cogl_matrix_stack_translate(). These operations will derive a new current transformation and will never affect a transformation that you have referenced using cogl_matrix_stack_get_entry().

Internally applying operations to a CoglMatrixStack builds up a graph of CoglMatrixEntry structures which each represent a single immutable transform.

CoglMatrixEntry

```
typedef struct _CoglMatrixEntry CoglMatrixEntry;
```

Represents a single immutable transformation that was retrieved from a CoglMatrixStack using cogl_matrix_stack_get_entry().

Internally a CoglMatrixEntry represents a single matrix operation (such as "rotate", "scale", "translate") which is applied to the transform of a single parent entry.

Using the CoglMatrixStack api effectively builds up a graph of these immutable CoglMatrixEntry structures whereby operations that can be shared between multiple transformations will result in shared CoglMatrixEntry nodes in the graph.

When a CoglMatrixStack is first created it references one CoglMatrixEntry that represents a single "load identity" operation. This serves as the root entry and all operations that are then applied to the stack will extend the graph starting from this root "load identity" entry.

Given the typical usage model for a CoglMatrixStack and the way the entries are built up while traversing a scenegraph then in most cases where an application is interested in comparing two transformations for equality then it is enough to simply compare two CoglMatrixEntry pointers directly. Technically this can lead to false negatives that could be identified with a deeper comparison but often these false negatives are unlikely and don't matter anyway so this enables extremely cheap comparisons.

> **Note** CoglMatrixEntrys are reference counted using cogl_matrix_entry_ref() and cogl_matrix_entry_unref() not with cogl_object_ref() and cogl_object_unref().

1.12.4 3 Component Vectors

3 Component Vectors — Functions for handling single precision float vectors.

Functions

void	cogl_vector3_init ()
void	cogl_vector3_init_zero ()
CoglBool	cogl_vector3_equal ()
CoglBool	cogl_vector3_equal_with_epsilon ()
float *	cogl_vector3_copy ()
void	cogl_vector3_free ()
void	cogl_vector3_invert ()
void	cogl_vector3_add ()
void	cogl_vector3_subtract ()
void	cogl_vector3_multiply_scalar ()
void	cogl_vector3_divide_scalar ()
void	cogl_vector3_normalize ()
float	cogl_vector3_magnitude ()
void	cogl_vector3_cross_product ()
float	cogl_vector3_dot_product ()
float	cogl_vector3_distance ()

Description

This exposes a utility API that can be used for basic manipulation of 3 component float vectors.

Functions

cogl_vector3_init ()

```
void
cogl_vector3_init (float *vector,
                   float x,
                   float y,
                   float z);
```

Initializes a 3 component, single precision float vector which can then be manipulated with the cogl_vector convenience APIs. Vectors can also be used in places where a "point" is often desired.

Parameters

vector	The 3 component vector you want to initialize	
x	The x component	
y	The y component	
z	The z component	

Since 1.4

Stability Level: Unstable

cogl_vector3_init_zero ()

```
void
cogl_vector3_init_zero (float *vector);
```

Initializes a 3 component, single precision float vector with zero for each component.

Parameters

vector	The 3 component vector you want to initialize

Since 1.4

Stability Level: Unstable

cogl_vector3_equal ()

```
CoglBool
cogl_vector3_equal (const void *v1,
                    const void *v2);
```

Compares the components of two vectors and returns TRUE if they are the same.

The comparison of the components is done with the '==' operator such that -0 is considered equal to 0, but otherwise there is no fuzziness such as an epsilon to consider vectors that are essentially identical except for some minor precision error differences due to the way they have been manipulated.

Parameters

v1	The first 3 component vector you want to compare
v2	The second 3 component vector you want to compare

Returns

TRUE if the vectors are equal else FALSE.

Since 1.4

Stability Level: Unstable

cogl_vector3_equal_with_epsilon ()

```
CoglBool
cogl_vector3_equal_with_epsilon (const float *vector0,
                                 const float *vector1,
                                 float epsilon);
```

Compares the components of two vectors using the given epsilon and returns TRUE if they are the same, using an internal epsilon for comparing the floats.

Each component is compared against the epsilon value in this way:

```
if (fabsf (vector0->x - vector1->x) < epsilon)
```

Parameters

vector0	The first 3 component vector you want to compare	
vector1	The second 3 component vector you want to compare	
epsilon	The allowable difference between components to still be considered equal	

Returns

TRUE if the vectors are equal else FALSE.

Since 1.4

Stability Level: Unstable

cogl_vector3_copy ()

```
float~*
cogl_vector3_copy (const float *vector);
```

Allocates a new 3 component float vector on the heap initializing the components from the given *vector* and returns a pointer to the newly allocated vector. You should free the memory using cogl_vector3_free()

Parameters

vector	The 3 component vector you want to copy	

Returns

A newly allocated 3 component float vector

Since 1.4

Stability Level: Unstable

cogl_vector3_free ()

```
void
cogl_vector3_free (float *vector);
```

Frees a 3 component vector that was previously allocated with cogl_vector3_copy()

Parameters

vector	The 3 component you want to free	

Since 1.4

Stability Level: Unstable

cogl_vector3_invert ()

```
void
cogl_vector3_invert (float *vector);
```

Inverts/negates all the components of the given *vector* .

Parameters

vector	The 3 component vector you want to manipulate	

Since 1.4

Stability Level: Unstable

cogl_vector3_add ()

```
void
cogl_vector3_add (float *result,
                  const float *a,
                  const float *b);
```

Adds each of the corresponding components in vectors *a* and *b* storing the results in *result* .

Parameters

result	Where you want the result written	
a	The first vector operand	
b	The second vector operand	

Since 1.4

Stability Level: Unstable

cogl_vector3_subtract ()

```
void
cogl_vector3_subtract (float *result,
                       const float *a,
                       const float *b);
```

Subtracts each of the corresponding components in vector *b* from *a* storing the results in *result* .

Parameters

result	Where you want the result written	
a	The first vector operand	
b	The second vector operand	

Since 1.4

Stability Level: Unstable

cogl_vector3_multiply_scalar ()

```
void
cogl_vector3_multiply_scalar (float *vector,
                              float scalar);
```

Multiplies each of the *vector* components by the given scalar.

Parameters

vector	The 3 component vector you want to manipulate	
scalar	The scalar you want to multiply the vector components by	

Since 1.4

Stability Level: Unstable

cogl_vector3_divide_scalar ()

```
void
cogl_vector3_divide_scalar (float *vector,
                            float scalar);
```

Divides each of the *vector* components by the given scalar.

Parameters

vector	The 3 component vector you want to manipulate	
scalar	The scalar you want to divide the vector components by	

Since 1.4

Stability Level: Unstable

cogl_vector3_normalize ()

```
void
cogl_vector3_normalize (float *vector);
```

Updates the vector so it is a "unit vector" such that the *vector* s magnitude or length is equal to 1.

Note It's safe to use this function with the [0, 0, 0] vector, it will not try to divide components by 0 (its norm) and will leave the vector untouched.

Parameters

vector	The 3 component vector you want to manipulate

Since 1.4

Stability Level: Unstable

cogl_vector3_magnitude ()

```
float
cogl_vector3_magnitude (const float *vector);
```

Calculates the scalar magnitude or length of *vector* .

Parameters

vector	The 3 component vector you want the magnitude for

Returns

The magnitude of *vector* .

Since 1.4

Stability Level: Unstable

cogl_vector3_cross_product ()

```
void
cogl_vector3_cross_product (float *result,
                            const float *u,
                            const float *v);
```

Calculates the cross product between the two vectors *u* and *v* .

The cross product is a vector perpendicular to both *u* and *v* . This can be useful for calculating the normal of a polygon by creating two vectors in its plane using the polygons vertices and taking their cross product.

If the two vectors are parallel then the cross product is 0.

You can use a right hand rule to determine which direction the perpendicular vector will point: If you place the two vectors tail, to tail and imagine grabbing the perpendicular line that extends through the common tail with your right hand such that you fingers rotate in the direction from *u* to *v* then the resulting vector points along your extended thumb.

Parameters

result	Where you want the result written	
u	Your first 3 component vector	
v	Your second 3 component vector	

Returns

The cross product between two vectors u and v .

Since 1.4

Stability Level: Unstable

cogl_vector3_dot_product ()

```
float
cogl_vector3_dot_product (const float *a,
                          const float *b);
```

Calculates the dot product of the two 3 component vectors. This can be used to determine the magnitude of one vector projected onto another. (for example a surface normal)

For example if you have a polygon with a given normal vector and some other point for which you want to calculate its distance from the polygon, you can create a vector between one of the polygon vertices and that point and use the dot product to calculate the magnitude for that vector but projected onto the normal of the polygon. This way you don't just get the distance from the point to the edge of the polygon you get the distance from the point to the nearest part of the polygon.

Note If you don't use a unit length normal in the above example then you would then also have to divide the result by the magnitude of the normal

---

The dot product is calculated as:

```
(a->x * b->x + a->y * b->y + a->z * b->z)
```

For reference, the dot product can also be calculated from the angle between two vectors as:

```
|a||b|cos&#x1d703;
```

Parameters

a	Your first 3 component vector	
b	Your second 3 component vector	

Returns

The dot product of two vectors.

Since 1.4

Stability Level: Unstable

cogl_vector3_distance ()

```
float
cogl_vector3_distance (const float *a,
                       const float *b);
```

If you consider the two given vectors as (x,y,z) points instead then this will compute the distance between those two points.

Parameters

a	The first point	
b	The second point	

Returns

The distance between two points given as 3 component vectors.

Since 1.4

Stability Level: Unstable

Types and Values

1.12.5 Eulers (Rotations)

Eulers (Rotations) — Functions for initializing and manipulating euler angles.

Functions

void	cogl_euler_init ()
void	cogl_euler_init_from_matrix ()
void	cogl_euler_init_from_quaternion ()
CoglBool	cogl_euler_equal ()
CoglEuler *	cogl_euler_copy ()
void	cogl_euler_free ()

Types and Values

	CoglEuler

Description

Euler angles are a simple representation of a 3 dimensional rotation; comprised of 3 ordered heading, pitch and roll rotations. An important thing to understand is that the axis of rotation belong to the object being rotated and so they also rotate as each of the heading, pitch and roll rotations are applied.

One way to consider euler angles is to imagine controlling an aeroplane, where you first choose a heading (Such as flying south east), then you set the pitch (such as 30 degrees to take off) and then you might set a roll, by dipping the left, wing as you prepare to turn.

They have some advantages and limitations that it helps to be aware of:

Advantages:

• Easy to understand and use, compared to quaternions and matrices, so may be a good choice for a user interface.

- Efficient storage, needing only 3 components any rotation can be represented.

Note Actually the CoglEuler type isn't optimized for size because we may cache the equivalent CoglQuaternion along with a euler rotation, but it would be trivial for an application to track the components of euler rotations in a packed float array if optimizing for size was important. The values could be passed to Cogl only when manipulation is necessary.

Disadvantages:

- Aliasing: it's possible to represent some rotations with multiple different heading, pitch and roll rotations.

- They can suffer from a problem called Gimbal Lock. A good explanation of this can be seen on wikipedia here: http://en.wikipedia.org/wiki/G but basically two of the axis of rotation may become aligned and so you loose a degree of freedom. For example a pitch of +-90° would mean that heading and bank rotate around the same axis.

- If you use euler angles to orient something in 3D space and try to transition between orientations by interpolating the component angles you probably wont get the transitions you expect as they may not follow the shortest path between the two orientations.

- There's no standard to what order the component axis rotations are applied. The most common convention seems to be what we do in Cogl with heading (y-axis), pitch (x-axis) and then roll (z-axis), but other software might apply x-axis, y-axis then z-axis or any other order so you need to consider this if you are accepting euler rotations from some other software. Other software may also use slightly different aeronautical terms, such as "yaw" instead of "heading" or "bank" instead of "roll".

To minimize the aliasing issue we may refer to "Canonical Euler" angles where heading and roll are restricted to +- 180° and pitch is restricted to +- 90°. If pitch is +- 90° bank is set to 0°.

Quaternions don't suffer from Gimbal Lock and they can be nicely interpolated between, their disadvantage is that they don't have an intuitive representation.

A common practice is to accept angles in the intuitive Euler form and convert them to quaternions internally to avoid Gimbal Lock and handle interpolations. See cogl_quaternion_init_from_euler().

Functions

cogl_euler_init ()

```
void
cogl_euler_init (CoglEuler *euler,
                 float heading,
                 float pitch,
                 float roll);
```

Initializes *euler* to represent a rotation of *x_angle* degrees around the x axis, then *y_angle* degrees around the y_axis and *z_angle* degrees around the z axis.

Parameters

euler	The CoglEuler angle to initialize	
heading	Angle to rotate around an object's y axis	
pitch	Angle to rotate around an object's x axis	
roll	Angle to rotate around an object's z axis	

Since 2.0

cogl_euler_init_from_matrix ()

```
void
cogl_euler_init_from_matrix (CoglEuler *euler,
                             const CoglMatrix *matrix);
```

Extracts a euler rotation from the given `matrix` and initializses `euler` with the component x, y and z rotation angles.

Parameters

euler	The CoglEuler angle to initialize	
matrix	A CoglMatrix containing a rotation, but no scaling, mirroring or skewing.	

cogl_euler_init_from_quaternion ()

```
void
cogl_euler_init_from_quaternion (CoglEuler *euler,
                                 const CoglQuaternion *quaternion);
```

Initializes a `euler` rotation with the equivalent rotation represented by the given `quaternion`.

Parameters

euler	The CoglEuler angle to initialize	
quaternion	A CoglEuler with the rotation to initialize with	

cogl_culor_oqual ()

```
CoglBool
cogl_euler_equal (const void *v1,
                  const void *v2);
```

Compares the two given euler angles `v1` and `v1` and it they are equal returns TRUE else FALSE.

Note This function only checks that all three components rotations are numerically equal, it does not consider that some rotations can be represented with different component rotations

---

Parameters

v1	The first euler angle to compare	
v2	The second euler angle to compare	

Returns

TRUE if *v1* and *v2* are equal else FALSE.

Since 2.0

cogl_euler_copy ()

```
CoglEuler~*
cogl_euler_copy (const CoglEuler *src);
```

Allocates a new CoglEuler and initilizes it with the component angles of *src* . The newly allocated euler should be freed using cogl_euler_free().

Parameters

src	A CoglEuler to copy

Returns

A newly allocated CoglEuler

Since 2.0

cogl_euler_free ()

```
void
cogl_euler_free (CoglEuler *euler);
```

Frees a CoglEuler that was previously allocated using cogl_euler_copy().

Parameters

euler	A CoglEuler allocated via cogl_euler_copy()

Since 2.0

Types and Values

CoglEuler

```
typedef struct {
  float heading;
  float pitch;
  float roll;
} CoglEuler;
```

Represents an ordered rotation first of *heading* degrees around an object's y axis, then *pitch* degrees around an object's x axis and finally *roll* degrees around an object's z axis.

Note It's important to understand the that axis are associated with the object being rotated, so the axis also rotate in sequence with the rotations being applied.

The members of a CoglEuler can be initialized, for example, with cogl_euler_init() and cogl_euler_init_from_quaternion(). You may also want to look at cogl_quaternion_init_from_euler() if you want to do interpolation between 3d rotations.

Members

float *heading*;	Angle to rotate around an object's y axis
float *pitch*;	Angle to rotate around an object's x axis
float *roll*;	Angle to rotate around an object's z axis

Since 2.0

1.12.6 Quaternions (Rotations)

Quaternions (Rotations) — Functions for initializing and manipulating quaternions.

Functions

void	cogl_quaternion_init_identity ()
void	cogl_quaternion_init ()
void	cogl_quaternion_init_from_angle_vector ()
void	cogl_quaternion_init_from_array ()
void	cogl_quaternion_init_from_x_rotation ()
void	cogl_quaternion_init_from_y_rotation ()
void	cogl_quaternion_init_from_z_rotation ()
void	cogl_quaternion_init_from_euler ()
CoglBool	cogl_quaternion_equal ()

CoglQuaternion *	cogl_quaternion_copy ()
void	cogl_quaternion_free ()
float	cogl_quaternion_get_rotation_angle ()
void	cogl_quaternion_get_rotation_axis ()
void	cogl_quaternion_normalize ()
float	cogl_quaternion_dot_product ()
void	cogl_quaternion_invert ()
void	cogl_quaternion_multiply ()
void	cogl_quaternion_pow ()
void	cogl_quaternion_slerp ()
void	cogl_quaternion_nlerp ()
void	cogl_quaternion_squad ()
const CoglQuaternion *	cogl_get_static_identity_quaternion ()
const CoglQuaternion *	cogl_get_static_zero_quaternion ()

Types and Values

| CoglQuaternion

Description

Quaternions have become a standard form for representing 3D rotations and have some nice properties when compared with other representation such as (roll,pitch,yaw) Euler angles. They can be used to interpolate between different rotations and they don't suffer from a problem called "Gimbal lock" where two of the axis of rotation may become aligned and you loose a degree of freedom. .

Functions

cogl_quaternion_init_identity ()

```
void
cogl_quaternion_init_identity (CoglQuaternion *quaternion);
```

Initializes the quaternion with the canonical quaternion identity [1 (0, 0, 0)] which represents no rotation. Multiplying a quaternion with this identity leaves the quaternion unchanged.

You might also want to consider using cogl_get_static_identity_quaternion().

Parameters

| quaternion | An uninitialized CoglQuaternion | |

Since 2.0

cogl_quaternion_init ()

```
void
cogl_quaternion_init (CoglQuaternion *quaternion,
                      float angle,
                      float x,
                      float y,
                      float z);
```

Initializes a quaternion that rotates *angle* degrees around the axis vector (x , y , z). The axis vector does not need to be normalized.

Parameters

quaternion	An uninitialized CoglQuaternion	
angle	The angle you want to rotate around the given axis	
x	The x component of your axis vector about which you want to rotate.	
y	The y component of your axis vector about which you want to rotate.	
z	The z component of your axis vector about which you want to rotate.	

Returns

A normalized, unit quaternion representing an orientation rotated *angle* degrees around the axis vector (x , y , z)

Since 2.0

cogl_quaternion_init_from_angle_vector ()

```
void
cogl_quaternion_init_from_angle_vector
                          (CoglQuaternion *quaternion,
                           float angle,
                           const float *axis3f);
```

Initializes a quaternion that rotates *angle* degrees around the given *axis* vector. The axis vector does not need to be normalized.

Parameters

quaternion	An uninitialized CoglQuaternion	
angle	The angle to rotate around *axis3f*	
axis3f	your 3 component axis vector about which you want to rotate.	

Returns

A normalized, unit quaternion representing an orientation rotated *angle* degrees around the given *axis* vector.

Since 2.0

cogl_quaternion_init_from_array ()

```
void
```

```
cogl_quaternion_init_from_array (CoglQuaternion *quaternion,
                                 const float *array);
```

Initializes a [w (x, y,z)] quaternion directly from an array of 4 floats: [w,x,y,z].

Parameters

quaternion	A CoglQuaternion	
array	An array of 4 floats w,(x,y,z)	

Since 2.0

cogl_quaternion_init_from_x_rotation ()

```
void
cogl_quaternion_init_from_x_rotation (CoglQuaternion *quaternion,
                                      float angle);
```

XXX: check which direction this rotates

Parameters

quaternion	An uninitialized CoglQuaternion	
angle	The angle to rotate around the x axis	

Since 2.0

cogl_quaternion_init_from_y_rotation ()

```
void
cogl_quaternion_init_from_y_rotation (CoglQuaternion *quaternion,
                                      float angle);
```

Parameters

quaternion	An uninitialized CoglQuaternion	
angle	The angle to rotate around the y axis	

Since 2.0

cogl_quaternion_init_from_z_rotation ()

```
void
cogl_quaternion_init_from_z_rotation (CoglQuaternion *quaternion,
                                      float angle);
```

Parameters

quaternion	An uninitialized CoglQuaternion	
angle	The angle to rotate around the z axis	

Since 2.0

cogl_quaternion_init_from_euler ()

```
void
cogl_quaternion_init_from_euler (CoglQuaternion *quaternion,
                                 const CoglEuler *euler);
```

Parameters

quaternion	A CoglQuaternion	
euler	A CoglEuler with which to initialize the quaternion	

Since 2.0

cogl_quaternion_equal ()

```
CoglBool
cogl_quaternion_equal (const void *v1,
                       const void *v2);
```

Compares that all the components of quaternions a and b are equal.

An epsilon value is not used to compare the float components, but the == operator is at least used so that 0 and -0 are considered equal.

Parameters

v1	A CoglQuaternion	
v2	A CoglQuaternion	

Returns

TRUE if the quaternions are equal else FALSE.

Since 2.0

cogl_quaternion_copy ()

```
CoglQuaternion~*
cogl_quaternion_copy (const CoglQuaternion *src);
```

Allocates a new CoglQuaternion on the stack and initializes it with the same values as src.

Parameters

src	A CoglQuaternion	

Returns

A newly allocated CoglQuaternion which should be freed using cogl_quaternion_free()

Since 2.0

cogl_quaternion_free ()

```
void
cogl_quaternion_free (CoglQuaternion *quaternion);
```

Frees a CoglQuaternion that was previously allocated via cogl_quaternion_copy().

Parameters

quaternion	A CoglQuaternion	

Since 2.0

cogl_quaternion_get_rotation_angle ()

```
float
cogl_quaternion_get_rotation_angle (const CoglQuaternion *quaternion);
```

Parameters

quaternion	A CoglQuaternion	

Since 2.0

cogl_quaternion_get_rotation_axis ()

```
void
cogl_quaternion_get_rotation_axis (const CoglQuaternion *quaternion,
                                   float *vector3);
```

Parameters

quaternion	A CoglQuaternion	
vector3	an allocated 3-float array.	[out]

Since 2.0

cogl_quaternion_normalize ()

```
void
cogl_quaternion_normalize (CoglQuaternion *quaternion);
```

Parameters

| quaternion | A CoglQuaternion | |

Since 2.0

cogl_quaternion_dot_product ()

```
float
cogl_quaternion_dot_product (const CoglQuaternion *a,
                             const CoglQuaternion *b);
```

Parameters

a	A CoglQuaternion	
b	A CoglQuaternion	

Since 2.0

cogl_quaternion_invert ()

```
void
cogl_quaternion_invert (CoglQuaternion *quaternion);
```

Parameters

| quaternion | A CoglQuaternion | |

Since 2.0

cogl_quaternion_multiply ()

```
void
cogl_quaternion_multiply (CoglQuaternion *result,
                          const CoglQuaternion *left,
                          const CoglQuaternion *right);
```

This combines the rotations of two quaternions into *result* . The operation is not commutative so the order is important because AxB != BxA. Cogl follows the standard convention for quaternions here so the rotations are applied *right* to *left* . This is similar to the combining of matrices.

Note It is possible to multiply the *a* quaternion in-place, so *result* can be equal to *a* but can't be equal to *b*.

Parameters

result	The destination CoglQuaternion	
left	The second CoglQuaternion rotation to apply	
right	The first CoglQuaternion rotation to apply	

Since 2.0

cogl_quaternion_pow ()

```
void
cogl_quaternion_pow (CoglQuaternion *quaternion,
                     float exponent);
```

Parameters

quaternion	A CoglQuaternion	
exponent	the exponent	

Since 2.0

cogl_quaternion_slerp ()

```
void
cogl_quaternion_slerp (CoglQuaternion *result,
                       const CoglQuaternion *a,
                       const CoglQuaternion *b,
                       float t);
```

Performs a spherical linear interpolation between two quaternions.

Noteable properties:

- commutative: No

- constant velocity: Yes

- torque minimal (travels along the surface of the 4-sphere): Yes

- more expensive than cogl_quaternion_nlerp()

Parameters

result	The destination CoglQuaternion	
a	The first CoglQuaternion	
b	The second CoglQuaternion	
t	The factor in the range [0,1] used to interpolate between quaternion a and b .	

cogl_quaternion_nlerp ()

```
void
cogl_quaternion_nlerp (CoglQuaternion *result,
                       const CoglQuaternion *a,
                       const CoglQuaternion *b,
                       float t);
```

Performs a normalized linear interpolation between two quaternions. That is it does a linear interpolation of the quaternion components and then normalizes the result. This will follow the shortest arc between the two orientations (just like the slerp() function) but will not progress at a constant speed. Unlike slerp() nlerp is commutative which is useful if you are blending animations together. (I.e. nlerp (tmp, a, b) followed by nlerp (result, tmp, d) is the same as nlerp (tmp, a, d) followed by nlerp (result, tmp, b)). Finally nlerp is cheaper than slerp so it can be a good choice if you don't need the constant speed property of the slerp() function.

Notable properties:

- commutative: Yes

- constant velocity: No

- torque minimal (travels along the surface of the 4-sphere): Yes

- faster than cogl_quaternion_slerp()

Parameters

result	The destination CoglQuaternion	
a	The first CoglQuaternion	
b	The second CoglQuaternion	
t	The factor in the range [0,1] used to interpolate between quaterion a and b .	

cogl_quaternion_squad ()

```
void
cogl_quaternion_squad (CoglQuaternion *result,
                       const CoglQuaternion *prev,
                       const CoglQuaternion *a,
                       const CoglQuaternion *b,
                       const CoglQuaternion *next,
                       float t);
```

Parameters

result	The destination CoglQuaternion	
prev	A CoglQuaternion used before a	
a	The first CoglQuaternion	
b	The second CoglQuaternion	
next	A CoglQuaternion that will be used after b	
t	The factor in the range [0,1] used to interpolate between quaternion a and b .	

Since 2.0

cogl_get_static_identity_quaternion ()

```
const CoglQuaternion~*
cogl_get_static_identity_quaternion (void);
```

Returns a pointer to a singleton quaternion constant describing the canonical identity [1 (0, 0, 0)] which represents no rotation.

If you multiply a quaternion with the identity quaternion you will get back the same value as the original quaternion.

Returns

A pointer to an identity quaternion

Since 2.0

cogl_get_static_zero_quaternion ()

```
const CoglQuaternion~*
cogl_get_static_zero_quaternion (void);
```

Returns

a pointer to a singleton quaternion constant describing a rotation of 180 degrees around a degenerate axis: [0 (0, 0, 0)]

Since 2.0

Types and Values

CoglQuaternion

```
typedef struct {
  float w;

  float x;
  float y;
  float z;
} CoglQuaternion;
```

A quaternion is comprised of a scalar component and a 3D vector component. The scalar component is normally referred to as w and the vector might either be referred to as v or a (for axis) or expanded with the individual components: (x, y, z) A full quaternion would then be written as [w (x, y, z)].

Quaternions can be considered to represent an axis and angle pair although sadly these numbers are buried somewhat under some maths...

For the curious you can see here that a given axis (a) and angle (θ) pair are represented in a quaternion as follows:

```
[w=cos(θ/2) ( x=sin(θ/2)*a.x, y=sin(θ/2)*a.y, z=sin(θ/2)*a. ↩
   x )]
```

Unit Quaternions: When using Quaternions to represent spatial orientations for 3D graphics it's always assumed you have a unit quaternion. The magnitude of a quaternion is defined as:

```
sqrt (w^2 + x^2 + y^2 + z^2)
```

and a unit quaternion satisfies this equation:

```
w$^2$ + x$^2$ + y$^2$ + z$^2$ = 1
```

Thankfully most of the time we don't actually have to worry about the maths that goes on behind the scenes but if you are curious to learn more here are some external references:

- http://mathworld.wolfram.com/Quaternion.html

- http://www.gamedev.net/reference/articles/article1095.asp

- http://www.cprogramming.com/tutorial/3d/quaternions.html

- http://www.isner.com/tutorials/quatSpells/quaternion_spells_12.htm

- 3D Maths Primer for Graphics and Game Development ISBN-10: 1556229119

- http://www.cs.caltech.edu/courses/cs171/quatut.pdf

- http://www.j3d.org/matrix_faq/matrfaq_latest.html#Q56

Members

float *w*;	based on the angle of rotation it is $\cos(\theta/2)$
float *x*;	based on the angle of rotation and x component of the axis of rotation it is $\sin(\theta/2) \cdot axis.x$

float y;	based on the angle of rotation and y component of the axis of rotation it is sin(𝜃/2)*axis.y
float z;	based on the angle of rotation and z component of the axis of rotation it is sin(𝜃/2)*axis.z

1.12.7 GPU synchronisation fences

GPU synchronisation fences — Functions for notification of command completion

Functions

void	(*CoglFenceCallback) ()
void *	cogl_fence_closure_get_user_data ()
CoglFenceClosure *	cogl_framebuffer_add_fence_callback ()
void	cogl_framebuffer_cancel_fence_callback ()

Types and Values

	CoglFence
	CoglFenceClosure

Description

Cogl allows notification of GPU command completion; users may mark points in the GPU command stream and receive notification when the GPU has executed to that point.

Functions

CoglFenceCallback ()

```
void
(*CoglFenceCallback) (CoglFence *fence,
                      void *user_data);
```

The callback prototype used with cogl_framebuffer_add_fence_callback() for notification of GPU command completion.

Parameters

fence	Unused. In the future this parameter may be used to pass extra information about the fence completion but for now it should be ignored.	
user_data	The private data passed to cogl_framebuffer_add_fence_callback()	

Since 2.0

Stability Level: Unstable

cogl_fence_closure_get_user_data ()

```
void~*
cogl_fence_closure_get_user_data (CoglFenceClosure *closure);
```

cogl_framebuffer_add_fence_callback ()

```
CoglFenceClosure~*
cogl_framebuffer_add_fence_callback (CoglFramebuffer *framebuffer,
                                     CoglFenceCallback callback,
                                     void *user_data);
```

Calls the provided callback when all previously-submitted commands have been executed by the GPU.

Returns non-NULL if the fence succeeded, or NULL if it was unable to be inserted and the callback will never be called. The user does not need to free the closure; it will be freed automatically when the callback is called, or cancelled.

Parameters

framebuffer	The CoglFramebuffer the commands have been submitted to	
callback	A CoglFenceCallback to be called when all commands submitted to Cogl have been executed.	*[scope notified]*
user_data	Private data that will be passed to the callback.	*[closure]*

Since 2.0

Stability Level: Unstable

cogl_framebuffer_cancel_fence_callback ()

```
void
cogl_framebuffer_cancel_fence_callback
                            (CoglFramebuffer *framebuffer,
                             CoglFenceClosure *closure);
```

Removes a fence previously submitted with cogl_framebuffer_add_fence_callback(); the callback will not be called.

Parameters

framebuffer	The CoglFramebuffer the commands were submitted to	
closure	The CoglFenceClosure returned from cogl_framebuffer_add_fence_callback()	

Since 2.0

Stability Level: Unstable

Types and Values

CoglFence

```
typedef struct _CoglFence CoglFence;
```

An opaque object representing a fence. This type is currently unused but in the future may be used to pass extra information about the fence completion.

Since 2.0

Stability Level: Unstable

CoglFenceClosure

```
typedef struct _CoglFenceClosure CoglFenceClosure;
```

An opaque type representing one future callback to be made when the GPU command stream has passed a certain point.

Since 2.0

Stability Level: Unstable

1.12.8 Versioning utility macros

Versioning utility macros — Macros for determining the version of Cogl being used

Functions

#define	COGL_VERSION_ENCODE()
#define	COGL_VERSION_CHECK()
#define	COGL_VERSION_GET_MAJOR()
#define	COGL_VERSION_GET_MINOR()
#define	COGL_VERSION_GET_MICRO()

Types and Values

#define	COGL_VERSION_MAJOR
#define	COGL_VERSION_MINOR
#define	COGL_VERSION_MICRO
#define	COGL_VERSION_STRING
#define	COGL_VERSION

Description

Cogl offers a set of macros for checking the version of the library at compile time.

Functions

COGL_VERSION_ENCODE()

```
#define                 COGL_VERSION_ENCODE(major, minor, micro)
```

Encodes a 3 part version number into a single integer. This can be used to compare the Cogl version. For example if there is a known bug in Cogl versions between 1.3.2 and 1.3.4 you could use the following code to provide a workaround:

```
#if COGL_VERSION >= COGL_VERSION_ENCODE (1, 3, 2) && \
    COGL_VERSION <= COGL_VERSION_ENCODE (1, 3, 4)
  /<!-- -->* Do the workaround *<!-- -->/
#endif
```

Parameters

major	The major part of a version number	

minor	The minor part of a version number	
micro	The micro part of a version number	

Since 1.12.0

COGL_VERSION_CHECK()

```
#define            COGL_VERSION_CHECK(major, minor, micro)
```

A convenient macro to check whether the Cogl version being compiled against is at least the given version number. For example if the function cogl_pipeline_frobnicate was added in version 2.0.1 and you want to conditionally use that function when it is available, you could write the following:

```
#if COGL_VERSION_CHECK (2, 0, 1)
cogl_pipeline_frobnicate (pipeline);
#else
/<!-- -->* Frobnication is not supported. Use a red color instead *<!-- -->/
cogl_pipeline_set_color_4f (pipeline, 1.0f, 0.0f, 0.0f, 1.0f);
#endif
```

Parameters

major	The major part of a version number	
minor	The minor part of a version number	
micro	The micro part of a version number	

Returns

TRUE if the Cogl version being compiled against is greater than or equal to the given three part version number.

Since 1.12.0

COGL_VERSION_GET_MAJOR()

```
#define            COGL_VERSION_GET_MAJOR(version)
```

Extracts the major part of an encoded version number.

Parameters

version	An encoded version number

Since 1.12.0

COGL_VERSION_GET_MINOR()

```
#define            COGL_VERSION_GET_MINOR(version)
```

Extracts the minor part of an encoded version number.

Parameters

| version | An encoded version number |

Since 1.12.0

COGL_VERSION_GET_MICRO()

```
#define              COGL_VERSION_GET_MICRO(version)
```

Extracts the micro part of an encoded version number.

Parameters

| version | An encoded version number |

Since 1.12.0

Types and Values

COGL_VERSION_MAJOR

```
#define COGL_VERSION_MAJOR COGL_VERSION_MAJOR_INTERNAL
```

The major version of the Cogl library (1, if COGL_VERSION is 1.2.3)
Since 1.12.0

COGL_VERSION_MINOR

```
#define COGL_VERSION_MINOR COGL_VERSION_MINOR_INTERNAL
```

The minor version of the Cogl library (2, if COGL_VERSION is 1.2.3)
Since 1.12.0

COGL_VERSION_MICRO

```
#define COGL_VERSION_MICRO COGL_VERSION_MICRO_INTERNAL
```

The micro version of the Cogl library (3, if COGL_VERSION is 1.2.3)
Since 1.12.0

COGL_VERSION_STRING

```
#define COGL_VERSION_STRING COGL_VERSION_STRING_INTERNAL
```

The full version of the Cogl library, in string form (suited for string concatenation)
Since 1.12.0

COGL_VERSION

```
#define          COGL_VERSION
```

The Cogl version encoded into a single integer using the COGL_VERSION_ENCODE() macro. This can be used for quick comparisons with particular versions.

Since 1.12.0

1.13 Binding and Integrating

1.13.1 SDL Integration

SDL Integration — Integration api for the Simple DirectMedia Layer library.

Functions

CoglContext *	cogl_sdl_context_new ()
void	cogl_sdl_renderer_set_event_type ()
int	cogl_sdl_renderer_get_event_type ()
void	cogl_sdl_handle_event ()
void	cogl_sdl_idle ()
SDL_Window *	cogl_sdl_onscreen_get_window ()

Description

Cogl is a portable graphics api that can either be used standalone or alternatively integrated with certain existing frameworks. This api enables Cogl to be used in conjunction with the Simple DirectMedia Layer library.

Using this API a typical SDL application would look something like this:

```
MyAppData data;
CoglError *error = NULL;

data.ctx = cogl_sdl_context_new (SDL_USEREVENT, &error);
if (!data.ctx)
  {
    fprintf (stderr, "Failed to create context: %s\n",
             error->message);
    return 1;
  }

my_application_setup (&data);

data.redraw_queued = TRUE;
while (!data.quit)
  {
    while (!data.quit)
      {
        if (!SDL_PollEvent (&event))
          {
            if (data.redraw_queued)
              break;

            cogl_sdl_idle (ctx);
            if (!SDL_WaitEvent (&event))
              {
```

```
                fprintf (stderr, "Error waiting for SDL events");
                return 1;
            }
        }

        handle_event (&data, &event);
        cogl_sdl_handle_event (ctx, &event);
      }

    data.redraw_queued = redraw (&data);
  }
```

Functions

cogl_sdl_context_new ()

```
CoglContext~*
cogl_sdl_context_new (int type,
                      CoglError **error);
```

This is a convenience function for creating a new CoglContext for use with SDL and specifying what SDL user event type Cogl can use as a way to interrupt SDL_WaitEvent().

This function is equivalent to the following code:

```
CoglRenderer *renderer = cogl_renderer_new ();
CoglDisplay *display;

cogl_renderer_set_winsys_id (renderer, COGL_WINSYS_ID_SDL);

cogl_sdl_renderer_set_event_type (renderer, type);

if (!cogl_renderer_connect (renderer, error))
  return NULL;

display = cogl_display_new (renderer, NULL);
if (!cogl_display_setup (display, error))
  return NULL;

return cogl_context_new (display, error);
```

Note SDL applications are required to either use this API or to manually create a CoglRenderer and call cogl_sdl_renderer_set_event_type().

Parameters

type	An SDL user event type between SDL_USEREVENT and SDL_NUMEVENTS - 1	
error	A CoglError return location.	

Since 2.0

Stability Level: Unstable

cogl_sdl_renderer_set_event_type ()

```
void
cogl_sdl_renderer_set_event_type (CoglRenderer *renderer,
                                  int type);
```

Tells Cogl what SDL user event type it can use as a way to interrupt SDL_WaitEvent() to ensure that cogl_sdl_handle_event() will be called in a finite amount of time.

Note This should only be called on an un-connected `renderer`.

Note For convenience most simple applications can use cogl_sdl_context_new() if they don't want to manually create CoglRenderer and CoglDisplay objects during initialization.

Parameters

renderer	A CoglRenderer	
type	An SDL user event type between `SDL_USEREVENT` and `SDL_NUMEVENTS - 1`	

Since 2.0

Stability Level: Unstable

cogl_sdl_renderer_get_event_type ()

```
int
cogl_sdl_renderer_get_event_type (CoglRenderer *renderer);
```

Queries what SDL user event type Cogl is using as a way to interrupt SDL_WaitEvent(). This is set either using cogl_sdl_context_new or by using cogl_sdl_renderer_set_event_type().

Parameters

renderer	A CoglRenderer	

Since 2.0

Stability Level: Unstable

cogl_sdl_handle_event ()

```
void
cogl_sdl_handle_event (CoglContext *context,
                       SDL_Event *event);
```

Passes control to Cogl so that it may dispatch any internal event callbacks in response to the given SDL *event* . This function must be called for every SDL event.

Parameters

context	A CoglContext	
event	An SDL event	

Since 2.0

Stability Level: Unstable

cogl_sdl_idle ()

```
void
cogl_sdl_idle (CoglContext *context);
```

Notifies Cogl that the application is idle and about to call SDL_WaitEvent(). Cogl may use this to run low priority book keeping tasks.

Parameters

context	A CoglContext	

Since 2.0

Stability Level: Unstable

cogl_sdl_onscreen_get_window ()

```
SDL_Window~*
cogl_sdl_onscreen_get_window (CoglOnscreen *onscreen);
```

Parameters

onscreen	A CoglOnscreen	

Returns

the underlying SDL_Window associated with an onscreen framebuffer.

Since 2.0

Stability Level: Unstable

Types and Values

1.13.2 Main loop integration

Main loop integration — Functions for integrating Cogl with an application's main loop

Functions

int	cogl_poll_renderer_get_info ()
void	cogl_poll_renderer_dispatch ()
GSource *	cogl_glib_source_new ()
GSource *	cogl_glib_renderer_source_new ()

Types and Values

| enum | CoglPollFDEvent |
| | CoglPollFD |

Description

Cogl needs to integrate with the application's main loop so that it can internally handle some events from the driver. All Cogl applications must use these functions. They provide enough information to describe the state that Cogl will need to wake up on. An application using the GLib main loop can instead use cogl_glib_source_new() which provides a GSource ready to be added to the main loop.

Functions

cogl_poll_renderer_get_info ()

```
int
cogl_poll_renderer_get_info (CoglRenderer *renderer,
                             CoglPollFD **poll_fds,
                             int *n_poll_fds,
                             int64_t *timeout);
```

Is used to integrate Cogl with an application mainloop that is based on the unix poll(2) api (or select() or something equivalent). This api should be called whenever an application is about to go idle so that Cogl has a chance to describe what file descriptor events it needs to be woken up for.

Note If your application is using the Glib mainloop then you should jump to the cogl_glib_source_new() api as a more convenient way of integrating Cogl with the mainloop.

After the function is called *poll_fds will contain a pointer to an array of CoglPollFD structs describing the file descriptors that Cogl expects. The fd and events members will be updated accordingly. After the application has completed its idle it is expected to either update the revents members directly in this array or to create a copy of the array and update them there.

When the application mainloop returns from calling poll(2) (or its equivalent) then it should call cogl_poll_renderer_dispatch() passing a pointer the array of CoglPollFDs with updated revent values.

When using the COGL_WINSYS_ID_WGL winsys (where file descriptors don't make any sense) or COGL_WINSYS_ID_SDL (where the event handling functions of SDL don't allow blocking on a file descriptor) *n_poll_fds is guaranteed to be zero.

timeout will contain a maximum amount of time to wait in microseconds before the application should wake up or -1 if the application should wait indefinitely. This can also be 0 if Cogl needs to be woken up immediately.

Parameters

| renderer | A CoglRenderer | |
| poll_fds | A return location for a pointer to an array of CoglPollFDs | |

n_poll_fds	A return location for the number of entries in *poll_fds	
timeout	A return location for the maximum length of time to wait in microseconds, or -1 to wait indefinitely.	

Returns

A "poll fd state age" that changes whenever the set of poll_fds has changed. If this API is being used to integrate with another system mainloop api then knowing if the set of file descriptors and events has really changed can help avoid redundant work depending the api. The age isn't guaranteed to change when the timeout changes.

Since 1.16

Stability Level: Unstable

cogl_poll_renderer_dispatch ()

```
void
cogl_poll_renderer_dispatch (CoglRenderer *renderer,
                             const CoglPollFD *poll_fds,
                             int n_poll_fds);
```

This should be called whenever an application is woken up from going idle in its main loop. The *poll_fds* array should contain a list of file descriptors matched with the events that occurred in revents. The events field is ignored. It is safe to pass in extra file descriptors that Cogl didn't request when calling cogl_poll_renderer_get_info() or a shorter array missing some file descriptors that Cogl requested.

> **Note** If your application didn't originally create a CoglRenderer manually then you can easily get a CoglRenderer pointer by calling cogl_get_renderer().

Parameters

renderer	A CoglRenderer	
poll_fds	An array of CoglPollFDs describing the events that have occurred since the application went idle.	
n_poll_fds	The length of the *poll_fds* array.	

Since 1.16

Stability Level: Unstable

cogl_glib_source_new ()

```
GSource~*
cogl_glib_source_new (CoglContext *context,
                      int priority);
```

Creates a GSource which handles Cogl's internal system event processing. This can be used as a convenience instead of cogl_poll_renderer_get_info() and cogl_poll_renderer_dispatch() in applications that are already using the GLib main loop. After this is called the GSource should be attached to the main loop using g_source_attach().

Applications that manually connect to a CoglRenderer before they create a CoglContext should instead use cogl_glib_renderer_source_new() so that events may be dispatched before a context has been created. In that case you don't need to use this api in addition later, it is simply enough to use cogl_glib_renderer_source_new() instead.

Note This api is actually just a thin convenience wrapper around cogl_glib_renderer_source_new()

Parameters

context	A CoglContext	
priority	The priority of the GSource	

Returns

a new GSource

Since 1.10

Stability Level: Unstable

cogl_glib_renderer_source_new ()

```
GSource~*
cogl_glib_renderer_source_new (CoglRenderer *renderer,
                               int priority);
```

Creates a GSource which handles Cogl's internal system event processing. This can be used as a convenience instead of cogl_poll_renderer_get_info() and cogl_poll_renderer_dispatch() in applications that are already using the GLib main loop. After this is called the GSource should be attached to the main loop using g_source_attach().

Parameters

renderer	A CoglRenderer	
priority	The priority of the GSource	

Returns

a new GSource

Since 1.16

Stability Level: Unstable

Types and Values

enum CoglPollFDEvent

A bitmask of events that Cogl may need to wake on for a file descriptor. Note that these all have the same values as the corresponding defines for the poll function call on Unix so they may be directly passed to poll.

Members

COGL_POLL_FD_EVENT_IN	there is data to read
COGL_POLL_FD_EVENT_PRI	data can be writ-ten (with-out block-ing)
COGL_POLL_FD_EVENT_OUT	there is ur-gent data to read.
COGL_POLL_FD_EVENT_ERR	error con-di-tion
COGL_POLL_FD_EVENT_HUP	hung up (the con-nec-tion has been bro-ken, usu-ally for pipes and sock-ets).
COGL_POLL_FD_EVENT_NVAL	invalid re-quest. The file de-scrip-tor is not open.

Since 1.10

Stability Level: Unstable

CoglPollFD

```
typedef struct {
  int fd;
  short int events;
  short int revents;
} CoglPollFD;
```

A struct for describing the state of a file descriptor that Cogl needs to block on. The `events` field contains a bitmask of CoglPollFDEvents that should cause the application to wake up. After the application is woken up from idle it should pass back an array of CoglPollFDs to Cogl and update the `revents` mask to the actual events that occurred on the file descriptor.

Note that CoglPollFD is deliberately exactly the same as struct pollfd on Unix so that it can simply be cast when calling poll.

Members

int *fd*;	The file descriptor to block on
short int *events*;	A bitmask of events to block on
short int *revents*;	A bitmask of returned events

Since 1.10

Stability Level: Unstable

1.13.3 GType Integration API

GType Integration API —

Functions

GType	cogl_gtype_matrix_get_type ()

Description

Functions

cogl_gtype_matrix_get_type ()

```
GType
cogl_gtype_matrix_get_type (void);
```

Returns

the GType for the registered "CoglMatrix" boxed type. This can be used for example to define GObject properties that accept a CoglMatrix value.

Types and Values

1.13.4   GLES 2.0 context

GLES 2.0 context — A portable api to access OpenGLES 2.0

Functions

#define	COGL_GLES2_CONTEXT_ERROR
CoglGLES2Context *	cogl_gles2_context_new ()
CoglBool	cogl_is_gles2_context ()
const CoglGLES2Vtable *	cogl_gles2_context_get_vtable ()
CoglBool	cogl_push_gles2_context ()
void	cogl_pop_gles2_context ()
CoglGLES2Vtable *	cogl_gles2_get_current_vtable ()
CoglTexture2D *	cogl_gles2_texture_2d_new_from_handle ()
CoglBool	cogl_gles2_texture_get_handle ()

Types and Values

	CoglGLES2Context
struct	CoglGLES2Vtable
enum	CoglGLES2ContextError

Description

Cogl provides portable access to the OpenGLES api through a single library that is able to smooth over inconsistencies between the different vendor drivers for OpenGLES in a single place.

The api is designed to allow Cogl to transparently implement the api on top of other drivers, such as OpenGL, D3D or on Cogl's own drawing api so even if your platform doesn't come with an OpenGLES 2.0 api Cogl may still be able to expose the api to your application.

Since Cogl is a library and not an api specification it is possible to add OpenGLES 2.0 api features to Cogl which can immidiately benefit developers regardless of what platform they are running on.

With this api it's possible to re-use existing OpenGLES 2.0 code within applications that are rendering with the Cogl API and also it's possible for applications that render using OpenGLES 2.0 to incorporate content rendered with Cogl.

Applications can check for OpenGLES 2.0 api support by checking for COGL_FEATURE_ID_GLES2_CONTEXT support with cogl_has_feature().

Functions

COGL_GLES2_CONTEXT_ERROR

```
#define COGL_GLES2_CONTEXT_ERROR (_cogl_gles2_context_error_domain ())
```

An error domain for runtime exceptions relating to the cogl_gles2_context api.

Since 2.0

Stability Level: Unstable

cogl_gles2_context_new ()

```
CoglGLES2Context~*
cogl_gles2_context_new (CoglContext *ctx,
                        CoglError **error);
```

Allocates a new OpenGLES 2.0 context that can be used to render to CoglOffscreen framebuffers (Rendering to CoglOnscreen framebuffers is not currently supported).

To actually access the OpenGLES 2.0 api itself you need to use cogl_gles2_context_get_vtable(). You should not try to directly link to and use the symbols provided by the a system OpenGLES 2.0 driver.

Once you have allocated an OpenGLES 2.0 context you can make it current using cogl_push_gles2_context(). For those familiar with using the EGL api, this serves a similar purpose to eglMakeCurrent.

Note Before using this api applications can check for OpenGLES 2.0 api support by checking for COGL_FEATURE_ID_GLES2_CONTEXT support with cogl_has_feature(). This function will return FALSE and return an COGL_GLES2_CONTEXT_ERROR_UNSUPPORTED error if the feature isn't available.

Parameters

ctx	A CoglContext	
error	A pointer to a CoglError for returning exceptions	

Returns

A newly allocated CoglGLES2Context or NULL if there was an error and *error* will be updated in that case.

Since 2.0

Stability Level: Unstable

cogl_is_gles2_context ()

```
CoglBool
cogl_is_gles2_context (void *object);
```

Gets whether the given object references a CoglGLES2Context.

Parameters

object	A CoglObject pointer	

Returns

TRUE if the object references a CoglGLES2Context and FALSE otherwise.

Since 2.0

Stability Level: Unstable

cogl_gles2_context_get_vtable ()

```
const CoglGLES2Vtable~*
cogl_gles2_context_get_vtable (CoglGLES2Context *gles2_ctx);
```

Queries the OpenGLES 2.0 api function pointers that should be used for rendering with the given `gles2_ctx` .

> **Note** You should not try to directly link to and use the symbols provided by any system OpenGLES 2.0 driver.

Parameters

gles2_ctx	A CoglGLES2Context allocated with cogl_gles2_context_new()

Returns

A pointer to a CoglGLES2Vtable providing pointers to functions for the full OpenGLES 2.0 api.

Since 2.0

Stability Level: Unstable

cogl_push_gles2_context ()

```
CoglBool
cogl_push_gles2_context (CoglContext *ctx,
                         CoglGLES2Context *gles2_ctx,
                         CoglFramebuffer *read_buffer,
                         CoglFramebuffer *write_buffer,
                         CoglError **error);
```

Pushes the given `gles2_ctx` onto a stack associated with `ctx` so that the OpenGLES 2.0 api can be used instead of the Cogl rendering apis to read and write to the specified framebuffers.

Usage of the api available through a CoglGLES2Vtable is only allowed between cogl_push_gles2_context() and cogl_pop_gles2_context() calls.

If there is a runtime problem with switching over to the given `gles2_ctx` then this function will return FALSE and return an error through `error` .

Parameters

ctx	A CoglContext	
gles2_ctx	A CoglGLES2Context allocated with cogl_gles2_context_new()	

read_buffer	A CoglFramebuffer to access to read operations such as glReadPixels. (must be a CoglOffscreen framebuffer currently)	
write_buffer	A CoglFramebuffer to access for drawing operations such as glDrawArrays. (must be a CoglOffscreen framebuffer currently)	
error	A pointer to a CoglError for returning exceptions	

Returns

TRUE if operation was successfull or FALSE otherwise and *error* will be updated.

Since 2.0

Stability Level: Unstable

cogl_pop_gles2_context ()

```
void
cogl_pop_gles2_context (CoglContext *ctx);
```

Restores the previously active CoglGLES2Context if there were nested calls to cogl_push_gles2_context() or otherwise restores the ability to render with the Cogl api instead of OpenGLES 2.0.

The behaviour is undefined if calls to cogl_pop_gles2_context() are not balenced with the number of corresponding calls to cogl_push_gles2_context().

Parameters

| ctx | A CoglContext | |

Since 2.0

Stability Level: Unstable

cogl_gles2_get_current_vtable ()

```
CoglGLES2Vtable~*
cogl_gles2_get_current_vtable (void);
```

Returns the OpenGL ES 2.0 api vtable for the currently pushed CoglGLES2Context (last pushed with cogl_push_gles2_context()) or NULL if no CoglGLES2Context has been pushed.

Returns

The CoglGLES2Vtable for the currently pushed CoglGLES2Context or NULL if none has been pushed.

Since 2.0

Stability Level: Unstable

cogl_gles2_texture_2d_new_from_handle ()

```
CoglTexture2D~*
cogl_gles2_texture_2d_new_from_handle (CoglContext *ctx,
                                       CoglGLES2Context *gles2_ctx,
                                       unsigned int handle,
                                       int width,
                                       int height,
                                       CoglPixelFormat format);
```

Creates a CoglTexture2D from an OpenGL ES 2.0 texture handle that was created within the given *gles2_ctx* via glGenTextures(). The texture needs to have been associated with the GL_TEXTURE_2D target.

Note This interface is only intended for sharing textures to read from. The behaviour is undefined if the texture is modified using the Cogl api.

Note Applications should only pass this function handles that were created via a CoglGLES2Vtable or via libcogl-gles2 and not pass handles created directly using the system's native libGLESv2 api.

Parameters

ctx	A CoglContext	
gles2_ctx	A CoglGLES2Context allocated with cogl_gles2_context_new()	
handle	An OpenGL ES 2.0 texture handle created with glGenTextures()	
width	Width of the texture to allocate	
height	Height of the texture to allocate	
format	The format of the texture	

Since 2.0

Stability Level: Unstable

cogl_gles2_texture_get_handle ()

```
CoglBool
cogl_gles2_texture_get_handle (CoglTexture *texture,
                               unsigned int *handle,
                               unsigned int *target);
```

Gets an OpenGL ES 2.0 texture handle for a CoglTexture that can then be referenced by a CoglGLES2Context. As well as returning a texture handle the texture's target (such as GL_TEXTURE_2D) is also returned.

If the CoglTexture can not be shared with a CoglGLES2Context then this function will return FALSE.

This api does not affect the lifetime of the CoglTexture and you must take care not to reference the returned handle after the original texture has been freed.

Note This interface is only intended for sharing textures to read from. The behaviour is undefined if the texture is modified by a GLES2 context.

Note This function will only return TRUE for low-level CoglTextures such as CoglTexture2D or CoglTexture3D but not for high level meta textures such as CoglTexture2DSliced

---

Note The handle returned should not be passed directly to a system OpenGL ES 2.0 library, the handle is only intended to be used via a CoglGLES2Vtable or via libcogl-gles2.

Parameters

texture	A CoglTexture	
handle	A return location for an OpenGL ES 2.0 texture handle	
target	A return location for an OpenGL ES 2.0 texture target	

Returns

TRUE if a handle and target could be returned otherwise FALSE is returned.

Since 2.0

Stability Level: Unstable

Types and Values

CoglGLES2Context

```
typedef struct _CoglGLES2Context CoglGLES2Context;
```

Represents an OpenGLES 2.0 api context used as a sandbox for OpenGLES 2.0 state. This is comparable to an EGLContext for those who have used OpenGLES 2.0 with EGL before.

Since 1.12

Stability Level: Unstable

struct CoglGLES2Vtable

```
struct CoglGLES2Vtable {
};
```

Provides function pointers for the full OpenGLES 2.0 api. The api must be accessed this way and not by directly calling symbols of any system OpenGLES 2.0 api.

Since 1.12

Stability Level: Unstable

enum CoglGLES2ContextError

Error codes that relate to the cogl_gles2_context api.

Members

COGL_GLES2_CONTEXT_ERROR_UNSUPPORTED	Creating GLES2 contexts isn't supported. Applications should use cogl_has_feature() to check for the COGL_FEATURE_ID_GLES2_CONTEXT.
COGL_GLES2_CONTEXT_ERROR_DRIVER	An underlying driver error occured.

Chapter 2

Glossaries

2.1 Annotation Glossary

A

allow-none

NULL is OK, both for passing and for returning.

array

Parameter points to an array of items.

C

closure

This parameter is a 'user_data', for callbacks; many bindings can pass NULL here.

I

in

Parameter for input. Default is transfer none.

inout

Parameter for input and for returning results. Default is transfer full.

O

out

Parameter for returning results. Default is transfer full.

out caller-allocates

Out parameter, where caller must allocate storage.

S

scope call

The callback is valid only during the call to the method.

scope notified

The callback is valid until the GDestroyNotify argument is called.

Stable

The intention of a Stable interface is to enable arbitrary third parties to develop applications to these interfaces, release them, and have confidence that they will run on all minor releases of the product (after the one in which the interface was introduced, and within the same major release). Even at a major release, incompatible changes are expected to be rare, and to have strong justifications.

T

transfer full

Free data after the code is done.

transfer none

Don't free data after the code is done.

U

Unstable

Unstable interfaces are experimental or transitional. They are typically used to give outside developers early access to new or rapidly changing technology, or to provide an interim solution to a problem where a more general solution is anticipated. No claims are made about either source or binary compatibility from one minor release to the next. The Unstable interface level is a warning that these interfaces are subject to change without warning and should not be used in unbundled products. Given such caveats, customer impact need not be a factor when considering incompatible changes to an Unstable interface in a major or minor release. Nonetheless, when such changes are introduced, the changes should still be mentioned in the release notes for the affected release.

Appendix A

License

This library is free software; you can redistribute it and/or modify it under the terms of the *GNU Library General Public License* as published by the Free Software Foundation; either version 2 of the License, or (at your option) any later version.

This library is distributed in the hope that it will be useful, but WITHOUT ANY WARRANTY; without even the implied warranty of MERCHANTABILITY or FITNESS FOR A PARTICULAR PURPOSE. See the *GNU Library General Public License* for more details.

You may obtain a copy of the *GNU Library General Public License* from the Free Software Foundation by visiting their Web site or by writing to:

```
Free Software Foundation, Inc.
59 Temple Place - Suite 330
Boston, MA 02111-1307
USA
```

Chapter 3

Index